Pro Office 2007 Development with VSTO

Ty Anderson

Apress®

Pro Office 2007 Development with VSTO

Copyright © 2009 by Ty Anderson

ISBN-13 (pbk): 978-1-4302-1072-6

ISBN-13 (electronic): 978-1-4302-1071-9

Lead Editor: Tony Campbell
Technical Reviewer: John Mueller
Editorial Board: Clay Andres, Steve Anglin, Mark Beckner, Ewan Buckingham, Tony Campbell, Gary Cornell, Jonathan Gennick, Michelle Lowman, Matthew Moodie, Jeffrey Pepper, Frank Pohlmann, Ben Renow-Clarke, Dominic Shakeshaft, Matt Wade, Tom Welsh
Project Manager: Sofia Marchant
Copy Editor: Nicole Abramowitz
Associate Production Director: Kari Brooks-Copony
Production Editor: Janet Vail
Compositor: Pat Christenson
Proofreader: Nancy Bell
Indexer: Broccoli Information Management
Artist: April Milne
Cover Designer: Kurt Krames
Manufacturing Director: Tom Debolski

Distributed to the book trade worldwide by Springer-Verlag New York, Inc., 233 Spring Street, 6th Floor, New York, NY 10013. Phone 1-800-SPRINGER, fax 201-348-4505, e-mail orders-ny@springer-sbm.com, or visit http://www.springeronline.com.

For information on translations, please contact Apress directly at 2855 Telegraph Avenue, Suite 600, Berkeley, CA 94705. Phone 510-549-5930, fax 510-549-5939, e-mail info@apress.com, or visit http://www.apress.com.

Apress and friends of ED books may be purchased in bulk for academic, corporate, or promotional use. eBook versions and licenses are also available for most titles. For more information, reference our Special Bulk Sales–eBook Licensing web page at http://www.apress.com/info/bulksales.

The source code for this book is available to readers at http://www.apress.com.

To Amy, Lilly, Hayden, and Evie

Contents at a Glance

Contents

About the Author

■**TY ANDERSON** is a partner at Cogent Company in Dallas, Texas. He spends his time consulting and building software using Microsoft technologies. In addition to consulting, Ty writes frequently about Microsoft products, including VSTO, SharePoint, Office, and SQL Server. His work has been published on MSDN, DevX, DevSource, Simple-Talk, and CIO. Those who know Ty best stand in awe and amazement of two things: 1) his incredible good looks and 2) his cynical and sarcastic (and sometimes offensive) behavior. Look for him at any tech conference; he will be wearing his yellow Oakland A's hat. Say hello, as he might just offer to buy you a pint.

In the meantime, you can read his latest ramblings on all things technical at his blog, `http://www.officedeveloper.net`. And if you need some great consultants who know Microsoft's stack inside and out, visit his company's web site at `http://www.cogentcompany.com`, and give them a ring.

About the Technical Reviewer

JOHN MUELLER is a freelance author and technical editor. He has writing in his blood, having produced 81 books and more than 300 articles to date. The topics range from networking to artificial intelligence and from database management to heads-down programming. His current project is *LINQ for Dummies* (Wiley Publishing, 2008). His technical editing skills have helped more than 58 authors refine the content of their manuscripts. You can reach John on the Internet at JMueller@mwt.net and on his web site at http://www.mwt.net/~jmueller/.

Acknowledgments

I love books and have surrounded myself with them throughout my office and my house. It's ridiculous, really, as I own more books than I could possibly read in the next few years. However, this fact doesn't prevent me from visiting the local bookstore to see what gems I can find. To me, books have always been a bit mysterious and magical. They calm my soul.

Likewise, the process of writing a book fascinates me. For example, what causes a writer to put words to paper (or whatever the equivalent phrasing is in the computer age)? How does a writer organize his thoughts and then have the discipline to sit at his desk, day after never-ending day, typing word after word to the point that his fingers cramp and ball into fists and his wrists ache and he wants to scream "Mama!"? Who would put up with the insufferable writer while he neglects all other responsibilities in favor of his beloved keyboard? Good questions all.

The answers to these questions have the potential of stripping the luster off the word *author*. Books are a bit magical, but there is absolutely nothing magical about the process of writing them. It is a long and lonely business meant for fools. I am such a fool.

What you hold in your hands is not mine alone. It was produced by the efforts of many, and I hold everyone involved in high esteem. To each of you, I extend my gratitude for your efforts on my behalf.

First of all, thanks to the great team at Apress, especially Tony Campbell for working to keep this project going despite my ever-changing schedule. Thanks for your understanding and flexibility to make it work.

Sofia Marchant did a wonderful job of managing everyone involved. She often provided the nudge I needed to finish a chapter and keep going. Thanks, Sofia, for knowing when to push.

John Mueller is the best technical editor an author could hope to work with. John provided great insights that made this book that much better. Thanks, John.

Nicole Abramowitz, as copy editor, ensured my prose conformed to grammatical standards. Thanks, Nicole, for your meticulous efforts.

Marc Hoppers, my partner at Cogent, helped clear time in my schedule for this project. He also has the benefit of being a frequent target of my incessant onslaught of sarcasm. Cheers, my friend; let's share a good scotch soon.

To my wife, Amy, who is my best friend and absolutely kicks it!

Introduction

The 2007 Microsoft Office system is ubiquitous. Or as they say in Lubbock, Texas, "It's everywhere!" No one disputes that Office is the de facto business productivity suite. Business people all over the world use Office every day. Most people are familiar with it, and even those who aren't can learn how to use it quickly. Given Office's popularity, it only makes sense to build solutions that extend Office applications and make the lives of Office users everywhere a bit easier.

Microsoft includes Visual Studio Tools for the Microsoft Office System (VSTO) as part of Visual Studio 2008. It's the preferred Office development tool of professionals, providing a way to write managed code and attach the resulting assemblies to Office applications and files (although only Word and Excel support document-level solutions).

Who Is This Book For?

This book is for anyone interested in building applications using managed code and Microsoft Office. This book is not intended for beginners, as I do not spend any time explaining the basics of using Office, Visual Studio, or the .NET Framework. A base level of knowledge regarding these topics is assumed. That said, I do not expect you to know anything about VSTO or the basics of Excel, Word, and Outlook development. I cover these topics and more in this book. So if you want to harness the power and goodness of the 2007 Microsoft Office system using VSTO, this book is for you.

How Is This Book Structured?

This book is written to allow you to move about freely and read the topics that interest you most. If you're new to Office development topics and VSTO, I recommend reading the initial two chapters first. The structure of the book is as follows.

Chapter 1: Introduction to VSTO 2008

This chapter introduces VSTO and discusses how to identify projects that fit VSTO. It explains the different VSTO project add-in types as well as VSTO's features.

Chapter 2: Getting Started with Excel, Word, and Outlook

This chapter provides a primer for understanding core development concepts related to Excel, Word, and Outlook. It covers the core objects in each application's object model, and it provides numerous code samples that illustrate how to perform common tasks with the objects.

Chapter 3: Understanding the Office Fluent User Interface and Action and Task Panes

Office offers a rich user interface for use in your projects. This chapter covers each of the UI elements VSTO and Office provide, such as the Fluent UI (aka, the Ribbon), action panes, task panes, and the traditional Office menu and toolbar. The chapter includes code examples for creating custom versions of each UI element.

Chapter 4: Building VSTO Excel Add-Ins

This chapter includes two sample VSTO add-in projects that illustrate how to work with Excel to build a solution. Both an application-level add-in sample and a document-level add-in sample are included. In addition, it covers the Excel host controls provided by VSTO.

Chapter 5: Building VSTO Word Add-Ins

This chapter also includes two sample VSTO add-in projects, but here the topic is Word-based solutions. An application-level add-in sample and a document-level add-in sample, as well as Word host controls, are included.

Chapter 6: Building VSTO Outlook Add-Ins

Completing the trio of chapters that provide in-depth sample code walk-throughs, this chapter includes four VSTO Outlook sample projects. Each project focuses on a separate Outlook topic, such as customizing form regions, using Outlook search, and integrating with other Office applications.

Chapter 7: Building SharePoint Workflows

VSTO provides the capability to build custom SharePoint workflows. This chapter explains how to build both sequential workflows and state machine workflows.

Chapter 8: Building Office Business Applications

Microsoft considers Office to be a development platform. Office Business Applications (OBAs) integrate data with Office and allow end users to work with data from external applications within Office. This chapter explains how to build an Outlook-based OBA that integrates data from a sales system and an accounting system.

Chapter 9: Deploying VSTO Solutions

This chapter explains VSTO's support of ClickOnce deployment. It provides a walkthrough of a sample VSTO project.

What Do You Need to Use This Book?

Office system 2007 and Visual Studio 2008 Professional Edition or Team System are all you need to build VSTO solutions. I recommend installing any available service packs for Office 2007 and Visual Studio as well. Chapter 7 covers building SharePoint workflows; you will need access to a SharePoint site (either Office SharePoint Server or Windows SharePoint Server) to work with that chapter's code.

CHAPTER 1

Introduction to VSTO 2008

Organizations of all types run their operations with the help of Microsoft Office. Since the initial release of Word, what has become the suite of applications known as Microsoft Office is no longer a tool only for the individual authoring documents. Today, the 2007 Microsoft Office system (Office 2007) is a business platform that allows teams of individuals to automate their complex business processes.

Enabling Office as a development platform for business is the reason Microsoft created Visual Studio Tools for the Microsoft Office System (VSTO). VSTO provides you with modern, .NET capabilities to build complicated, enterprise-class solutions using managed code with Office as the underlying platform. In this chapter, you will learn

- How to identify projects that fit VSTO

- The difference between application-level and document-level add-ins

- How to create application-level and document-level add-ins

- The development features VSTO provides

- The purpose of the `ThisAddin`, `ThisDocument`, and `ThisWorkbook` classes

- The purpose of deployment and application manifests

An Overview of VSTO 2008

The official product name is Visual Studio Tools for the Microsoft Office System 2008. Microsoft certainly does not have the best imagination when naming its products, but its names rarely leave you wondering what it is that the product does. This couldn't be truer with VSTO, as it does exactly what the name implies. VSTO extends Visual Studio's toolset to Office and allows you to build Office-based solutions using managed code (Visual Basic .NET or C# only).

VSTO relies on the .NET Framework, which means all the power and features available with .NET are available to you when programming with Office. For example, when creating an Excel worksheet solution, you can add WinForm controls to the worksheet. Also, if you want to create a custom action pane in an Office application, the form you will use is a .NET WinForm user control, which has all the features you expect from WinForm controls. These tools are a serious improvement over the control set available using Visual Basic for Applications (VBA)—the traditional Office scripting or macro language.

VBA: NOT DEAD YET!

VBA has had a long and good life and will continue its life for the foreseeable future as the macro language for Office. However, it will eventually fade into the sunset, because Microsoft does not have a road map for future VBA language enhancements. It has not added any features to the core VBA language or the Office Visual Basic Editor since Office XP. In fact, the initial VSTO team included many of the existing VBA team members. Despite VBA's stunted growth, Office 2007 contains hundreds of new objects and methods related to Office's new features, such as the RibbonX application programming interface (API). You can build complete solutions with VBA, but you don't have access to the features provided by VSTO.

The first version of VSTO allowed for the creation of custom Word and Excel document solutions in Visual Basic .NET (VB .NET) and C#. This initial version of VSTO implemented a simple model that relied on custom document properties. These properties told VSTO the location of the .NET assembly and the name of the startup class to call within it. This model separated the code from the document by calling the linked .NET assembly and took full advantage of the .NET code-access security model. This release established a .NET beachhead within the Office development community, as it allowed developers to build *document-level* add-ins with managed code. Prior to VSTO, document-level add-ins were only possible using VBA.

The second version of VSTO included two releases: VSTO 2005 and VSTO 2005 Second Edition (VSTO 2005 SE). These two versions combined to extend the VSTO feature set to include application-level add-ins for Excel, Word, Outlook, PowerPoint, InfoPath, and Visio. Beyond including support for these new types of add-ins, Microsoft made other improvements to the existing document-level add-ins. These two versions of VSTO together provided support for Office 2003 and Office 2007.

As the third major release of VSTO, VSTO 2008 rolls up all the features from the previous VSTO versions and includes many new features for Office 2007 development. The preexisting Office 2003 features still remain, making VSTO 2008 the most powerful set of development tools for Office.

Existing Features Prior to VSTO 2008

I want to start the discussion of VSTO's features by talking about the feature set that already existed prior to VSTO 2008. I'll then explain the new tools and capabilities included with VSTO 2008. It's important to understand the existing feature set, as it is the foundation for everything in VSTO 2008. The combination of the old and new features has caused VSTO 2008 (the third major release of VSTO) to leave its infancy and join the ranks of mature development tools.

Application-Level Add-Ins

An application-level add-in is a class-library project that produces an assembly associated with a supported Office application. This assembly runs as an add-in within the host application's domain. Using this type of project, you have access to all of the .NET namespaces as well as the target Office application's object model. In fact, the project provides a class named ThisApplication, which gives you easy access to the Office application object.

The project type is a simplified version of the Shared Add-in that was once the recommended framework for building Office add-ins with managed code. With this version, however, you don't need to worry about creating a Component Object Model (COM)-based wrapper—or shim—for final deployment with Office, as VSTO does this for you.

■**Note** A shim is complex and requires a C++ wrapper class. I recommend reading "Implementing IDTExtensibility2 in an Automation Add-in" by Andrew Whitechapel (http://blogs.officezealot.com/whitechapel/archive/2005/06/09/4756.aspx).

Document-Level Add-Ins

Document-level add-ins are the original VSTO add-in type. Like application-level add-ins, a document-level add-in produces an assembly. The difference, however, is this assembly attaches to an Office document. Currently, only Word documents, Word templates, Excel worksheets, and Excel templates are supported. Whichever type you choose, the document stores a link to the assembly, and the assembly remains external to the document. This deployment strategy is different from VBA macros, which are embedded inside the document. Document-level add-ins give you access to all .NET namespaces and the target document's objects. Instead of ThisApplication, the class name is either ThisWorkbook or ThisDocument.

With document-level add-ins, you have the ability to write code that reads and writes data related to the business objects represented by the document. You don't need to worry about finding the value in cell A2 in Excel or, worse, the customer name typically found on page 2, paragraph 2 in Word. Instead, you can reference data using WinForm data-binding objects to access the data directly without messing with the Office objects.

Custom Task Panes and Action Panes

Custom Task Pane forms and Action Pane forms are the task-oriented vertical windows that typically display next to a document (see Figure 1-1). Task panes are associated with an application-level add-in, while action panes are associated with document-level add-ins. Besides this one contextual difference, they are basically the same. These panes allow you to build context-sensitive user interfaces for your supported task or scenario using Windows Forms and WinForm controls. For example, you can build a custom pane that connects to your company's sales data, lists current contacts, allows the user to select a value, and inserts the data into the document.

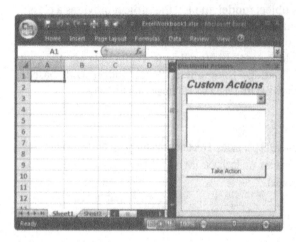

Figure 1-1. *A custom VSTO action pane filled with WinForm controls*

Outlook Form Regions

Outlook is one of the more popular Office development targets, because it acts as the operation hub for millions of Office users every day. VSTO allows you to create custom form regions to extend the various Outlook forms with additional layout regions. These regions display as part of the targeted Outlook form (see Figure 1-2). Form regions provide the abilities to extend the default page area and replace standard forms.

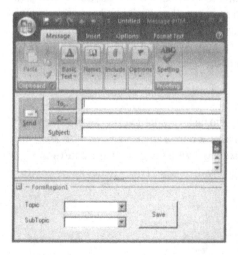

Figure 1-2. *A custom form region displaying within an Outlook mail item*

Customizing the Default Page Area

You can extend the default page area of any Outlook item's standard form, including e-mail, appointments, and tasks. Previously, the default page for most Outlook forms was not open to developer customization. Now, you have the ability to extend Outlook forms to capture and display those missing fields your users have been clamoring to see. For those who require a plethora of customizations, VSTO supports adding up to 30 extra pages to any of the standard Outlook forms.

Replacing Standard Forms

You now have the ability to replace Outlook forms with your customized version. The ability to perform this trick was previously possible but definitely not supported by Microsoft.

OUTLOOK FORM REPLACEMENT PRIOR TO VSTO 2008

Replacing standard Outlook forms with your own custom version is possible without VSTO 2008, but it is unsupported by Microsoft. In fact, if you were to attempt to replace the standard Contact form, for example, you would be required to implement all the features required by the form without any help from VSTO. The secret is to capture the event that opens an Outlook form (NewInspector), cancel the opening of the form, and instead, open your custom version. Although possible, this strategy requires a lot of work to reimplement the features your users would expect a Contact form to include. To see how to implement the old, unsupported method for replacing Outlook forms, read an article I wrote on the topic: "Outlook the Way You Want It—Build Custom Outlook GUIs with WinForms & VSTO" (http://www.devx.com/MicrosoftISV/Article/29261).

Ribbon Customizations

Office 2007 includes a new toolbar user interface for Word, Excel, PowerPoint, and Outlook (only partially implemented in Outlook) known as the Office Fluent User Interface, or Ribbon (see Figure 1-3). VSTO allows you to customize the Ribbon by adding your own tabs, groups, and buttons. This is much like creating new command bars in previous versions of Office. VSTO 2008 provides a Ribbon Designer, which greatly improves the developer experience for creating Ribbon customizations. I'll explain the designer later in this chapter.

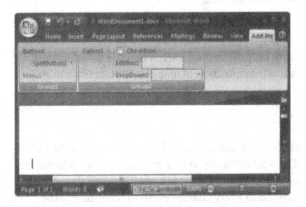

Figure 1-3. *A customized Ribbon displayed in Word*

Smart Tags

A smart tag is a class library attached to a Word or Excel document. Smart tags scan for defined strings of text that have actions attached to them. VSTO allows you to maintain a list of actionable values and recognize them when they appear in either a Word or Excel document. Anytime a desired value is recognized, VSTO displays a menu of actions that you have defined for that type of string. Because you can define the various types of strings the VSTO add-in should identify, you can display different actions for each value type.

VSTO smart tags affect only the targeted document. This means the smart tag only reacts to identified values in its associated document. It doesn't react to any other document, as it isn't in scope. The ability to attach a smart tag to a single document (*single-document scoping*) is a key distinction from Office smart tags that operate at the application level and respond to identified values across all open documents.

You can implement smart tags to provide easy access to contextual actions within the document window. For example, a proposal document could scan for known client names and provide a menu that allows a user to view additional client data, such as contact details and financial details.

Host Controls

Host controls extend Office objects for interaction with managed code. They are based on native, COM-based Office controls and behave like their native Office counterparts. However, host controls add properties and methods that allow you to respond to that instance of the control.

Bookmark

The Bookmark control, supported by Word, identifies a placeholder inside a Word document. You can bind this control to a data source. This control automatically reflects any changes to the underlying data source.

XMLNode

The XMLNode control, supported by Word, only exists if an Extensible Markup Language (XML) schema is attached and mapped to the document. It also supports data binding to a data source. You can manipulate this object directly with code.

XMLNodes

The XMLNodes control, supported by Word, only exists if an XML schema is attached and mapped to the document. This control contains a collection of mapped XMLNode objects. It does not support data binding.

NamedRange

The NamedRange control, supported by Excel, contains a Range object and supports data binding. A range is a collection of Excel cells. The NamedRange control provides you with the ability to access the range directly and code against its events. This is not possible with the Office-based Range object, where you need to respond to every change event to determine if the desired range triggered the change.

ListObject

The ListObject control, supported by Excel, contains an Excel list and supports data binding. It exposes properties and methods that allow you to reference the list and code directly against it.

Chart

The Chart control, supported by Excel, contains a Chart object, supports data binding, and exposes properties and methods that allow you to reference the list and code directly against it.

XMLMappedRange

The XMLMappedRange control, supported by Excel, contains a range with an XML schema mapped against it. This range supports data binding and direct manipulation through code via its exposed properties and methods.

Visual Document Designers

VSTO provides full-featured designers for Word and Excel (see Figure 1-4). These designers open Word and Excel documents within Visual Studio and treat the documents as a design surface similar to a Windows form. You can drag and drop controls, edit properties, and switch between Code and Design views to your heart's delight. This feature greatly enhances the Office development experience, as you can write code behind the document as you build its corresponding interface. In addition, the full Office menus integrate within Visual Studio, so you can edit the underlying document as you normally would in Word or Excel.

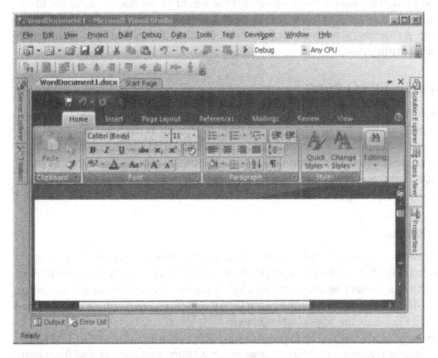

Figure 1-4. *A Word-based VSTO solution displaying the Word visual designer*

Data Programming

VSTO allows you to access and manipulate data within Office documents directly, without relying on the Office object models. VSTO employs the model-view-controller (MVC) pattern to separate the data from the Office document user interfaces. (See `http://en.wikipedia.org/wiki/Model-view-controller` for more information.)

VSTO stores the data as an XML data island. Since the data is XML-based, you can create typed datasets to access the underlying data schema by name. This strategy removes a major source of pain with traditional Office development methods that require navigating the user interface to access data. With VSTO, data access is direct and simple due to VSTO's data-caching features and the `ServerDocument` object.

Data Caching

The data contained in the XML data island enables offline data caching. Data retrieved externally to the document fills the data island. After the document closes, the data island remains filled with the data, enabling offline usage. Think of the classic airplane example, where the data cache is offline, and the account executive is downloading sales spreadsheets and reviewing them on the plane trip to meet the client.

ServerDocument

The XML data island also exposes methods for manipulating supported Office document data directly. The `ServerDocument` object provides the APIs for reading and writing data with server-side code. This doesn't require the code to execute in Windows Server; instead this refers to the location of the execution code—either the server or the client, which could be one and the same.

The data-programming features are available with document-level add-ins, meaning only Word and Excel are supported.

What's New in VSTO 2008

VSTO 2008 targets solutions developed with Office 2007. The new features included in this version largely correspond with the new features in Office 2007, such as the new Office XML file formats, the Ribbon user interface, Outlook form regions, and Word content controls. However, this release does more than support Office's new features; it also adds support for .NET technologies like ClickOnce deployment. Each tool helps you build powerful, Office-based solutions in less time and with less effort.

ClickOnce Deployment

Finally, ClickOnce deployment exists for Office development. ClickOnce is a self-updating deployment technology that allows for deployment of applications with minimal user interaction. The idea is to make installing and updating applications as easy as clicking a link . . . once. Once deployed, the add-in checks the server each time it initializes to determine if an updated version exists; if it finds one, the add-in self-updates.

.This deployment model has not been possible with Office solutions due to the COM architecture of Office and its reliance upon the Windows registry. Office applications read the registry to load any associated add-ins on application startup. ClickOnce does not support writing keys to the registry, making ClickOnce an impossibility.

VSTO 2008 changes this dire situation by supporting ClickOnce installations for application-level add-ins. VSTO provides a Publish Wizard (see Figure 1-5) to guide you through the creation of a deployment package (called a ClickOnce manifest). This is a powerful and much needed tool for Office development.

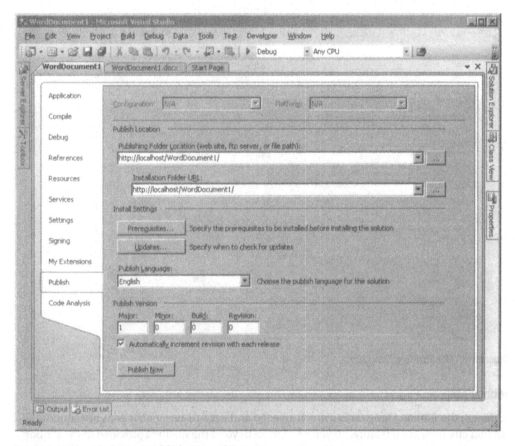

Figure 1-5. *The ClickOnce Publish Wizard in action*

Unfortunately, document-level add-ins are not supported and continue to use the VSTO 2005 deployment model.

Ribbon Designer

Customizing the Ribbon is now supported with a design-time control known as the Ribbon Designer (see Figure 1-6). This designer allows you to create custom Ribbon tabs in the same manner as designing Windows Forms. With this tool, you can quickly create new tabs, extend Office's built-in tabs, add control groups, and draw controls within them. The Ribbon controls function similarly to Windows Forms controls with familiar objects, properties, and events.

The Ribbon user interface is XML-based, so peculiarities exist. For example, you can't double-click the Ribbon control to attach an event. Instead, you assign the name of the method you want to execute as an attribute of the control.

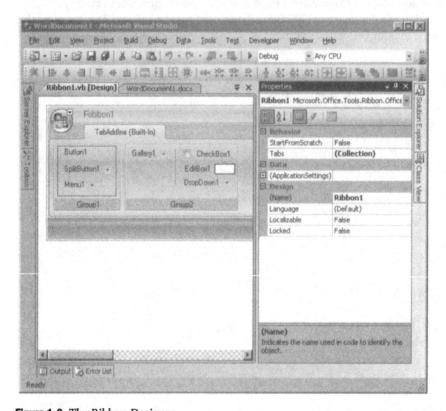

Figure 1-6. *The Ribbon Designer*

Ribbon XML

Although the Ribbon Designer is a much-needed and easy-to-use tool, it does not support all Ribbon customization features. If you need to go beyond the features provided in the Ribbon Designer, you will need to write Ribbon XML manually. Fortunately, VSTO 2008 provides a Ribbon (XML) project template to support these needs.

Use the Ribbon (XML) template if you want to

- Include standard Ribbon groups in your custom tab or another standard Ribbon tab

- Add standard controls to your custom group

- Add buttons to the Quick Access Toolbar (the button in the upper left-hand corner of Ribbon-supported Office applications, as shown in Figure 1-7)

- Override default event handlers for standard controls with your custom code

- Share your Ribbon (XML) customizations among multiple add-ins

Figure 1-7. *A customized Quick Access Toolbar*

Word Content Controls

Word 2007 includes a new set of controls known as *content controls*. These controls add structure to Word documents by defining a data region and its data type. These controls ease the effort required to edit the typed data within a Word document. In addition, they allow for better support of data types, as you can limit what type of data you can input within the control.

VSTO provides the developer experience expected within Windows Forms. You draw content controls onto the document surface (see Figure 1-8). You can write code to respond to the control's events, set its properties, and so on.

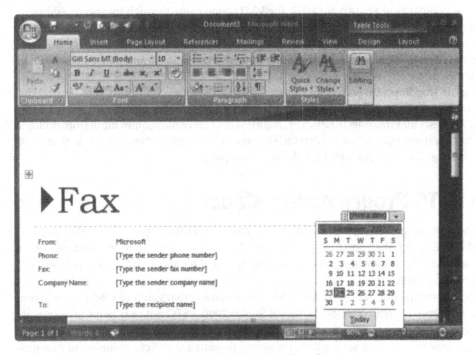

Figure 1-8. *A Word content control containing a DateTime data type*

Outlook Form Region Wizard

VSTO automates the creation of custom Outlook form regions with the Form Region Wizard. This wizard eliminates the need for you to manually create the XML required for custom form regions. Once added to your Outlook add-in project, this wizard takes you through a five-step process for creating the shell for your custom region. Utilizing the wizard, you can

- Create new form regions or import the Outlook Form Storage (.ofs) file created within Outlook's form designer

- Specify the form region's location

- Specify display preferences

- Associate the region to Outlook items, including mail, tasks, and the calendar

After the wizard creates the form region, you code against it as if it were a Windows form by drawing controls, setting properties, attaching event handlers, and more.

SharePoint Workflow

Given the popularity of SharePoint 2007, the VSTO team came through for you by adding support for building custom SharePoint workflows. These project templates allow you to build custom processes that control the life cycle of documents and lists. Support for both sequential (a series of actions) and state-machine (a set of states, transitions, and actions) workflows exists.

Custom workflows are perfect for business processes whose complexity goes beyond the standard SharePoint workflows. A good example is the process of responding to government-related Requests for Proposals (RFPs). This business process could require input from multiple individuals and external partners. With VSTO, you can create a complex, state-machine work-flow to manage the various stages of building the proposal.

The VSTO Programming Model

The beauty of using Office to build solutions is that it is familiar to your users. They use it every day and even if they don't necessarily love it, they are accustomed to it and know how to accomplish their work with it. This familiarity is one of the more compelling reasons to build VSTO solutions.

Another compelling reason to create VSTO solutions is that you build them using a tool known and loved by .NET developers, Visual Studio 2008. VSTO not only helps take care of your users, but it also provides the tools you need in a familiar environment. Your VSTO learning curve is low, because you're not required to learn a significant number of new programming skills.

Enabling .NET Development

Each Office application is a COM-based program and is completely unaware of the .NET Framework. COM was Microsoft's specification for providing object interoperability prior to

.NET. All of Office's interfaces are based on the COM specification, which means COM remains a key component of Office development.

Traditionally, you would build Office solutions with Office's embedded macro language, VBA, or you would use classic Visual Basic to automate Office applications from your custom application. Also, you would need to pick from a plethora of Office add-in technologies such as COM add-ins (managed or unmanaged), smart tags, Excel file add-ins (.xla files), Word file add-ins (.dot files), and many more.

Each of these pre-VSTO add-in technologies were great, because they provided flexibility in how you extended Office. The problem, however, was that Office lacked a single development model. Each technology provided its own interface and development model. Building Office solutions in pre-VSTO days required a large amount of patience and a desire to learn a multitude of interfaces.

VSTO 2008 still supports the previous methods for building Office add-ins. It doesn't replace them or consolidate them into a single, overarching programming model. Instead, it provides the Office extensibility architecture for Office 2007 and beyond. If you want to extend Office with VSTO, you only need to know how to build an add-in. You no longer need to determine whether or not you should customize a menu using an Excel add-in instead of managed-code, COM add-in (also known by its Visual Studio template name, Shared Add-in). Using VSTO, you only need to know which project template to select and how to work within the VSTO framework. In the remainder of this chapter, I'll discuss the VSTO programming model along with the key objects and classes you will use when building VSTO-based Office solutions.

Model Overview

VSTO supports both Office 2003 and Office 2007, with the latter receiving more support and features. To build a VSTO solution, begin by opening Visual Studio and selecting the project template appropriate for your development needs. VSTO provides templates for building both application-level and document-level solutions to varying degrees. For example, document-level add-in templates are only available for Word and Excel. In addition, Access, Publisher, and Groove lack application-level add-in support. Table 1-1 lists the application support for each project type.

Table 1-1. *Application Support by Project Type*

Add-In Types	Supported Office 2007 Applications	Supported Office 2003 Applications
Application-level add-ins	Outlook Excel Word InfoPath PowerPoint Project Visio	Outlook Excel Word PowerPoint Project Visio
Document-level add-ins	Word Excel	Word Excel
SharePoint workflows	SharePoint Server 2007	Not supported

Once you create a new project and Visual Studio loads it into the editor, building with VSTO is similar to building a Windows Forms application. However, having Office in the mix does add to the complexity of your solution, and the inner workings of how you move from a VSTO project template to an executing assembly working with Office applications or documents require further explanation.

First, let me explain the main development paradigms of VSTO.

Office Objects Are .NET Classes

VSTO provides custom classes for each supported Office application and document. These classes (`ThisAddin`, `ThisDocument`, and `ThisWorkbook`) are fully typed .NET classes that incorporate and extend the Office object model. They provide the interfaces for the VSTO managed code to call Office's COM-based objects.

Managed Controls Hosted Within Documents

Managed controls (also called *host controls*) are .NET controls that connect to their actual Office counterpart. They are not the same as the object they represent; instead, they provide a reference to the actual object and provide the ability to extend its class, as you would expect to do with a .NET class.

Separation of Business Logic and View

VSTO provides .NET controls for objects such as the Excel NamedRange control and the Word Bookmark control. These controls provide direct access to their related objects in the actual document. You no longer have to navigate the document and parse values until you find the one you want. Simply drop these controls onto the document (or workbook) and manipulate them by name, just as you would expect to do with a WinForm application.

Now that you understand the main developer benefits of VSTO and understand that, more or less, building a VSTO add-in is much like building a Windows Forms application, it is time to learn how to build each type of add-in. In this chapter, I'm concerned only with application-level and document-level add-ins. I'll cover SharePoint workflow projects in Chapter 15.

Understanding Application Add-Ins

The best method to learn how VSTO works is to build with it. In this section and the next, you will learn the basic developer workflow for building VSTO solutions. As you build each add-in, I will explain each of the main components and the role they play within the overall solution.

As mentioned earlier, a VSTO application-level add-in is an assembly executing against a VSTO-supported Office application such as Outlook, Excel, or PowerPoint. Open Visual Studio, and let's walk through how to build an add-in that targets Outlook.

Creating an Outlook Application Add-In

Since Outlook is one of the most popular target applications for VSTO add-ins, let's use it to walk through building our first sample add-in. Complete the following steps:

1. Open Visual Studio.

2. Open the New Project dialog box (File ➤ New ➤ Project) and select Visual Basic ➤ Office ➤ 2007 in the Project Types section (see Figure 1-9).

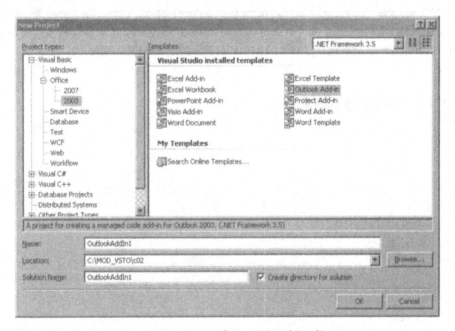

Figure 1-9. *Selecting a VSTO project template in Visual Studio*

Since VSTO supports both Office 2003 and Office 2007, two nodes exist to make it easy for you to select a project type that supports your targeted version of Office. The available project types follow the data presented Table 1-1.

3. Select the Outlook Add-in template from the Templates section and click OK. Make things easy on yourself, and accept the default values for the Name, Location, and Solution Name, as this is a sample application.

With this blank add-in ready to go, let's review the main components that make it function.

Main Add-In Components

After Visual Studio creates the project, take a look at the Solution Explorer window to review the objects that make up the add-in project (see Figure 1-10). Application add-ins initially consist of a single class and references to the host application, which in this case is Outlook. The class implements the IDTExtensibility2 interface required for Office add-ins.

Note VSTO dramatically simplifies the implementation of the IDTExtensibility2 interface. In short, with VSTO, you only need to implement two of the five interface methods. Behind the scenes, VSTO implements the other three methods. You can learn more by reading "VSTO support for Outlook" by Eric Carter (http://blogs.msdn.com/eric_carter/archive/2005/06/06/423986.aspx).

Figure 1-10. *The contents of the Outlook add-in displayed in Solution Explorer*

The ThisAddin Class Every VSTO application add-in contains a class named ThisAddin. This class acts as the entry point to the add-in and is the starting point for implementing your code. Listing 1-1 contains the full code stub for the newly created ThisAddin.

Listing 1-1. *A Stubbed-Out ThisAddin Class*

```
Public Class ThisAddIn

    Private Sub ThisAddIn_Startup(ByVal sender As Object, ByVal e As _
      System.EventArgs) Handles Me.Startup

    End Sub
```

```
Private Sub ThisAddIn_Shutdown(ByVal sender As Object, ByVal e As _
    System.EventArgs) Handles Me.Shutdown

End Sub
```

```
End Class
```

The class contains two methods: Startup and Shutdown. These are appropriate for initializing and cleaning up your add-in, respectively. The Startup event executes when the host application loads the add-in into memory. This means the host application has completed its initialization process and all of its objects are available for you to access and manipulate with your code. The Shutdown method executes just prior to the host application unloading it from memory. Use the Shutdown method to perform any required cleanup.

Both methods contain the same arguments. For application add-ins, the sender argument passes a reference to the add-in, providing you with access to the classes' properties and methods.

Perhaps the most important property of ThisAddin is the Application property. This property is a reference to the current instance of the host application, which is important to Office development. The Application object is always the parent object within Office applications; all other objects are linked as child objects. Thus, if you have access to the Application object, you have access to every other object in the application.

Office Primary Interop Assemblies Within Solution Explorer, click the Show All Files button to view the project's References folder (see Figure 1-11). VSTO automatically includes a reference to the host application Outlook (Microsoft.Office.Interop.Outlook). This is a reference to Outlook's Primary Interop Assembly (PIA), which is just one of the Office PIAs. Interop is short for interoperability and in the context of VSTO, refers to the managed assemblies that wrap the Office COM-based interfaces for use within .NET development. A full listing of all Office PIAs is available on the Microsoft Developer Network (MSDN) site at http://msdn2.microsoft.com/en-us/library/15s06t57(VS.90).aspx.

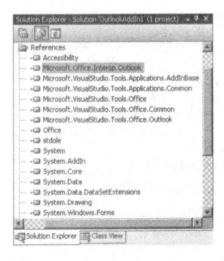

Figure 1-11. *The project's References folder for a VSTO Outlook add-in*

The Office PIAs contain the Office type definitions for each Office application and are what make coding Office with managed code a possibility. In order for managed code to communicate with COM-based code, it needs to understand the types of objects it is calling. The PIAs provide these descriptions and let the managed code know what object types and data types it should use to call the referenced COM object.

A SET OF PIAS FOR EVERY VERSION OF OFFICE

Microsoft publishes a version of PIAs for each new version of Office starting with Office 2003. It is important to make sure you use the Microsoft version of the PIAs and not allow Visual Studio to generate one by creating a reference to an Office application. Although this will work, Microsoft doesn't support it, and it will most likely cause problems that you could easily avoid by using the correct PIAs for your targeted version of Office.

Manifest Files VSTO utilizes two types of XML-based manifest files for deploying and updating add-ins. The first manifest is the application manifest, which contains the information that VSTO needs to locate the assemblies included within the add-in. The application manifest stores such information as the add-in's name, version, public key token, and language. It also stores information about assembly dependencies and prerequisites, as well as the name of the class that serves as the application entry point. Basically, if an add-in needs a file to execute properly, this manifest will include the needed information. Listing 1-2 contains a sample application manifest.

Listing 1-2. *A Sample VSTO Application Manifest*

```
<?xml version="1.0" encoding="utf-8"?>
<asmv1:assembly xsi:schemaLocation="urn:schemas-microsoft-com:asm.v1
 assembly.adaptive.xsd" manifestVersion="1.0" xmlns:asmv3=
"urn:schemas-microsoft-com:asm.v3" xmlns:dsig=
"http://www.w3.org/2000/09/xmldsig#" xmlns="urn:schemas-microsoft-com:asm.v2"
 xmlns:asmv1="urn:schemas-microsoft-com:asm.v1" xmlns:asmv2=
"urn:schemas-microsoft-com:asm.v2" xmlns:xsi=
"http://www.w3.org/2001/XMLSchema-instance"
xmlns:co.v1="urn:schemas-microsoft-com:clickonce.v1">
<asmv1:assemblyIdentity name="OutlookAddIn1.dll" version="1.0.0.0"
  publicKeyToken="b213866c46f1a387" language="en" processorArchitecture=
"msil" type="win32" />
<description xmlns="urn:schemas-microsoft-com:asm.v1">
OutlookAddIn1 - Outlook add-in created with Visual Studio Tools
for Office</description>
<application />
<entryPoint>
<co.v1:customHostSpecified />
```

```
</entryPoint>
<trustInfo>
<security>
<applicationRequestMinimum>
<PermissionSet Unrestricted="true" ID="Custom" SameSite="site" />
<defaultAssemblyRequest permissionSetReference="Custom" />
</applicationRequestMinimum>
<requestedPrivileges xmlns="urn:schemas-microsoft-com:asm.v3">
<requestedExecutionLevel level="asInvoker" />
</requestedPrivileges>
</security>
</trustInfo>
<dependency>
<dependentAssembly dependencyType="preRequisite" allowDelayedBinding="true">
<assemblyIdentity name="Microsoft.Office.Interop.Outlook" version="12.0.0.0"
 publicKeyToken="71E9BCE111E9429C" language="neutral" />
</dependentAssembly>
</dependency>
<vstav1:addIn xmlns:vstav1="urn:schemas-microsoft-com:vsta.v1">
<vstav1:entryPoints>
<vstav1:entryPoint class="OutlookAddIn1.ThisAddIn">
<assemblyIdentity name="OutlookAddIn1" version="1.0.0.0" language="neutral"
processorArchitecture="msil" />
</vstav1:entryPoint>
</vstav1:entryPoints>
<vstav1:update enabled="true">
<vstav1:expiration maximumAge="7" unit="days" />
</vstav1:update>
<vstav1:application>
<vstov3:customization xmlns:vstov3="urn:schemas-microsoft-com:vsto.v3">
<vstov3:appAddIn application="Outlook" loadBehavior="3" keyName="OutlookAddIn1">
<vstov3:friendlyName>OutlookAddIn1</vstov3:friendlyName>
<vstov3:description>OutlookAddIn1 - Outlook add-in created with
Visual Studio Tools for Office</vstov3:description>
</vstov3:appAddIn>
</vstov3:customization>
</vstav1:application>
</vstav1:addIn>
```

The second manifest is the deployment manifest, which serves to identify the current version of the application that should be deployed to the user's machine. The information included in this manifest largely matches that of the application manifest, as it contains the name, version, language, and so on, but in much less detail. It does not list all of the add-in's assemblies and other required files. This file only serves to identify the current version and point to the application manifest associated with that version. Listing 1-3 contains a sample of a deployment manifest.

Listing 1-3. *A Sample VSTO Deployment Manifest*

```
<?xml version="1.0" encoding="utf-8"?>
<asmv1:assembly xsi:schemaLocation="urn:schemas-microsoft-com:asm.v1
  assembly.adaptive.xsd" manifestVersion="1.0" xmlns:asmv3=
"urn:schemas-microsoft-com:asm.v3" xmlns:dsig=
http://www.w3.org/2000/09/xmldsig#" xmlns:co.v1="urn:schemas-microsoft-
com:clickonce.v1" xmlns="urn:schemas-microsoft-com:asm.v2" xmlns:asmv1=
"urn:schemas-microsoft-com:asm.v1" xmlns:asmv2=
"urn:schemas-microsoft-com:asm.v2" xmlns:xrml=
"urn:mpeg:mpeg21:2003:01-REL-R-NS" xmlns:xsi=
"http://www.w3.org/2001/XMLSchema-instance">
<assemblyIdentity name="OutlookAddIn1.vsto" version="1.0.0.0"
publicKeyToken="b213866c46f1a387" language="en"
processorArchitecture="msil" xmlns="urn:schemas-microsoft-com:asm.v1" />
<description asmv2:publisher="Microsoft" asmv2:product="OutlookAddIn1"
xmlns="urn:schemas-microsoft-com:asm.v1" />
<deployment install="false" mapFileExtensions="true" />
<dependency>
<dependentAssembly dependencyType="install" codebase=
"OutlookAddIn1_1_0_0_0\OutlookAddIn1.dll.manifest" size="11993">
<assemblyIdentity name="OutlookAddIn1.dll" version="1.0.0.0"
publicKeyToken="b213866c46f1a387"
language="en" processorArchitecture="msil" type="win32" />
<hash>
<dsig:Transforms>
<dsig:Transform Algorithm="urn:schemas-microsoft-com:HashTransforms.Identity" />
</dsig:Transforms>
<dsig:DigestMethod Algorithm="http://www.w3.org/2000/09/xmldsig#sha1" />
<dsig:DigestValue>9oVorZqzS8vRJFnPSCNnjHIiXo4=</dsig:DigestValue>
</hash>
</dependentAssembly>
</dependency>
```

CLICKONCE AND VSTO

Both the application and the deployment manifests are based on the ClickOnce manifest schemas. However, they do not support the full ClickOnce schemas and ignore any nonsupported element.

To understand how the two manifest files work together at runtime, see the "VSTO Runtime Overview" section later in this chapter.

Windows Registry Entries Office utilizes the Windows registry to discover if any add-ins should be loaded when an Office applications loads. In order for an Office application to know of an add-in, a special key must exist that tells the host how to locate the add-in. When the host application loads, it checks the registry for any settings under this node to determine the add-in's entry point. The data entered here depends on the targeted version of Office, but the registry node for each version is HKEY_CURRENT_USER\Software\Microsoft\Office\ APPLICATION NAME\Addins\ADDIN ID node.

For Office 2007, the registry stores the location of the add-in's deployment manifest. The name of the key is Manifest, and it stores the location of the add-in's deployment manifest.

For Office 2003, both the Manifest Name and Manifest Location values must exist in the registry. In addition, the manifest in this case is the application manifest, not the deployment manifest.

AS WITH ALL THINGS IN LIFE, EXCEPTIONS EXIST

I have no idea why Visio's add-in registry key does not share the same location as its Office brethren. The registry key for Visio add-ins is stored in the HKEY_CURRENT_USER\Software\Microsoft\Visio*APPLICATION NAME*\Addins*ADDIN ID* node.

Also, an Office 2003 add-in can become a machine-level add-in if you change the first node to HKEY_LOCAL_MACHINE. For Office 2007, this strategy causes Office to ignore the add-in. That said, strategies exist for creating a machine-level add-in installation. If enabling your add-in for use by all users of a single machine is important to your Office 2007 development efforts, I suggest that you read "Deploying your VSTO Add-In to All Users" by Misha Shneerson (http://blogs.msdn.com/mshneer/archive/ 2007/09/04/deploying-your-vsto-add-in-to-all-users-part-i.aspx).

Understanding Document Add-Ins

Document add-ins are managed assemblies attached to an Office document (Excel or Word only). The code is not embedded as part of the document but instead resides in a separate location such as a URL, a network share, or another location available to the end user. This scenario allows for a development experience that resembles Windows Forms development. Here, the form canvas is the Word or Excel document. The managed code resides *behind* the document and provides for true separation between your code and the form. When a user opens the document, the Office application locates and loads the assembly, enabling your code to respond to the document's events and manipulate its objects. Just like application add-ins, document level add-ins utilize the Office PIAs to communicate with the COM-based types found within the Office object model.

For the sake of this discussion, I will walk through a Word document add-in. The structure is largely the same for a Word and Excel object. Where they diverge, I will point out their differences, but suffice it to say, the developer model for each is similar. If you understand one, you understand the other.

Creating a Word Document Add-In

For this sample, you will create a Word document VSTO project in Visual Studio. Complete the following steps to build the add-in:

1. Open Visual Studio and open the New Project dialog box.

2. Select the Word Document project template and click the OK button.

3. The Office Project Wizard displays to guide you through creating the add-in project's shell. The first step requires you to either create a new Word document or specify an existing one (see Figure 1-12).

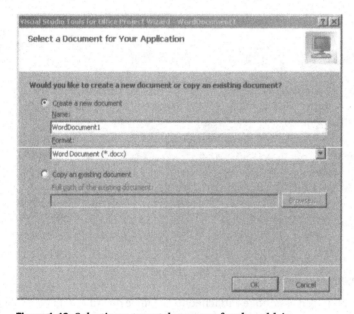

Figure 1-12. *Selecting a target document for the add-in*

If you had an existing document in use by your organization already, you could copy it to the add-in project by selecting the second option and specifying its path. The original would remain where it is, and you would code against a copy.

4. For our purposes, we want to use a new document, so keep the selection with "Create a new document" and click OK. Visual Studio will create the project.

Once created, Visual Studio will display the WordDocument.docx file within a Visual Studio designer (see Figure 1-13). This designer is one of the killer features of developing with VSTO, as it enables Office development from the comfy confines of Visual Studio. You can draw

WinForm controls, data controls, common controls, and more. Anything available to you in a Windows Forms application is available to you as you build document add-ins.

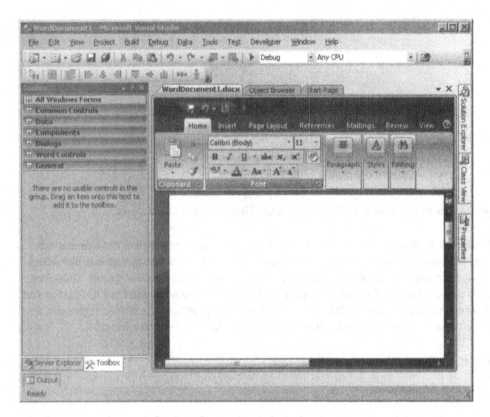

Figure 1-13. *The VSTO document designer for a Word document*

Main Add-In Components

Just like the application add-ins, a VSTO document add-in contains a single stubbed-out class that acts as the entry point for the add-in and serves as the starting point of your customization efforts. Unlike the application add-ins, document add-ins contain either a Word or Excel document (these could be either document or template types) that acts as the target, or *host document.*

The Host Document (WordDocument1.docx) The host document is the target document that the add-in attaches to during runtime. It has the ThisDocument class attached as a child node in Solution Explorer (see Figure 1-14). You can perform all normal Word document functions to build out the document structure as needed. This includes applying formatting, inserting tables, and attaching the XML structure. Since the Ribbon is available within the designer, all Word menus are available.

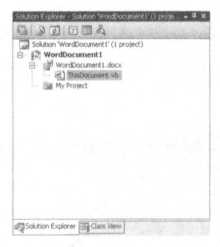

Figure 1-14. *The WordDocument1.docx node with ThisDocument.vb attached*

The ThisDocument Class The ThisDocument class functions almost exactly like the application add-ins' ThisAddin class (see Listing 1-4). It contains two methods for startup and shutdown. This class functions exactly like ThisAddin, except it executes against a document. Therefore, events in this class occur after the host application has already loaded and fired its Startup and Shutdown events. Another key difference is the object type passed in the sender argument. For document add-ins, sender is a reference to the host application (Word or Excel).

Listing 1-4. *A Stubbed-Out ThisDocument Class*

```
Public Class ThisDocument

    Private Sub ThisDocument_Startup(ByVal sender As Object, ByVal e As _
        System.EventArgs) Handles Me.Startup

    End Sub

    Private Sub ThisDocument_Shutdown(ByVal sender As Object, ByVal e As _
        System.EventArgs) Handles Me.Shutdown

    End Sub

End Class
```

These events are the ideal location for code that initializes the object needed by your add-in—for example, menu customizations, data objects, user interfaces, and project-level references to the host application object.

EXCEL'S MAIN DOCUMENT ADD-IN OBJECTS

Following Excel's nomenclature, the main class's name is ThisWorkbook, which represents the entire Excel file and all its contents. In addition, the Worksheet class represents a single tab included in ThisWorkbook. Each of these classes has Startup and Shutdown events that work as you would expect.

Upon starting up the add-in, the ThisWorkbook.Startup method executes. Then, each individual worksheet within the Excel workbook executes its Worksheet.Startup method. The sequence follows the order of worksheets in the physical file—for example, Sheet1, Sheet2, Sheet3, and so on. The shutdown sequence follows the same order as the Startup method.

Custom Document Properties and Manifest Files Instead of registry entries, document add-ins rely on custom document properties named _AssemblyName and _AssemblyLocation. The _AssemblyName stores a Globally Unique Identifier (GUID) string that refers to the entry point of the VSTO loader. The _AssemblyLocation stores the location of the deployment manifest. There isn't anything too special about these properties except for the data they contain. Otherwise, they are just typical document properties that you could create and edit as you would any custom document property. The good news is VSTO handles the creation and editing for you as part of the solution publishing process.

Document add-ins also utilize deployment and application manifests. These function in the same manner as application add-ins with the deployment manifest containing version information and the location of the application manifest. The application manifest contains all the information required to install and run the add-in.

VSTO Runtime Overview

The VSTO runtime performs two functions. First, it provides the set of classes used to extend the host application and host documents with your custom code. The classes included in the runtime are managed assemblies. These assemblies handle all communication between your code and the COM-based Office applications. Assemblies for error handling, caching data offline, and hosting controls in Office documents, as well as those providing VSTO's internal functions, are all part of the runtime. This is true for both application-level and document-level add-ins. (For full details on every VSTO assembly, check out MSDN at http://msdn2.microsoft.com/en-us/library/bb608603(VS.90).aspx.)

Second, the runtime includes a runtime loader that loads the correct version of the VSTO runtime for the executing Office application. For Office 2007–based projects, VSTO utilizes version 3.0 of the VSTO runtime (VSTOEE.dll). Projects targeting Office 2003, however, load the VSTO 2005 SE runtime. That said, solutions originally built for Office 2003 will load in Office 2007, as the VSTO 2005 SE runtime is supported by Office 2007 applications.

In addition to the runtime loader, the VSTO runtime has a solution loader (VSTOLoader.dll) whose job it is to load the solution assembly. The solution loader performs numerous tasks as outlined.

Implementing the IDTExtensibility2 Interface

The IDTExtensibility2 is the COM add-in interface introduced with Office 2000. This interface is still part of the foundation of Office add-ins no matter which technology (Visual Basic 6, .NET, VSTO, Delphi, et al.) you use to develop them. The fact is IDTExtensibility2 (http://msdn2.microsoft.com/en-us/library/extensibility.idtextensibility2(VS.80).aspx) must be implemented for an Office add-in, and the solution loader handles this for you.

Implementing the IManagedAddin Interface

IManagedAddin is a new interface with Office 2007 applications that you must implement for any assembly that loads a managed add-in with Office 2007. The IManagedAddin (http://msdn2.microsoft.com/en-us/library/aa942112(VS.90).aspx) interface exists specifically to work with the VSTO runtime, but since it is an interface, you could theoretically create your own add-in loader.

Creating a Separate Application Domain for the Add-In

One of the main criticisms of Office add-ins built with older technologies (i.e., COM add-ins) was due to the fact that Office add-ins all shared the same application domain. This meant that if one add-in misbehaved and corrupted in memory space, then all other loaded add-ins were taken out as well. VSTO corrects this flaw by loading each VSTO add-in into a separate application domain. This ensures that your solidly architected, well-behaved add-in will remain unaffected by the lesser-built add-ins.

Checking Security Levels

VSTO applications run under a strict model of full trust by the Global Assembly Cache (GAC) in order to execute. The solution loader checks the GAC to determine if the add-in has the appropriate level of permissions to run from its location.

Summary

VSTO is a tool for professional developers building enterprise-level applications with Office 2007. An ideal example of when you would use VSTO is with a business process, where the data within an Office application or document represents an actual business object, such as an invoice, a proposal, or a work order.

VSTO implements two models for building Office add-ins: application-level add-ins and document-level add-ins. Although these two models are similar, their intended use is different. Application-level add-ins attach to the targeted host Office application object and can access all documents and objects. The main class is ThisApplication. Document-level add-ins attach to a single document and work with objects and data within the document. The main class is either ThisDocument or ThisWorkbook (for Word or Excel, respectively).

VSTO provides several features that make building applications with Office more enjoyable. These features bridge the divide between Office and Visual Studio and enable you to work with Office in a manner similar to building Windows Forms–based applications.

■ ■ ■

CHAPTER 2

Getting Started with Excel, Word, and Outlook

Microsoft Office has long supported writing code to automate tasks and processes. As a result, each Office application exposes an object model that allows you to automate via custom code what users can do with the various Office application user interfaces (UIs). In order to be proficient at building add-ins with Visual Studio Tools for the Microsoft Office System (VSTO), you need to have a solid understanding of the main objects you will code against in the Office object models.

This chapter will cover foundational topics that are key to developing with Excel, Word, and Outlook. After reading this chapter, you should have the understanding required to begin working with each of these applications in the context of developing VSTO solutions.

This is a long chapter because it covers three application object models and a plethora of code listings showing how to achieve common tasks in Excel, Word, and Outlook. This chapter will serve as a handy reference you can refer to often as you develop with VSTO.

Getting Started with Excel Programming

Excel 2007 is a powerful tool that you can use to analyze, communicate, and manage information and to make informed decisions. Whether you're publishing a financial forecast for an executive review or providing a business report to an external auditor, Excel 2007 helps you communicate your analysis in professional-looking reports and charts that are easier to create.

Excel is a popular development tool because of its large feature set. It exposes a robust calculation engine, charting capabilities, customizable task panes, and a large object model. You can use VSTO to rapidly develop Excel solutions that support Windows Forms controls and smart tags.

In this chapter, you will learn

- How to iterate through and access workbooks using the Workbooks collection

- How to create a NamedRange object at runtime

- The difference between a NamedRange and a ListObject object

Understanding the Excel Object Model

Excel supports three VSTO project types: workbook, template, and add-in projects. These project types enable you to choose exactly the right option for your VSTO customization. Workbooks and templates are good for specific instance projects, while add-ins let you change the fundamental Excel experience.

One of the great things about Excel spreadsheets is the flexibility available. You can use Excel to pose various *what-if* scenarios with your data and see its corresponding graphical representation. Figures are updated dynamically, so you can see changes without the tedium of calculating them all yourself. Excel also provides a large number of formatting options that can improve the quality of your overall presentation.

All of these features are available to you as a VSTO developer. The Excel objects that you manipulate with VSTO will be familiar to you if you have previous experience using Excel from a user perspective. The Excel objects correspond logically to objects found in the UI. Let's take a look at the main Excel objects that you'll use to build Excel solutions.

Working with the Application Object

The logical starting point for Excel customizations is the Application object. The Application object is the root object within the Excel object model (OM) and provides access to all the other objects in the OM. In addition, the Application object contains the largest number of properties, methods, and events of any object in Excel. You can access all the other Excel objects by qualifying them with *Application* and traversing the object hierarchy as needed.

As you'll see, the Application object also contains a number of global settings that can affect your user's runtime experience. You can also perform basic functionality such as file manipulation and printer activities by using the Application object. Let's begin by taking a look at some of the Application object's most frequently used properties.

FULL OBJECT MODEL EXPLANATIONS AVAILABLE ON MSDN

If you want to take a deep look at the ins and outs of the Excel object model, you can find all the information that you desire on Microsoft Developer Network (MSDN). The full object model is available at http://msdn2.microsoft.com/en-us/library/bb149081.aspx. This link contains documentation for every object available to you when you develop against Excel.

I also suggest visiting the Excel Developer Portal at http://msdn2.microsoft.com/en-us/office/aa905411.aspx. This site is a great place to get started learning additional Excel development topics. For a good example of the content available on any of the Office application development portals, read "Understanding the Excel Object Model from a .NET Developer's Perspective" by Ken Getz (http://msdn.microsoft.com/library/aa168292(office.11).aspx).

Active Objects

The `Application` object has seven properties that return *active* objects. Active objects are objects currently selected or in use while the code executes (see Table 2-1).

Table 2-1. *Excel's Active Objects*

Active Object	Description
ActiveCell	Returns a Range object representing the selected cell
ActiveChart	Returns a chart representing the selected chart
ActivePrinter	Returns or sets the name of the selected printer
ActiveSheet	Returns an object representing the selected sheet
ActiveWindow	Returns a Window object representing the current window
ActiveWorkbook	Returns a Workbook object representing the workbook residing in the ActiveWindow

In each case, the return object is what you would expect (`Cell`, `Chart`, `Printer`, `Sheet`, `Window`, and `Workbook`). These objects provide a convenient way to know where a user is at any given time. For instance, you might want to change the font color of a cell at a given time to provide a visual cue. The following code snippet changes the current cell to red:

```
Application.ActiveCell.Font.Color = vbRed
```

You can also declare variables to hold these objects. Doing so can be a convenient way to avoid typing the fully qualified name each time you access the object in code. For instance, you can create a variable of type `Sheet` and assign the `ActiveSheet` object to it.

```
Dim mySheet as Excel.Sheet
mySheet = Application.ActiveSheet
```

Collection Objects

The `Application` object also has several properties that return `Collection` objects. `Collection` objects provide a convenient way to refer to a related group of items as a single object. The items, or members, in a collection need only be related because they exist in the same collection. Table 2-2 lists some of the most commonly used `Collection` objects in Excel.

Table 2-2. *Excel's Collection Objects*

Collection Object	Object Contained in Collection	Description
Charts	Chart	Returns a Sheets object containing all charts in the ActiveWorkbook
Cells	Cell	Returns a Range object containing all cells in the ActiveWorksheet
Columns	Column	Returns a Range object containing all columns in the ActiveWorksheet
Names	Name	Returns a Names collection containing all names in the ActiveWorkbook
Rows	Row	Returns a Range object containing all rows in the ActiveWorksheet
Sheets	Worksheet or Chart	Returns a Sheets collection containing all sheets in the ActiveWorkbook
Workbooks	Workbook	Returns a Workbooks collection containing all open workbooks
Worksheets	Worksheet	Returns a Sheets collection containing all worksheets in the ActiveWorkbook

Each Collection object contains one or more items of their kind (for example, the Charts collection contains one or more Chart objects, the Cells collection contains one or more Cell objects, and so forth). Two exceptions do exist: the Worksheets collection contains only Worksheet objects, and the Sheets collection contains sheets of any type.

A Collection object provides access to all the items it contains, allowing you to iterate through the collection items and perform actions against several objects at one time. For example, you can use the Workbooks collection to execute your custom code against all files open in Excel, as shown in Listing 2-1.

Listing 2-1. *Looping Through the Worksheets Collection*

```
Dim objSingleWorksheet As Excel.Worksheet
For Each objSingleWorksheet In Globals.ThisWorkbook.Worksheets
 'Your code here
Next objSingleWorksheet
```

The Globals Class and Excel Host Items

VSTO provides easy access to all host items contained within the add-in. Host items are the host application or the host document as well as any controls included in the add-in project. The Globals class is static and instantiates during the add-in's initialization.

For Excel, the Globals class includes the host items listed as follows.

ThisWorkbook

You use ThisWorkbook to gain access to a document-level add-in's target workbook. You can access the workbook from anywhere within the add-in with a call to Globals.ThisWorkbook.

Sheetx

The Globals class provides access to each sheet in a workbook by name. For example, a call to a worksheet named Sheet1 would be Globals.Sheet1. If the name were MyCustomSheet, the call would be Globals.Sheet1.

ThisApplication

ThisApplication provides access to an application-level add-in's target host application. You can call Globals.ThisApplication to gain access to all objects within the host's object model.

ThisAddin

ThisAddin is a reference to the VSTO add-in. You can call Globals.ThisAddin to gain access to all objects within the application add-in from anywhere in your code.

The Globals class simplifies calls within the various Office applications' object models by allowing you to access your desired objects without having to know where they reside within the document or application.

Working with a Workbook

I briefly discussed the Workbooks collection in the "Collection Objects" section. Now, let's take a closer look to see how this important object works in practice. A Workbook object is a single element of a Workbooks collection. A Workbook object contains Sheets collections, which contain Sheet objects. The Sheet object can contain any of the supported Excel Sheet objects.

Each code snippet in this section should be placed in the Excel workbook VSTO project's ThisWorkbook_Startup method. The remainder of the chapter contains several code snippets intended to teach you how to work with Excel's more commonly used objects. Before you read these sections, create a new Excel workbvtook VSTO project with Visual Studio.

Creating a New Workbook

Creating a new workbook requires a call to the Add method of the Workbooks collection:

```
Application.Workbooks.Add([Template])
```

The Add method accepts an optional Template argument that allows you to specify the location of an existing Excel template to use as the basis for the new workbook. If you omit the Template argument, the method will add a blank workbook to the Workbooks collection.

The Template argument also accepts Excel constant values that represent the different sheet types. The syntax is as follows:

```
Application.Workbooks.Add(Excel.xlWBATemplate.SheetType)
```

WHAT'S NEW IN EXCEL 2007

Before diving deep into Excel programming, it's worth pointing out some of the new features introduced with Excel 2007. Excel is one of the Office applications utilizing the new, *results-oriented* Office Fluent User Interface (Fluent UI). The new Fluent UI receives most of the attention, but Excel includes many powerful updates and features.

Increased Spreadsheet Real Estate

Excel 2007 now supports more rows and columns—another improvement that is sure to please those who work with large amounts of data. Excel 2007 supports up to 1 million rows and 16,000 columns per worksheet. Specifically, the Excel 2007 grid is 1,048,576 rows by 16,384 columns, which provides you with 1,500% more rows and 6,300% more columns than you had available in Excel 2003.

Simplified Formatting

Excel 2007 supports more themes and lets you view them on the fly. It also has greatly improved support for working with multidimensional databases, such as SQL Server Analysis Services. New cube functions are used to extract Online Analytical Processing (OLAP) data (sets and values) from Analysis Services and display it in a cell. OLAP formulas can be generated when you convert pivot-table formulas to cell formulas or when you use AutoComplete for cube function arguments when you type formulas.

Enhanced Charting Capabilities

The Chart object has been expanded and is now truly shared between all the different applications in Office. Pivot tables are now much easier to use than in earlier versions of Excel. Pivot charts also went through an upgrade process and are much easier to create. All of the filtering improvements are also available for pivot charts. When you create a pivot chart, specific pivot chart tools and context menus are available so that you can analyze the data in the chart.

Simplified Database Management

Excel 2007 introduces a new database feature called *Quicklaunch*, which allows you to select from a list of data sources so that you no longer need to know exact names to connect to databases. It also introduces a new file format known as the Office Open XML format. Finally, you can save an Excel workbook as a PDF or XPS file from an Office 2007 system program only after you install an add-in, which is available at http://www.microsoft.com/downloads/details.aspx?FamilyID=4d951911-3e7e-4ae6-b059-a2e79ed87041.

These are just some of the new features introduced in Excel 2007. Most of these features are also available for your VSTO projects.

Sheet types reside within the XLWBATemplate class within the Excel namespace. To create a blank worksheet, use this syntax:

```
Application.Workbooks.Add()
```

To create a new worksheet from a template residing at a specific file location (for example, `C:\Templates\Budget.xlt`), use this syntax:

```
Application.Workbooks.Add("C:\Templates\Budget.xlt")
```

To create a new workbook using one of the `xlWBATemplate` constants (in this case, the `Chart` constant), follow this syntax:

```
Application.Workbooks.Add(Excel.XLWBATemplate.xlWBATChart)
```

After your code creates the new workbook, it becomes the `ActiveWorkbook` object, and you can access it directly from the `Application` object (`Application.ActiveDocument`).

REAL-WORLD SCENARIO: FINDING EXCEL CONSTANTS FOR USE WITHIN VSTO

I frequently find it difficult within Visual Studio to discover where a particular constant resides within the Excel object model (or any Office application's object model). It could be due to my Visual Basic for Applications (VBA) roots, but I find it easier to open Excel's Visual Basic Editor and use its Object Browser to search for the class that contains the constants that I need. Once found, I can either access them directly within VSTO (for example, `Excel.XLWBATemplate.SheetType`), or I can add them to the namespace declaration by using the `Imports` keyword. If you experience trouble finding Office objects within Visual Studio, don't be afraid to open the related Office application's VB Editor to search for them.

Saving a Workbook

As with any file, three situations exist for saving. One: you have a new file and the Save method requires you to provide a file name and location before you output the file to the file system. Two: you have an existing file with a known name and location, and all that is required is for the file to write its contents back to the file system. Three: you have an existing file, but you want to create a copy of it with a new name and file system location.

If this is the first time saving your workbook or if you want to save a copy of the open workbook, call the `SaveAs` method of the workbook.

```
Globals.ThisWorkbook.SaveAs("C:\Book1.xml", _
    FileFormat:=Excel.XlFileFormat.xlXMLSpreadsheet)
```

Simply saving an existing file requires the following syntax:

```
Globals.ThisWorkbook.Save()
```

Opening a Workbook

You can use the `Workbooks` collection's `Open` method to open an existing workbook. This method returns a `Workbook` object that represents the file you told Excel to open. The `Open` method only requires a single parameter—the name of the file to open.

```
Application.Workbooks.Open(C:\Book1.xlsx)
```

Thirteen optional parameters exist in addition to the required file name. The parameters allow you to open a file as read-only, specify the way links within the file are treated, and specify passwords when opening protected workbooks.

Closing a Workbook

You can use the Workbooks collection's Close method to close an existing workbook. This method closes the specified Workbook object and does not require any parameters.

```
Globals.ThisWorkbook.Close()
```

The Close method contains two optional parameters of note: SaveChanges and FileName. SaveChanges is a Variant type used to specify if changes should be saved or discarded. FileName is also a Variant type that you can use to specify the file name and location for saving (assuming you specified SaveChanges = true). The syntax for these two options variables is as follows:

```
Globals.ThisWorkbook.Close(SaveChanges:=False, _
    Filename:="C:\Book1.xlsx")
```

This method saves the host workbook. If no changes are made to the document, then the SaveChanges parameter has no effect.

Protecting and Unprotecting a Workbook

You can prevent users from changing the data or changing the display by using Excel's built-in file protection. Excel provides three ways that you can use the Protect method to protect a workbook.

Requiring a Password to Open the Workbook

Requiring a password is the simplest form of protection. With a single password, you can lock the contents of the workbook. To read and edit the file, users are forced to enter the password when they open the workbook. The syntax for locking a workbook with a password only is as follows:

```
Globals.ThisWorkbook.Protect([Password], [Structure],[Window])
```

Preventing Users from Adding, Deleting, Hiding, and Unhiding Sheets

The Protect method allows you to prevent users from editing the workbook and its contents. This includes preventing them from adding, deleting, and hiding/unhiding sheets. The protection also ensures that the order of sheets in the workbooks is maintained. The syntax for protecting the workbook structure is as follows:

```
Globals.ThisWorkbook.Protect("Password", True)
```

Preventing Users from Changing the Size or Position of Windows

You can use the Protect method to prevent users from resizing workbook windows, thus ensuring that the windows are the same size anytime anyone opens the workbook. The syntax to protect window size and positioning is as follows:

```
Globals.ThisWorkbook.Protect("Password", True, True)
```

A password is not required to protect a workbook. If you omit the password, the workbook will be protected, but the user will be able to unprotect it without needing a password. Also, keep in mind that passwords are case-sensitive, so be sure to store your passwords somewhere safe and secure in case you ever need to refer to them.

Removing protection works in the opposite direction as the Protect method and contains only the Password argument.

```
Globals.ThisWorkbook.Unprotect("Password")
```

Working with Worksheets, Charts, and Sheets

The worksheet is the area in which users do most of their work on a spreadsheet. Each intersection of a column and a row forms a cell that can be identified by its address using the column letter and row number. Examples of the cell address, or cell reference, are A4, B32, and C3.

The name box, shown in Figure 2-1, displays the address for the active cell, which is always surrounded by a thick, dark border. The formula bar (to the right of the name box) is where data appears as you type. You also use the formula bar to edit numeric data, text, and formulas. As soon as you start typing something that looks like a function, the Function Wizard in Excel appears.

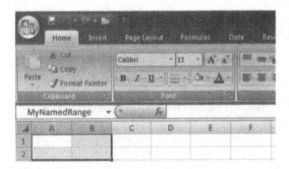

Figure 2-1. *The worksheet's name box*

The Worksheets, Charts, and Sheets collection objects are all remarkably similar. This section covers these three objects together, as the properties and methods are shared across each object. The distinguishing feature of each object is whether it contains a worksheet, a chart, or both. The Sheets collection object is the only type of object that can contain both Worksheet and Chart objects.

Each code snippet in this section should be placed in the Excel workbook VSTO project's Sheet1_Startup method.

Creating New Worksheets or Charts

The Worksheet and Chart objects each have an Add method that you can use to add either worksheets or charts to their respective collections. The Add method has four optional parameters for worksheets and sheets and three for charts. Table 2-3 summarizes these parameters.

Table 2-3. *Workbooks.Add Parameters*

Parameter	Description	Applicable To
Before	Set to either a sheet or chart to which the newly added object should appear before	Worksheet and Chart
After	Set to either a sheet or chart to which the newly added object should appear after	Worksheet and Chart
Count	Set to the number of objects you wish to add	Worksheet and Chart
Type	Set to either a Worksheet or Chart	Worksheet only

Listing 2-2 shows two different ways to use the Add method of the Workbook object. The variable c is defined as a Chart object, while the variable ws is set to a worksheet. In both cases, the Count parameter is used to insert multiples of each object.

Listing 2-2. *Using the Add Method*

```
Private Sub ThisWorkbook_Startup(ByVal sender As Object, _
  ByVal e As System.EventArgs) Handles Me.Startup
        Dim c As Excel.Chart
        Dim ws As Excel.Worksheet
        c = Me.Charts.Add(, , 4)
        ws = Me.Worksheets.Add(, , 3)
End Sub
```

Activating and Hiding Worksheets

Because worksheets reside within a workbook, opening them doesn't really make sense because you can't access them without opening a workbook first. Instead, if your desired worksheet is not visible in the Excel window, you only need to activate it by using the following syntax:

```
Globals.Sheet3.Activate()
```

The Activate method does not have any required or optional parameters. After executing, the specified worksheet becomes the ActiveSheet.

Hiding a worksheet works similarly to activating a worksheet. All that is required is to set the worksheet's Visible property to hidden.

```
Globals.Sheet3.Visible = Excel.XlSheetVisibility.xlSheetHidden
```

Looping Through Worksheets

One of the most common tasks when working with a workbook is to iterate through its Worksheets collection and execute code against each Worksheet object. Fortunately, each of these objects utilizes a GetEnumerator method that allows you to use a For...Each loop. Listing 2-3 shows two examples applicable to each individual type of Sheet object.

Listing 2-3. *Looping Through Sheet Objects*

```
Public Class ThisWorkbook
  Private Sub ThisWorkbook_Startup(ByVal sender As Object, _
    ByVal e As System.EventArgs) Handles Me.Startup
      Dim ws As Excel.Worksheet
      Dim c As Excel.Chart
      For Each ws In Me.Worksheets
        MsgBox(ws.Name)
      Next
      For Each c In Me.Charts
        MsgBox(c.Name)
      Next
  End Sub

  Private Sub ThisWorkbook_Shutdown(ByVal sender As Object, _
    ByVal e As System.EventArgs) Handles Me.Shutdown
  End Sub
End Class
```

Moving Worksheets

You change worksheet positions within Excel workbooks by calling a worksheet's Move method. As shown in Listing 2-4, this method moves the specified worksheet to a new location, either before or after another specified worksheet.

Listing 2-4. *Changing Worksheet Positions Within a Workbook*

```
Private Sub MoveWorksheets()
  Dim allSheetsCount As Integer = _
    Application.ActiveWorkbook.Sheets.Count

  Globals.Sheet1.Move(After:= _
    Globals.ThisWorkbook.Sheets(allSheetsCount))
End Sub
```

This custom method moves Sheet1 to the last position in the workbook. The Move method accepts the Before and After optional arguments. Both arguments are Variant types, and you should pass the name of a worksheet as the argument value.

You cannot use both arguments. If you do, you will receive an error. If you do not pass either, Excel will create a new workbook and move the specified worksheet to it.

Moving Worksheets to a Separate Workbook

If you want to take complete control of how a worksheet moves to a workbook (new or existing), you can use the Move method but include the location of a workbook.

```
Globals.ThisWorkbook.Sheets("Sheet1").Move _
  Before:=Workbooks("Book2").Sheets("Sheet3")
```

As you see, the syntax is similar to moving a worksheet within a workbook. Here, however, the fully qualified reference to the target workbook must be utilized.

Protecting and Unprotecting Worksheets

You are not limited to only protecting the entire workbook. Excel provides worksheet-level protection that operates separately from workbook protection. You can protect a worksheet and leave the entire workbook unprotected. You can also protect worksheets and the workbook independently of each other. The syntax for protecting worksheets is as follows:

```
Globals.Sheet1.Protect("PaSSword",True, True)
```

The syntax for the Protect method is the same for both worksheets and workbooks. When you want to remove protection, call the Unprotect method, as shown here:

```
Globals.ThisWorkbook.Unprotect("PaSSword")
```

The Unprotect method has only the Password argument. It is only needed if the worksheet is password-protected.

Working with Ranges

A *range* is a group of cells within a worksheet. Range objects provide you with the ability to manipulate groups of cells as a single object. In addition, you can give a range a name, enabling you to refer to it in your code by its given name. This type of range is known as a *named range*. Calling a NamedRange object allows you to code against a named range without having to know its Column and Row position within the worksheet (for example, Column A, Row 1—or A1).

Within the Excel UI, you can create a named range by selecting a group of cells and inputting a name for them within Excel's name box (see Figure 2-1). After you create a named range, manipulating the range's cells and values is straightforward.

Each code snippet in this section should be placed in the Excel workbook VSTO project's ThisWorkbook_Startup method.

Adding and Deleting a Named Range

To add a named range at runtime, you call the AddNamedRange method of the worksheet's Controls collection. Listing 2-5 shows the Startup event for a worksheet named Sheet1 and shows how to add a named range when the worksheet initializes at runtime.

Listing 2-5. *The Sheet1_Startup Event Adds a Named Range to a Worksheet*

```
Private Sub Sheet1_Startup(ByVal sender As Object, _
        ByVal e As System.EventArgs) Handles Me.Startup

    Dim objNamedRange As Microsoft.Office.Tools.Excel.NamedRange
    objNamedRange = Me.Controls.AddNamedRange(Me.Range("B10"), _
        "NamedRangeName")
    objNamedRange.Value2 = "Value for Named range"
End Sub
```

In this example, I create a NamedRange object and pass the B10 cell to the AddNamedRange method. In addition, I store a reference to the newly created range and change its value. The syntax for the AddNamedRange method is AddNamedRange (range, name).

The range is a Microsoft.Office.Interop.Excel.Range object. This type is the specialized interoperability Range object that the Office Primary Interop Assemblies (PIAs) provide. The name is the string type and becomes the name of the range after it is created. AddNamedRange requires both arguments.

If you decide you no longer need a range, you can delete it by using the following line of code:

```
Globals.Sheet1.Range("NamedRangeName").Delete()
```

Here you use the Globals class to call the named range residing in Sheet1 and delete it.

Binding a DataTable to a NamedRange

A great feature of NamedRange objects in VSTO is the ability to bind them to a data source. Listing 2-6 shows how to bind a DataTable object to a NamedRange object.

Listing 2-6. *Binding a DataTable to a NamedRange Object*

```
Dim objNamedRange As Microsoft.Office.Tools.Excel.NamedRange
objNamedRange = Me.Controls.AddNamedRange(Me.Range("F1"), "StudentRange")

Dim objDataTable As New DataTable("Test")
    objDataTable.Columns.Add("Subject")
    objDataTable.Columns.Add("Mark")

    objDataTable.Rows.Add("English", 70)
    objDataTable.Rows.Add("Maths", 90)
    objDataTable.Rows.Add("History", 80)

objNamedRange.DataBindings.Add("Value2", objDataTable, _
    "Subject")
```

After creating a named range, you can build a DataTable object and add a few rows. Then call the Add method of the named range's DataBindings collection. The DataBindings collection is the same object available within Windows Forms used to define the relationship between the data and the object presenting the data.

A named range only shows a single record at a time and is not intended for displaying multiple rows.

Working with Lists

A ListObject is a VSTO object that allows you to define a range of worksheet cells as a list. You can access a ListObject directly in code and bind a data source to it. ListObject objects correspond to Excel table objects and are best suited for displaying data sets that contain several rows.

Each code snippet in this section should be placed in the Excel workbook VSTO project's ThisWorkbook_Startup method.

Adding ListObjects to Worksheets

Use the code in Listing 2-7 to add a ListObject to a worksheet.

Listing 2-7. *Adding a ListObject to a Worksheet*

```
'Option 1: Create ListObject first, then add it to
'worksheet by calling AddListObject
Dim objListObj As Microsoft.Office.Tools.Excel.ListObject
objListObj = Globals.Sheet1.Controls.AddListObject(Me.Range("I14", "J16"), _
  "ListObject1")

'Option 2: Call AddListObject and pass a range of cells.
Globals.Sheet1.Controls.AddListObject(Me.Range("$A$1:$D$4"), "ListObject1")
```

In either case, the code adds a new ListObject to the Sheet1 worksheet.

Binding a Data Source to a ListObject

Binding a ListObject to a data source requires setting the ListObject's DataSource property to a valid data object, as shown in Listing 2-8.

Listing 2-8. *Binding Data to a ListObject*

```
Dim objListResult As Microsoft.Office.Tools.Excel.ListObject = _
  Globals.Sheet1.Controls.AddListObject(Globals.Sheet1.Range( _
  "A1:B4"), "MarkSheet")

Dim objDataTable As New DataTable("Test")
objDataTable.Columns.Add("Subject")
objDataTable.Columns.Add("Mark")
```

```
objDataTable.Rows.Add("English", 70)
objDataTable.Rows.Add("Maths", 90)
objDataTable.Rows.Add("History", 80)

objListResult.DataSource = objDataTable
```

You can bind any data source that .NET supports. ListObject objects also support the ability to edit the data in the control. Changes made within the control are written back to the data bound by the object. If you want to prevent edits, you can call the ListObject's Disconnect method after the list fills with data. Doing so disconnects from the bound data source, and any edits only save to the worksheet without affecting the source data.

Excel Summary

This section covered Excel's main objects and how to perform common tasks using VSTO. VSTO-based solutions include using the Globals class, which provides access to the add-in itself. In addition, Globals provides easy access to the Excel Application object from any class in your solution. VSTO also provides host controls that allow you to visually add NamedRange and ListObject objects to an Excel worksheet. These controls allow you to refer to the Range and List they create by name in your Excel solutions.

The next section covers VSTO's support for Word as well as how to use Word objects to perform common Word-related tasks with code.

Getting Started with Word Programming

Microsoft Word 2007 is one of the most powerful and popular word processors ever released. It has an enormous feature set and provides a great deal of flexibility and customization options for the end user; you, the developer, can access almost all of these features by using VSTO. You have access to more than 295 objects (with more than 4,500 properties and methods) at your programming disposal when you start a Word project. To see a comprehensive list of the objects and their relative properties and methods, visit the Word Object Model Reference at http://msdn2.microsoft.com/en-us/library/bb244515.aspx.

In this section, you will learn how to

- Create new documents and open existing documents

- Create Word bookmarks

- Differentiate between built-in document properties and custom document properties

Understanding the Word Object Model

Despite the large number of objects in the Word OM, learning the Word object hierarchy is not too difficult a task. The reason for the low learning curve is that you only need to fully understand a handful of objects to meet most requirements. Let's take a look at the most commonly used properties, methods, and collections of the four most important Word objects:

The Application Object

The Application object represents the Word application and is the parent of all the other objects. Its members usually apply to Word as a whole. You can use its properties and methods to control the Word environment.

The Document Object

The Document object is central to programming Word. When you open an existing document or create a new document, you create a new Document object, which is added to the Word Documents collection. The document that is the focus is called the active document and is represented by the Application object's ActiveDocument property.

The Range Object

The Range object contains a section of a document along with all the content within it. Range objects have a single starting character position and a single ending character position. A single document can have multiple Range objects. Range objects can be anything from a single character to the entire document. In addition, you can create variables to represent a range and have numerous Range variables overlapping within the same document.

The Selection Object

The Selection object represents the area of the document that is currently selected. When you select an area of the document with the Word UI, you are actually setting the boundary of the Selection object. A Selection always exists, and there might only be a single Selection object at any given time. If you or the user don't select anything, the Selection object represents the insertion point where the cursor is located. The Selection object can also be multiple, noncontiguous blocks of text when several different items are highlighted.

Understanding Word Templates and Documents

Every Word document is based on a template. Templates are distinguished in the file system by their extension—either .dot, .dotm, or .dotx, depending on the version of Word. Documents have a .doc, .docm, or .docx extension. Every time you create a new document, it maintains a link to the template Word used to create it. You can change this template association, but a document cannot exist without an accompanying template. In most cases, unless you specify a custom template, Word will create new documents based on the Normal.dotx default template. Office installs this template file during the installation of Word. If you delete the Normal.dotx template, Word will re-create it.

Understanding Global and Document Templates

Word uses two basic types of templates: global templates and document templates. Global templates are available to all documents. The most common global template is the Normal.dotx template. This file is the default template from which all blank documents are created. Document templates contain settings that are available only to documents attached to that template. A document created from a template can use the settings from both the document template as well as the settings available in any global template. Word provides numerous document templates as part of its installation. Good examples of Word's template files are fax cover sheets, letters, and résumés. If the templates Word provides do not suit your needs, you can always find thousands more, available free of charge, with a Google search for *word template*. And if all else fails, you can create your own templates.

Global Templates

Global templates are typically referred to as template add-ins. To use settings from another template, you must either load the other template as a global template or attach a reference to the other template. If you load a template as a global template, items stored in that template will be available to all documents. Figure 2-2 illustrates how a document can access both its associated parent template and numerous potential add-in templates.

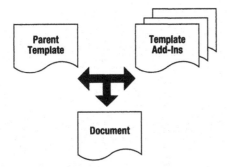

Figure 2-2. *The interaction of documents and templates*

Document Templates

Templates reside within two areas in the New Document dialog box, as shown in Figure 2-3.

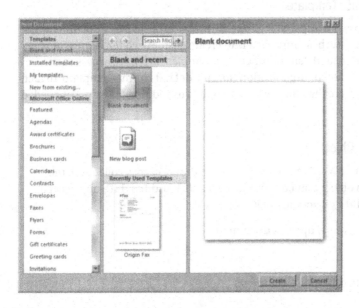

Figure 2-3. *The Word 2007 New Document dialog box*

The "User templates" and "Workgroup templates" directories are specified in Microsoft Office Button ➤ Word Options ➤ Advanced ➤ File Locations. These directories, and any subdirectories that contain templates, appear in Word's New Document dialog box. This directory is the location for any organizational templates. The File Locations dialog box displays templates that appear in both locations, as shown in Figure 2-4.

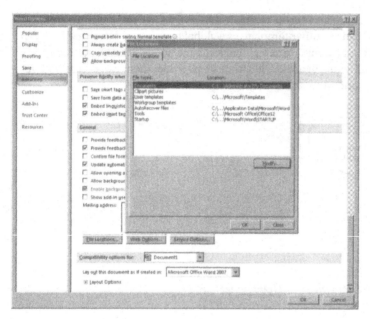

Figure 2-4. *The File Locations dialog box*

Understanding the Normal.dotx Template

The Normal.dotx (Normal) template is global in scope and is available to every document that you create. For VSTO solutions, the best approach is to create customized templates for specific applications. Documents created using your custom template still have access to the settings contained in any corporate- or organization-specific default Normal template. In fact, you can attach a document to more than one custom template in addition to Normal if needed to meet your requirements.

Understanding the Template Object

The Template object represents a Word template. Much like the Documents collection, the Template object is a collection object that contains all available Word Template objects at a given point in time. The Template object includes

- All templates that are currently open as documents

- All global templates

- All templates attached to any open documents

- The Normal template

Templates only have two methods: OpenAsDocument and Save. The OpenAsDocument method is important, as it allows you to access certain properties and methods not available when a template is *acting like a template* (vs. a document created from a template*)*. The following line of code displays the currently attached template of the ActiveDocument object:

```
Msgbox(Application.ActiveDocument.AttachedTemplate())
```

The Template object provides a way for you to work with a Word template. The Template object is the foundation object for a Word document. The Document object is one level beneath the Application object, but is the most utilized object in Word programming.

Using Documents as Templates

You are not limited to templates as containers for customized styles and code. You can also create a Word document project to customize and write code in individual documents without affecting the content of the parent template. When Word invokes your code, it uses the fully qualified reference of the source, so the choice of a Document or Template project is based entirely upon the actual usage rather than a technical limitation of either type.

The Globals Class and Word Host Items

As with Excel workbooks and templates, VSTO supports document-level add-ins for Word documents and templates. In addition, you can use VSTO to build Word application-level add-ins. VSTO provides easy access to all host item objects contained within the add-in through host items and host controls that provide .NET capabilities to their corresponding Component Object Model (COM) objects. The Globals class is the gateway to accessing the host items. For Word, the Globals class includes the host items listed as follows.

ThisDocument

You use ThisDocument to gain access to a document-level add-in's target document. You can access the document from anywhere within the add-in with a call to Globals.ThisDocument.

ThisApplication

ThisApplication provides access to an application-level add-in's target host application. You can call Globals.ThisApplication to gain access to all objects within the host's object model.

ThisAddin

ThisAddin is a reference to the VSTO add-in. You can call Globals.ThisAddin to gain access to all objects within the application add-in from anywhere in your code.

The Globals class simplifies calls within the various Office applications' object models by allowing you to access your desired objects without having to know where they reside within the document or application.

WHAT'S NEW IN WORD 2007

Word 2007 offers a plethora of new features to developers. In addition to the Fluent UI, Word 2007 includes powerful features that can help you build solutions that simplify your users' document-authoring processes.

Improved Control over Document Structure

My favorite new feature is *content controls*. These controls represent blocks of content that you define and position within a Word document. Available content controls include calendar drop-downs, combo boxes, text boxes, drop-down menus, and pictures. You can manipulate content controls by name in your code and even map them to XML data that is contained within the document.

Reusable Content Reduces Effort to Build Documents

Building blocks are another type of content-related control. Building blocks are reusable content blocks that allow you to quickly insert preformatted pieces of content into the current document. Examples of building blocks include cover pages, headers, and footers.

Improved Data Mapping Provides Separation Between a Document's Data and Its Formatting

XML mapping allows you to attach XML data to Word documents and link XML elements to placeholders in the document. Combined with content controls, XML mapping becomes a powerful tool for developers. These features provide you with the capability to position content controls in the document and then link them to XML elements. This type of data and view separation allows you to access Word document data to repurpose and integrate with other systems and applications.

Working with the Application Object

Before looking at the `Application` object, let's create a simple starter project that you can use for building the following code snippets that I discuss in the remainder of this chapter. Follow these steps:

1. Open Visual Studio and create a new Word 2007 Document project. Name the project anything you like, and accept the defaults until you complete the project wizard.

2. Open the `WordDocument1.docx` designer (the file name will be different if you gave your project a different name and did not accept the defaults).

3. Drag a button from the Visual Studio toolbox onto the Word document surface, as shown in Figure 2-5.

4. Create the event stub (a placeholder for event-driven code) for the `Click` event by double-clicking the button within the Visual Studio Integrated Development Environment (IDE). After you double-click the button, you are taken to the `ThisDocument.vb` file, which shows the code shown in Listing 2-9.

Figure 2-5. *A button that resides directly within a Word document*

Listing 2-9. *The ThisDocument Class*

```
Public Class ThisDocument

    Private Sub ThisDocument_Startup(ByVal sender As Object, _
    ByVal e As System.EventArgs) Handles Me.Startup

    End Sub

    Private Sub ThisDocument_Shutdown(ByVal sender As _
        Object, ByVal e As System.EventArgs) Handles Me.Shutdown

    End Sub

    Private Sub Button1_Click(ByVal sender As System.Object, _
        ByVal e As System.EventArgs) Handles Button1.Click

        'Your Button1 code will go here

    End Sub
End Class
```

Understanding the ActiveDocument Property

One of the most frequently used starting points when programming against Word is the ActiveDocument property of the Application object. This property returns a Document object that represents the currently active document in a Word session. Using this property can be tricky sometimes: keep in mind that what you think might be the current document might not actually be if a user is switching back and forth between documents. The better practice is to control the creation or addition of documents programmatically and then use a Document object variable as the focal point.

To illustrate the simple usage of the ActiveDocument property, enter the code shown in Listing 2-10 behind the Click event that you created in the previous section. This code snippet is subtly different from the similar VBA syntax. In VSTO, you're forced to use the Application qualifier even though ActiveDocument is a global property within Word. In this case, however, you're working outside the context of Word (inside Visual Studio), and you need to qualify your property call. Your Click event should now look like the code shown in Listing 2-10.

Listing 2-10. *The Button1_Click Event*

```
Private Sub Button1_Click(ByVal sender As System.Object, _
  ByVal e As System.EventArgs) Handles Button1.Click
     'your code will go here
     MsgBox(Application.ActiveDocument.Name)
End Sub
```

Now test the sample VSTO project to see the code in action. Press F5 to build the project and open an instance of Word with your document project executing. The button that you've created should be the only item visible on the document. After you press the button, you are greeted with a message box that displays the name of the active document, as shown in Figure 2-6.

Figure 2-6. *Displaying the ActiveDocument.Name property*

Creating a New Document Object

You create new Document objects by accessing the Application object's Documents collection and adding a new Document to the collection.

```
Dim objNewWordDoc As Word.Document
objNewWordDoc = Application.Documents.Add()
```

You can pass the location of a template file, and the Add method creates a new document based on the specified template.

Opening a Document

You also use the Documents collection to open an existing document. The Open method requires you to pass a FileName parameter, as the following code shows:

```
Application.Documents.Open("C:\Specify Your Path\Filename.docx")
```

After it opens, the document becomes an item in the Documents collection. Keep in mind that the file path must be valid or Word will raise an error.

Saving a Document

To save a document, call the ActiveDocument object's Save method if you want to save the currently active document.

```
Application.ActiveDocument.Save()
```

You can also call the Documents collection's Save method and pass either the Document object's file name or index to identify it as the document to save.

```
Application.Documents("Specify File Name").Save()
Application.Documents(1).Save()
```

Closing a Document

You close a document by calling the Application.ActiveDocument.Close method. Because VSTO provides access to the document through the Me object, you can close a VSTO targeted document with the following code snippet:

```
Me.Close()
```

For application add-ins, you can call the Close method of the ActiveDocument object or of the Documents collection:

```
Application.ActiveDocument.Close()
Application.Documents(1).Close()
```

The Close method allows you to specify if you want to save changes automatically, discard changes, or prompt the user to decide upon closing by passing the appropriate constant (wdSaveChanges, wdDoNotSaveChanges, or wdPromptToSaveChanges) to the SaveChanges argument.

Working with the Document Object

The Document object represents a Word document and resides inside the Documents collection that represents all open documents at a given point in time. You can access members of a collection by name or by the index value. You can also iterate over the entire Documents collection easily by using a For…Each loop. You really can't get deep into Word programming by using the Application object alone. The Document object is so fundamental to Word programming that you really can't avoid using it. You need to understand the basics such as adding, deleting, opening, and accessing documents just to get by. In this section, I cover the basics of the Document object's most commonly used objects and properties.

Using Bookmarks as Placeholders

The Word bookmark is a name associated with a specific range of text or a single insertion point. This distinction is perhaps the most important thing to understand when working with bookmarks. Word has two types of bookmarks: *placeholder* bookmarks and *enclosure* bookmarks. When working with bookmarks, you want to turn on the display of bookmarks. Follow these steps to enable bookmark displaying:

1. Open the Word Options dialog box (Microsoft Office Button ➤ Word Options).

2. Select the Advanced section on the left side of the dialog box and scroll down to the "Show document content" section, as shown in Figure 2-7.

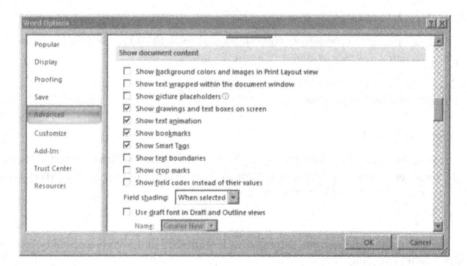

Figure 2-7. *The "Show document content" section of the Word Options dialog box*

3. Check the "Show bookmarks" check box and click OK.

Enabling bookmark visibility makes it easier to see what's actually happening as a result of your code.

Placeholder bookmarks look like a beam, while enclosure bookmarks appear enclosed in square brackets. The following line illustrates a simple use of the bookmark for document assembly. You can set the Text property of a bookmark's Range object to insert text at the bookmark's location, as shown here:

```
Application.ActiveDocument.Bookmarks("name").Range.Text = "Paul Hewson"
```

You can add a bookmark to the Bookmarks collection by using the following syntax:

```
Application.[Document].Bookmarks.Add(Name, Range)
```

Bookmarks are probably the most utilized method of programmatically inserting text into a document. Bookmarks are flexible in that they can mark either a single insertion point or an entire paragraph (or more) if necessary. If you're using bookmarks as placeholders for dynamic text in a boilerplate document, you'll want to create a subroutine that inserts the appropriate text so that you don't have to write unnecessary code each time you want to insert text.

The best way to insert text at a bookmark without losing the bookmark is to set a range variable to the bookmark's range. Listing 2-11 provides an UpdateBookmark procedure that you can utilize to insert text into a document. The function takes the name of the bookmark and the text to be inserted as parameters.

Listing 2-11. *Sample UpdateBookmark Procedure*

```
Sub UpdateBookmark(ByVal bookmarkName As String, ByVal insertText As String)
    Dim rngBookmark As Word.Range
    rngBookmark = Application.ActiveDocument.Bookmarks(bookmarkName).Range
    rngBookmark.Text = insertText
    Application.ActiveDocument.Bookmarks.Add(bookmarkName, rngBookmark)
End Sub
```

This procedure works well if you know that the bookmark parameter is valid (that it actually occurs in the document). The Exists method is the appropriate method to check for the existence of a given bookmark. If you attempt to access bookmarks that do not exist, you will trigger an error. The Exists method follows a simple syntax, so you could use the conditional statement shown in Listing 2-12 to update the UpdateBookmark procedure.

Listing 2-12. *Updating the Bookmark*

```
If Application.ActiveDocument.Bookmarks(bookmarkName).Exists Then
'code to execute
End If
```

Using the BuiltInDocumentProperties Object

The purpose of document properties is to provide a common way to describe any document. Document properties are details, or *metadata*, about a file that help identify it, such as a descriptive title, the author's name, the subject, and keywords that identify topics or other important information in the file. Custom properties extend this functionality by allowing you to define your own properties.

Document properties belong to the following four main property categories:

- *Automatically updated properties*: These include statistics that Office programs maintain for you, such as file size and the dates that files were created and last modified.

- *Preset properties*: These already exist (such as author, title, and subject), but you must add a text value.

- *Custom properties*: These are properties that you define. You can assign a text, time, or numeric value to custom properties, and you can assign them the values yes or no. You can choose from a list of suggested names or define your own.

- *Document library properties*: These are for files in a document library on a web site or public folder. When you design a document library, you define one or more document library properties and set rules on their values.

Listing 2-13 illustrates how to use the BuiltInDocumentProperties object to display the list of authors for each document in a given directory.

Listing 2-13. *Displaying a List of Authors*

```
Private Sub Button1_Click(ByVal sender As System.Object, _
  ByVal e As System.EventArgs) Handles Button1.Click
    'your code will go here
    Dim sDir As String = "C:\mastering_office_vsto\c06\testdocs\"
    Dim dDir As New System.IO.DirectoryInfo(sDir)
    Dim docFile As System.IO.FileInfo
    Dim s As String
    For Each docFile In dDir.GetFiles()
        Dim tempDoc As New Word.Document
        tempDoc = wrdApp.Documents.Open(sDir & docFile.Name, False, True)
        s = s & vbNewLine & tempDoc.BuiltInDocumentProperties( _
          Word.WdBuiltInProperty.wdPropertyAuthor).Value
    Next
    MsgBox(s)
End Sub
```

You might need to edit the path defined in the sDir string to match the actual location on your system. If you download the companion files and install them to their default location, you should be able to run this code in your current project and see the message box that Figure 2-8 displays.

Figure 2-8. *A message box that displays the built-in Author property for multiple documents*

In this example, the sDir variable holds a hard-coded path to the test documents. You use a fully qualified call to the System.IO.DirectoryInfo class and iterate the files in that directory using a For…Each loop. The results are concatenated into a single string variable using the vbNewLine constant to display a list. As you can see, you must programmatically open the Document object in order to access the BuiltInDocumentProperties object.

Several different constants are associated with the BuiltInDocumentProperties collection. Keep in mind that these properties are different from the CustomDocumentProperties and use the appropriate object for your organization. The syntax and behavior of the two objects are similar, except that CustomDocumentProperties uses an arbitrary name, while BuiltInDocumentProperties uses predefined constants. Table 2-4 shows the constants that Word uses.

Table 2-4. *The BuiltInDocumentProperties Constants*

Member Name	Description
wdPropertyAppName	The name of the Office application
wdPropertyAuthor	The document author
wdPropertyBytes	The size of the document measured in bytes
wdPropertyCategory	The document category
wdPropertyCharacters	The number of characters in the document
wdPropertyCharsWSpaces	The number of characters in the document including spaces
wdPropertyComments	The document comments
wdPropertyCompany	The company name of the document author
wdPropertyKeywords	The listing of metadata keywords used to categorize the document
wdPropertyLastAuthor	The name of the last author to edit the document
wdPropertyLines	The number of lines in the document
wdPropertyManager	The name of the author's manager
wdPropertyNotes	The document notes

Member Name	Description
wdPropertyPages	The number of pages in the document
wdPropertyParas	The number of paragraphs in the document
wdPropertyRevision	The document's revision number
wdPropertySecurity	The document's security setting
wdPropertySubject	The document subject
wdPropertyTemplate	The attached template file name
wdPropertyTimeCreated	The time and date that represent when the document was created
wdPropertyTimeLastPrinted	The time and date that represent the last printing
wdPropertyTimeLastSaved	The time and date that represent the last save
wdPropertyTitle	The document's title
wdPropertyWords	The number of words in the document

DOCUMENT PROPERTIES IN THE REAL WORLD

My company has a law firm as a client. This firm had grown exponentially over the years, but it had never instituted a document management system. Word documents were scattered over the entire network. Each attorney named, stored, and versioned a document differently. Some attorneys used simple templates, and some used none and at all, preferring to cut and paste documents together from scratch each time the need arose.

After several years (and the departure of several attorneys), the firm wanted to clean up its files and get an accurate listing of the documents that existed on the network. Fortunately, most users preferred the network to their desktops, as the network was routinely archived. This way, they could avoid the costly loss of time if their desktop failed.

It was relatively easy to write a recursive routine to traverse the network and search for the appropriate file extensions. It was not easy, however, to create and destroy a document variable each time a document was found. The program could trace the network structure in a matter of minutes. When we introduced the code to instantiate a Document object and retrieve built-in and custom document properties as well as run several search functions, the time the program required to run exploded exponentially.

We finally convinced the law firm to work with a smaller set of data and use the file system to retrieve basic information about the file. Our suggestion provided the starting point for the project. We were able to deliver a solution that could quickly identify and retrieve the desired files by searching a small collection of properties. This situation illustrates that although something might be technically feasible, it might not make sense in the larger scheme of things.

Using Custom Document Properties

Custom document properties look and function much like built-in properties except that they belong to a document's CustomDocumentProperties collection. Custom document properties are useful anytime you need to track additional information not included as part of the built-in property collection. A great scenario for custom property usage is a professional services company that desires to track documents by client and project. You can track additional information by implementing custom properties. Listing 2-14 shows how to create a custom property in Word.

Listing 2-14. *Creating a Custom Property*

```
Dim objCustomProps As Object
Dim tempStr As String
'Get the CustomDocumentProperties collection.
    objCustomProps = Globals.ThisDocument.CustomDocumentProperties
'Added a custom property
objCustomProps.Add("MyCustomProperty", False, _
  Office.MsoDocProperties.msoPropertyTypeString, _
  "MyCustomDataForProperty")
```

Listing 2-15 shows how to delete a custom property in Word.

Listing 2-15. *Deleting a Custom Property*

```
Dim objBuiltInProps As Object
Dim objCustomProps As Object
Dim tempStr As String
'Get the CustomDocumentProperties collection.
objCustomProps = Globals.ThisDocument.CustomDocumentProperties
'Delete the Custom Document Property.
objCustomProps.Item("MyCustomProperty").Delete()
```

In both examples, you use the Globals class to navigate to the add-in document's CustomDocumentProperties collection. Adding a new property requires calling the Add method of the collection and providing a property name, data type, and value. Deleting a custom property requires passing the name of the custom property to be deleted as the index of the CustomDocumentProperties collection.

Using the Fields Collection

The most robust set of items available to a Word document is the Fields collection. The Field object represents an individual field in a Word document, while the Fields property returns a Fields collection that contains all of the fields that currently exist in a document.

You can use fields in much the same manner as bookmarks for inserting text into a document. These fields also populate information without requiring you to write code. Take the Date field for instance. You can use it to easily add the current date to a document without writing a single line of Visual Basic.

You can also use fields to build intelligence into the document by using conditional statements. This technique covers adding additional documents, if necessary, and using language dependencies. Table 2-5 shows the methods associated with Word Field objects.

Table 2-5. *Methods of the Word Field Object*

Method Name	Description
Select	Selects a field in the document. This method returns a Selection object, which represents the document's current selection.
Copy	Places a copy of the field contents to the Windows clipboard that makes the Field object.
Cut	Creates a copy of the field on the clipboard and removes the field from the document.
Delete	Deletes a field in the document.
DoClick	Performs the equivalent of a click from the document user. You can use this method to move the document insertion point, trigger a macro, or jump to a link within the document.
Unlink	Replaces a field with its current value and removes the Field object. Once unlinked, a field no longer supports updating.
Update	Performs an update of the specified field.
UpdateSource	Updates the source file that the field displays in the document. This method is for IncludeText fields only. This type of field displays text from a separate text file within the document.

Table 2-6 shows the properties associated with Word Field objects.

Table 2-6. *Popular Properties of the Word Field Object*

Property Name	Description
Kind	Specifies what type of link the field contains: Cold, Hot, None, or Warm. A Cold field doesn't have a result. A Hot field does have a result and updates automatically anytime it becomes visible. A None field doesn't have valid results (for example, it might be blank). A Warm field has a result and can be updated either automatically or manually.
Locked	Specifies if the field can or cannot receive updates.
Result	The field's result. This property returns a Word Range object, and you can access a Field object's results by using the returned Range object's Text property.
ShowCodes	Specifies if the field displays its field code or its field results.

Adding Fields

You can add a `Field` object to a document by using the `Add` method of the `Fields` collection. The syntax is straightforward with the following two notes: (1) the `Type` parameter is the type of field as defined by the `Word.WdFieldType` constant, and (2) the optional `Text` parameter is any additional text necessary for a particular field. `PreserveFormatting` is set to `True` to have the formatting preserved when the field is inserted.

```
FieldObject.Add(Range, Type, Text, PreserveFormatting)
```

While adding fields is important, a far more common situation involves the deletion of fields from a document in order to cleanse metadata.

Deleting Fields

Keep in mind that fields are actually metadata, and you must avoid using them to contain sensitive information. If you do use them to contain metadata, make sure that you clear them out before sharing the document with others. Visual Basic does not have an equivalent of the `Replace` method for globally deleting all fields in a document. You can accomplish the same thing by using Visual Basic code, but you must iterate through each `StoryRange` object of the document to delete every field. `StoryRange` objects are a collection of `Range` objects that represent *stories* in a document. Stories are simply a mechanism by which Word organizes a document into its associated components.

Use the sample procedure in Listing 2-16 to delete all of the fields in a document.

Listing 2-16. *The DeleteAllFields Procedure*

```
Sub DeleteAllFields()
    Dim rngDel As Word.Range
    rngDel = Application.ActiveDocument.Range
    Do
        With rngDel.Fields
        While .Count > 0
                .Item(1).Delete()
            End While
        End With
        rngDel = rngDel.NextStoryRange
    Loop Until rngDel Is Nothing
End Sub
```

Now, let's say that you only want to delete a particular type of field. The `DocVariable` field is probably the number-two method of inserting text into a document (behind bookmarks), but `DocVariable` fields can contain a great deal of metadata that is not visible on the *face* of the document. From an end user's perspective, Search and Replace don't work because the `DocVariable` information can be created programmatically and might not exist on the actual document itself. The procedure in Listing 2-17 deletes all `DocVariable` fields in a document.

Listing 2-17. *The DeleteDocVariables Procedure*

```
Sub DeleteDocVariables()
    Dim rngDel As Word.Range
    Dim oFld As Word.Field

    For Each rngDel In Application.ActiveDocument.StoryRanges
        Do
            For Each oFld In rngDel.Fields
                Select Case oFld.Type
                    Case Word.WdFieldType.wdFieldDocVariable
                        oFld.Delete()
                    Case Else
                        'Do nothing
                End Select
            Next
            rngDel = rngDel.NextStoryRange
        Loop Until rngDel Is Nothing
    Next
End Sub
```

Using the FormFields Collection

You can use the FormFields property to return the FormFields collection. Quite a few documents exist out in the world that use FormFields, even though InfoPath and web forms have greatly diminished the value of Word's simple FormFields collection. Listing 2-18 counts the number of text-box form fields in the active document.

Listing 2-18. *Counting the Number of Text-Box Form Fields*

```
Dim count As Integer
    For Each aField In Application.ActiveDocument.FormFields
        If aField.Type = _
            Word.WdFieldType.wdFieldFormTextInput Then count = count + 1
    Next aField
    MsgBox("There are " & count & " text boxes in this document")
```

You can programmatically add a FormField by using the Add method with the FormFields collection. Listing 2-19 adds a check box at the beginning of the active document.

Listing 2-19. *Adding a Check Box*

```
Application.ActiveDocument.FormFields.Add( _
    Range:=ActiveDocument.Range(Start:=0, End:=0), _
    Type:=wdFieldFormCheckBox)
```

Using Shape and InlineShape Objects

Each Word document has two graphical layers: the *text layer* and a *drawing layer*. If you've ever used Adobe Photoshop, you undoubtedly understand virtual layers. If not, think of them as transparent sheets over a white background. A Shape object is a Word object that is placed on the drawing sheet that lies on top of the text sheet.

Shape objects are anchored to a specific range, which results in the often frustrating experience of changing nearby text and inadvertently moving the shape. InlineShape objects, on the other hand, are shapes that are placed onto the text sheet of the document.

Shapes utilize a Z-order property in much the same way as controls on a form. You can use the Z-order to

- Move the shape to the front

- Move the shape to the back

- Move the shape one step forward

- Move the shape one step backward

You can programmatically convert shapes from one type to another. Listing 2-20 converts each inline shape in the active document to a Shape object.

Listing 2-20. *Converting InLineShapes Objects to Shape Objects*

```
For Each iShape In Application.ActiveDocument.InlineShapes
    iShape.ConvertToShape()
Next iShape
```

You can use the New method to create a new picture as an inline shape. You can use the AddPicture and AddOLEObject methods to add pictures or Object Linking and Embedding (OLE) objects and link them to a source file. The Count property for this collection in a document returns the number of items in the main story only. To count items in other stories, use the collection with the Range object. When you open a document created in an earlier version of Word, pictures are converted to inline shapes.

Using the Paragraphs Collection

The Paragraphs collection is one of the most convenient mechanisms when you work with the organization or structure of a Word document. You can add paragraphs programmatically, or you can manipulate their text by using either the Range or the Selection objects.

Word also provides *styles* to format both paragraphs and individual characters in your document. These styles can greatly simplify the consistent application of formatting across an entire document. You might need to determine the name of the style that is applied to a particular paragraph. You can do that by using the Style property with a Paragraph object, where (i) represents the numeric identifier of an individual paragraph in the Paragraphs collections.

```
sStyle = Application.ActiveDocument.Paragraphs(i).Style
```

You can achieve useful tasks in code that have no Word UI equivalent. For instance, let's say a user wants to find all bulleted paragraphs in a lengthy document. This task seems easy enough, but you cannot use Word's search feature to find bulleted paragraphs. Word doesn't provide a way to search for a *bulleted* attribute. Word also doesn't allow you to search for the actual bullet character.

One approach is to make sure that you always use styles to apply your bullets to paragraphs. This approach allows you to quickly search for paragraphs formatted with a specific style. Listing 2-21 provides a quick mechanism to search for the first occurrence of such paragraphs and take the user directly to it. You'll see how you can easily extend this type of functionality to match your needs.

Listing 2-21. *Finding Bulleted Paragraphs*

```
Sub FindBulletedParagraphs()
    Dim rngTarget As Word.Range
    Dim oPara As Word.Paragraph

    rngTarget = Application.ActiveDocument.Range
    With rngTarget
        Call .Collapse(Word.WdCollapseDirection.wdCollapseEnd)
        .End = Application.ActiveDocument.Range.End

        For Each oPara In .Paragraphs
            If oPara.Range.ListFormat.ListType = Word.WdListType.wdListBullet Then
                oPara.Range.Select()
                Exit For
            End If
        Next
    End With
End Sub
```

Working with the Range Object

Word solutions often utilize more than one Range object at a time. You can create Range type variables, and they can even overlap if necessary. (However, this isn't a good practice, because it's prone to causing unintended results.) This is one of the advantages the Range object has over the Selection object. Only one Selection object can exist at any given time. (Actually, it is one per window pane, but working with multiple window panes is uncommon.)

You have numerous methods of accessing a Range object. Table 2-7 shows the common ways of creating a Range object. In the following sections, I'll show you how to create a Range object and then utilize it to perform common tasks, such as inserting text and applying formatting.

Table 2-7. *Ways to Retrieve a Range Object*

Range Object	Description	Code Example
Characters, words, sentences, and paragraphs	Each of these provides a Range property.	`ActiveDocument.Paragraphs(Index).Range()`
`ConvertToText` method	This method belongs to the Table object and some of its children. It returns a Range object that represents the resultant text.	`ActiveDocument.Tables(Index).ConvertToText()`
Entire document	Range is a child of a Document object and can return a Range that consists of the document as a whole.	`ActiveDocument.Range()`
`Field` object	Using either Code or Result returns a Range object.	`ActiveDocument.Fields(Index).Code()` `ActiveDocument.Fields(Index).Result()`
`Find` object	This is a method of the Range object. If executed successfully, a Range object will be returned.	`ActiveDocument.Range.Find()`
`FormattedText` property	This property returns a Range object that represents both the formatting and the text of a particular object.	`ActiveDocument.Range.FormattedText()`
`GoTo` method	This is a Range object method. It returns a Range object that corresponds with the insertion point of the GoTo result.	`ActiveDocument.Range.GoTo(What, Which, Count, Name)`
`Range` method and `Range` property	Both of these return a Range object for the parent object that calls them.	`ObjectType.Range()`
`TextRange` property	This property belongs to the `TextFrame` object associated with an Office Shape object.	`ActiveDocument.Shapes(Index).TextFrame.TextRange()`

Inserting Text with the Range Object

The Range object provides a great way to insert text into a document. You can set the Range.Text property as well as retrieve it. When you insert text with this method, you probably want to make sure that the range represents a single insertion point in the document; otherwise, it will replace the entire range that you chose. You can easily move to the beginning or end of a Range object by using the Collapse method.

```
Range.Collapse(Direction)
```

As you'll see, Word provides several ways to accomplish essentially the same thing. For example, the Insert method can provide similar results. The Collapse method allows you to collapse to either the end or start of the current range by using the following constants:

```
Word.WdCollapseDirection.wdCollapseStart
Word.WdCollapseDirection.wdCollapseEnd
```

After you collapse the Range object, you can use a variable assignment to the Text property to insert the text that you choose. Let's take a look at this in the context of the project that you created earlier in the chapter. Follow these steps:

1. With this chapter's project open, add a new button to the WordDocument1.docx canvas.

2. Enter the code as shown in Listing 2-22.

Listing 2-22. *Using the Range Object*

```
Private Sub Button1_Click(ByVal sender As System.Object, _
  ByVal e As System.EventArgs) Handles Button1.Click
        'your code will go here
        Dim rngDoc As Word.Range
        rngDoc = Application.ActiveDocument.Range
        rngDoc.Collapse(Word.WdCollapseDirection.wdCollapseStart)
        rngDoc.Text = "VSTO Document Assembly" & Chr(13)
    End Sub
```

This code declares a Range variable and assigns the ActiveDocument.Range object to it. The assignment causes the variable to contain the entire document. You can then either collapse the range to the back or move its start position and assign some text to the variable's Text property.

3. Run the code; you should see something similar to that shown in Figure 2-9. For fun, you can comment out the line that collapses the range and run the code. The entire document will be replaced—even the button that you created in the IDE.

Figure 2-9. *Text inserted within a Range object*

Setting the Bold, Italic, and Underline Properties

Most of the properties that I'm discussing apply to both the Range and Selection objects. However, the Range object has a few format-related properties that the Selection object does not have. Both objects have a Font object that you can use to control the font details, but the Range object can also access the Bold, Italic, and Underline properties directly.

You can set the Bold and Italic properties to True, False, or Word. The return value for Bold and Italic can be True, False, or Undefined (if there is a mixture in the current range).

The Underline property has several associated constants:

- wdUnderlineDash

- wdUnderlineDashHeavy

- wdUnderlineDashLong

- wdUnderlineDashLongHeavy

- wdUnderlineDotDash

- wdUnderlineDotDashHeavy

- wdUnderlineDotDotDash

- wdUnderlineDotDotDashHeavy

- wdUnderlineDotted

- wdUnderlineDottedHeavy

- wdUnderlineDouble

- wdUnderlineNone

- wdUnderlineSingle

- wdUnderlineThick

- wdUnderlineWavy

- wdUnderlineWavyDouble

- wdUnderlineWavyHeavy

- wdUnderlineWords

The following code snippet and Figure 2-10 demonstrate how to apply the different possible values for underlining:

```
oPara.Range.Underline = Word.WdUnderline.wdUnderlineDashLong
```

Notice that these same options are available when you work through the Word UI.

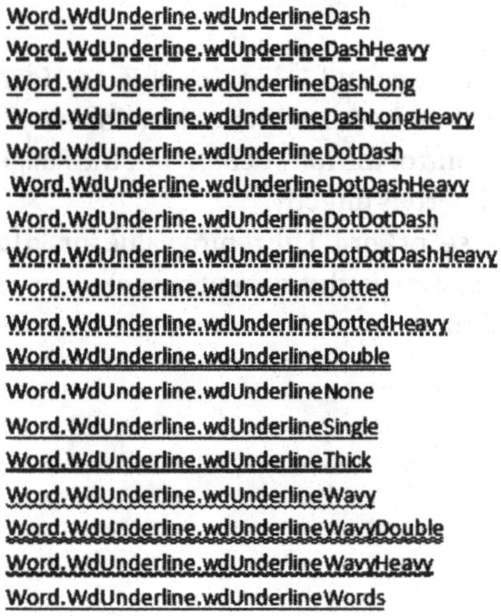

Word.WdUnderline.wdUnderlineDash
Word.WdUnderline.wdUnderlineDashHeavy
Word.WdUnderline.wdUnderlineDashLong
Word.WdUnderline.wdUnderlineDashLongHeavy
Word.WdUnderline.wdUnderlineDotDash
Word.WdUnderline.wdUnderlineDotDashHeavy
Word.WdUnderline.wdUnderlineDotDotDash
Word.WdUnderline.wdUnderlineDotDotDashHeavy
Word.WdUnderline.wdUnderlineDotted
Word.WdUnderline.wdUnderlineDottedHeavy
Word.WdUnderline.wdUnderlineDouble
Word.WdUnderline.wdUnderlineNone
Word.WdUnderline.wdUnderlineSingle
Word.WdUnderline.wdUnderlineThick
Word.WdUnderline.wdUnderlineWavy
Word.WdUnderline.wdUnderlineWavyDouble
Word.WdUnderline.wdUnderlineWavyHeavy
Word.WdUnderline.wdUnderlineWords

Figure 2-10. *The Underline property's format options*

Accessing Characters, Words, and Sentences

One of the neatest things about working with Word is that an individual character in a Word document is actually an object. Characters, Words, and Sentences are all collection objects in Word. As shown in Listing 2-23, the syntax for accessing each is remarkably simple.

Listing 2-23. *Accessing Characters, Words, and Sentences Collections*

```
Application.ActiveDocument.Range.Characters.[property]
Application.ActiveDocument.Range.Words.[property]
Application.ActiveDocument.Range.Sentences.[property]
```

As Collection objects, these collections can utilize all the typical collection properties. You can access an individual instance of them by using the Item method. You can iterate through them by using a Loop up until the Count is reached. You can also easily access the First and Last properties. The following list gives the general properties and methods of these Collection objects:

- Application
- Count
- Creator
- First

- Item

- Last

- Parent

Using the GoTo Methods

Both the Range and Selection objects have a GoTo method. The Document object also has a GoTo method. GoTo returns a Range object that represents the starting position of the GoTo target. The syntax of GoTo is as follows, with Expression being either a Range, Selection, or Document object.

Expression.GoTo(What, Which, Count, Name)

The What parameter identifies the type of object that the GoTo method is trying to find. The following list identifies the constants of the GoTo method. Keep in mind that these constants need to be preceded by the appropriate qualifier (Word.WdGoToItem.[constant]) so that VSTO knows exactly what you are working with.

- *wdGoToBookMark

- wdGoToComment

- wdGoToEndNote

- wdGoToEquation

- wdGoToField

- wdGoToFootnote

- wdGoToGrammaticalError

- wdGoToGraphic

- wdGoToHeading

- wdGoToLine

- wdGoToObject

- wdGoToPage

- wdGoToPercent

- wdGoToProofreadingError

- wdGoToSection

- wdGoToSpellingError

- wdGoToTable

The Which parameter is optional. It identifies the specific target among the potentially numerous items that the previous constants identify. It has six potential constants that help identify the target. The following list shows these constants. These constants are preceded by the curiously named syntax, Word.WdGoToDirection.[constant]. The Count parameter identifies the relative number among a series of potential targets. The Name parameter pertains to those items (Bookmarks, Fields, Comments, and Objects) that have relative names.

- wdGoToAbsolute
- wdGoToFirst
- wdGoToLast
- wdGoToNext
- wdGoToPrevious
- wdGoToRelative

Using the Find Object

One of the most common operations in Word is to search and replace text in the body of a document. Word provides a robust interface that allows your VSTO project to utilize this same functionality. You have several properties to work with when you use the Find method. You might find that it is easier to obtain the correct syntax by recording a macro in VBA and converting the code to Visual Basic syntax.

The actual process of searching for text or formatting is as simple as assigning values to the appropriate Find object properties and launching the Execute object. Keep in mind that Find is an object and not a method. The Find object has 25 properties that you can set for any given search. Listing 2-24 shows the Find object searching for all instances of the word *[Company]* and replacing it with *Microsoft*.

Listing 2-24. *Using the Range's Find Object*

```
Private Sub Button1_Click(ByVal sender As System.Object, _
    ByVal e As System.EventArgs) Handles Button1.Click
        'your code will go here
        Dim rng as Word.Range

        rng.Find.ClearFormatting()
        rng.Find.Replacement.ClearFormatting()
        With rng.Find
            .Text = "[Company]"
            .Replacement.Text = "Microsoft"
            .Forward = True
            .Wrap = wdFindContinue
            .Format = False
            .MatchCase = False
            .MatchWholeWord = False
            .MatchWildcards = False
```

```
        .MatchSoundsLike = False
        .MatchAllWordForms = False
      End With
rng.Find.Execute(Replace:=wdReplaceAll)
```

```
End Sub
```

If you've ever searched for something in Word, you've undoubtedly encountered the Wrap property. In a manual search, you're prompted with a dialog box that mentions that you reached the end of the document and asks you whether you want to continue searching from the beginning. This dialog box is the Wrap property in action. It takes the following constants: wdFindAsk, wdFindContinue, and wdFindStop.

You might not want to actually replace the text that you're searching for. An old Word trick to find the count of all instances of a particular word is to search and replace the same word and see the number of occurrences. Figure 2-11 shows the resultant message box when I searched and replaced the word *the* in the current document. Programmatically, Find returns a Boolean value to show the result of the search. If the search is successful, the Range variable is updated so that it now contains the result of the search. If Find is being used from a Selection object, the selection will be changed (the actual highlighting in the Word document or template will change) to include the results of the search.

Figure 2-11. *Counting instances of a particular word*

Working with the Selection Object

The Selection object is conceptually similar to the Range object, but the procedure for creating a Selection object is a bit different. You can create Selection variables just as you can Range variables, but keep in mind that there can only be one Selection variable at a time. To set the Selection object, use the Select method of the appropriate object (Paragraph, Bookmark, Field, and so on), which sets the Selection object. For instance, Application.ActiveDocument.Select causes the Selection to represent the entire document, just as the Range object did.

The Selection property applies only to the Application, Pane, and Window objects. At first, this restriction might seem a bit strange, but it is because there can only be a single selection at any given point in time (per window). As a practical matter, you'll work with the Application object's Selection object most of the time. Several objects have a Select method, and each one sets the Selection object. The following list shows the objects that have the Select method:

- Bookmark

- Cell

- Column

- Columns

- Document

- Field

- FormField

- Frame

- InlineShape

- MailMergeField

- OLEControl

- PageNumber

- Range

- Row

- Rows

- Selection

- Shape

- ShapeRange

- Subdocuments

- Table

The Selection object has most of the same functionality that I discussed for the Range object. However, the following important differences exist:

- The Selection object can be important when interacting with a user, as it contains whatever the user highlighted.

- The Selection object has the following several sub Select methods that the Range object does not:

  - SelectColumn

  - SelectCurrentAlignment

  - SelectCurrentColor

  - SelectCurrentFont

  - SelectCurrentIndent

  - SelectCurrentSpacing

  - SelectCurrentTabs

  - SelectRow

- The Selection object has the following Type methods that the Range object does not.

  - TypeBackspace

  - TypeParagraph

  - TypeText

Word Summary

This section covered the core objects of the Word object model. As with Excel, the Word-based VSTO solution includes a Globals class that provides access to the VSTO add-in as well as the Application object. VSTO provides host controls for native Word objects like content controls and bookmark controls. And as with the VSTO Excel solutions, these host controls allow you to access the document content by name.

The next section covers Outlook and how to utilize its object model when building Outlook solutions with VSTO.

Getting Started with Outlook Programming

You use Office applications to create different types of files. You use Excel to create spreadsheets, you use Word to create documents, and you use PowerPoint to create presentations. Almost every Office application has an associated file type that serves as the user's creative product. Outlook is the lone exception. Even though Outlook does have associated file types, such as .pst and .ost files, they serve as data storage systems and do not act as typical Office files, such as .docx, .xlsx, and .pptx files.

Microsoft built Outlook to serve as the activity hub for the Office user. By using Outlook, you can manage your e-mail, stay current with your contacts, track notes, manage your calendar, and keep a list of tasks. You can do all of this and much more, thanks to Outlook's customization options.

Given Outlook's multiple purposes, you might have already realized that Outlook stores multiple types of data and is not restricted to only a single type. To begin building applications built with Outlook, it is important to understand how Outlook manages the plethora of data types and objects available to you and the user.

In this section, you will learn

- The purpose of the Explorer and Inspector objects

- How to access the current Outlook session

- How to create default Outlook item objects

Understanding the Outlook Object Model

Outlook's OM is unique among the Office applications, as it is really a type of database that contains several tables and data types. Outlook provides a series of objects to help you manage the data stored within Outlook and automate the user experience (see Figure 2-12). Outlook stores data within a hierarchy of folders, and the folders don't all store the same

Outlook data types. As a result, finding and manipulating your desired item can sometimes be a difficult task.

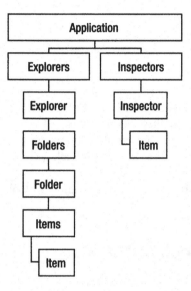

Figure 2-12. *Outlook's core objects*

Like Word and Excel, you can use a small number of key objects to meet the majority of your coding requirements. Five objects provide the Outlook OM foundation for developing with Outlook (see Figure 2-13).

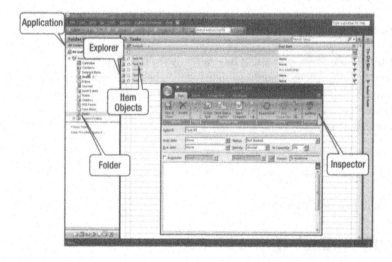

Figure 2-13. *Each of the core Outlook objects as seen in the Outlook UI*

Application Object

The Application object represents the Outlook application (see Figure 2-13). You can utilize this object to perform almost any action that a user can perform with the Outlook UI. Also, as the top-level object in the OM, you can use the Application object as the starting point to traverse the entire OM. This object provides you with access to the Explorer and Inspector objects used for navigating the Outlook folder structure and displaying items. In addition, you use the Application object to create new Outlook items, such as mail, task, contact, and so forth.

Explorer Object

The Explorer object and its parent collection object, Explorers, work a lot like Windows Explorer. You utilize the Explorer object to gain access to a particular Outlook folder and work with the items stored in the folder. This object represents the actual Outlook window that displays all folder items. With the Explorer object, you can change the current folder, change the folder view, filter the view, and more. At any time, you can reference the Explorer displayed in the Outlook UI through the Application.ActiveExplorer property.

Inspector Object

If you *explore* for multiple items at a time, it does make some sense that you *inspect* individual items. The Inspector object represents the active item that is displayed in Outlook. Outlook tracks all individual Inspector objects within the Inspectors collection. Anytime that you create a new task, e-mail, or any Outlook item, the form that you see is an Inspector. The Inspector that receives the user's focus in the UI is the active Inspector and can be accessed through the Application.ActiveInspector property. You can use the Inspector object to manipulate its underlying Outlook item as well as to control its display properties.

Folder Object

A Folder object is a folder. It works like a folder in the Windows file system in that you can store Outlook items and additional folders within it. You use the Folder object to gain access to folder items as well as to perform common folder tasks like copying, moving, and deleting items. Outlook contains a special set of folders known as *default folders*. The default folders are the folders that are specified in Outlook's user settings as the default location for storing each type of Outlook item. The Folder object is the child object of the Folders collection, and you can reference a folder by using the Application.Session.Folders object or the Application.Session.GetDefaultFolder() method.

Item Object

The Item object represents an individual Outlook item. Outlook has several types that will be familiar to you if you've worked with Outlook; MailItem, ContactItem, CalendarItem, and TskItem are the most commonly used. Item objects can contain any of the Outlook item types, such as MailItem, TaskItem, and AppointmentItem. This means that you need to be careful when you access a Folder object's Items property. The Items property returns an Items collection that contains all Item objects that reside in the folder. You need to recast Item objects when enumerating within an Items collection if you want to take advantage of IntelliSense in Visual Studio. Each Item object type provides you with properties and events for the individual item.

INTELLISENSE: THE LIFESAVER FOR THOSE OF US LACKING A PHOTOGRAPHIC MEMORY

IntelliSense provides you with the ability to complete object calls without knowing every property or method an object contains. As you type, Visual Studio provides you with a listing of the object and properties for the current object. You can select the one that you need, and Visual Studio inserts the required text for the call and provides visual cues for any required arguments.

Outlook has one of the largest sets of objects in the Office suite. For a full map of the Outlook object model, go to http://msdn.microsoft.com/en-us/library/bb176619.aspx.

Understanding the ThisAddin and Globals VSTO Classes in Outlook Add-Ins

VSTO provides the ThisAddin class, which represents your Outlook application-level add-in. You have global access to this class from anywhere in your VSTO Outlook add-in through the special VSTO Globals class. In VSTO Outlook projects, Globals is a static class with only one property: ThisAddin. Having this type of access to the add-in's main class makes ThisAddin a great place to add any methods that you want to have access to across your project.

ThisAddin contains a reference to the Outlook Application object as well. Given that the Application object is the root object of the Outlook OM, you will want to use both Globals and ThisAddin frequently to reference Outlook objects.

WHAT'S NEW FOR THE DEVELOPER IN OUTLOOK 2007?

Outlook 2007 provides many new features to the Outlook developer. The new features simplify Outlook add-in development as well as enable scenarios that Microsoft has not supported previously.

Form Regions Simplify Outlook Form Customizations

Outlook form regions provide the long-awaited and much-requested ability to extend the Outlook default forms. You can now create form regions that display additional controls for capturing and displaying custom data elements. For example, you can now capture additional fields specific to your business-related contacts, or you can display related contacts for an opened contact item. The possibilities are limited only by your imagination and business rules. Form regions provide you with the ability to extend a form, add pages to a form, or replace a form in its entirety.

Consolidated Object Model Simplifies Development Tasks

With Outlook 2007, you can finally rely completely on the Outlook OM alone for all development tasks. With previous versions of Outlook, you needed to rely on several libraries, such as Collaboration Data Objects (CDO) and Exchange Client Extensions to perform many e-mail-related tasks. This situation was particularly true when attempting to successfully work within Outlook's strict security rules. Thankfully, you no longer need to utilize CDO or other third-party application programming interfaces (APIs). The Outlook object model provides you with a consolidated object model that includes objects from CDO 1.21, Exchange Client Extensions, and Extended Messaging Application Programming Interface (MAPI). MAPI is the underlying messaging system that allows you to access and program against the Outlook data store.

Improved Searching Performance

Outlook has famously suffered performance issues when someone has attempted to automate searches or navigate deep into the folder structure to return Outlook items. To rectify this known issue, Outlook 2007 includes the read-only `Table` object. You can use the `Table` object to return a set of Outlook items such as the table's row set.

Ability to Easily Store Application Settings

You can now take advantage of the new `StorageItem` object to store solution data in Outlook folders as hidden objects. Instead of storing the settings as an external XML file, text file, database, and so forth, the `StorageItem` gives you the ability to store your application settings in Outlook to take advantage of Outlook's synchronization and offline features. Thanks to this object, you can easily support a scenario in which a user has your solution installed on more than one machine.

A (More) Realistic View Toward Security

Outlook's OM Guard has been the bane of the Outlook developer's existence for years. Guard is Microsoft's solution to the plethora of viruses that have targeted Outlook over the years. Guard limits the objects that you can manipulate without user approval. For more information related to the OM Guard, go to `http://msdn2.microsoft.com/library/bb176874.aspx`.

Just about any task that you would like to automate, such as editing a contact, would trigger the OM Guard with previous versions of Outlook. This strict lockdown of Outlook most likely only made sense to Microsoft's executives. My hunch is that it greatly reduced Microsoft's legal risk resulting from viruses that target Outlook, so I don't really blame Microsoft for making life difficult for Outlook solution developers given the risks involved to Microsoft and the user.

The good news is that Microsoft now allows you to automate Outlook from external applications without triggering the OM Guard. Two caveats exist however. First, the user's system must have antivirus software installed. Second, the installed antivirus software's virus definitions must be current. If either of these two caveats is not met, you will be forced to deal with the strict policies of the OM Guard.

Over 80 New Objects to Explore

My list of new features covers only the main highlights. For a full understanding of the new features resulting from Outlook 2007's new objects, go to `http://msdn2.microsoft.com/en-us/library/bb176827.aspx`.

Working with the Application Object

The starting point for accessing any object in the Outlook OM is the `Application` object. Table 2-8 lists the common properties and methods for the `Application` object.

Table 2-8. *The Commonly Used Application Object's Properties and Methods*

Application Property or Method Name	Description	VSTO Code
`ActiveExplorer`	This property returns the currently selected `Explorer` object in the Outlook UI.	`Application.ActiveExplorer`
`ActiveInspector`	This property returns the currently selected `Inspector` object in the Outlook UI.	`Application.ActiveInspector`
`CreateItem`	This method creates an Outlook item using the specified item type. This method returns the item as the specified `ItemType`.	`Application.CreateItem(ItemType)`
`CreateItemFromTemplate`	This method creates an Outlook item using the specified template. The method returns a corresponding `ItemType`.	`Application.CreateItemFromTemplate (TemplatePath, InFolder)`
`Explorers`	This property returns an `Explorers` collection containing all open `Explorer` objects.	`Application.Explorers`
`GetNamespace`	This method returns a `Namespace` object. Outlook only supports the MAPI namespace. The Outlook `Session` object is also a `Namespace` object.	`Application.GetNamespace("MAPI")`
`Inspectors`	This property returns an `Inspectors` collection containing all open `Inspector` objects.	`Application.Inspectors`
`Session`	This property returns the `Namespace` object for the current user's Outlook session. This property and the `GetNamespace` method both return the current user's session.	`Application.Session`

You use the Application object to gain access to any object in Outlook as well as to create new items. Using VSTO's ThisAddin object, you can grab objects as you need them from anywhere in your project.

In the remainder of this chapter, I will provide code samples for common code tasks required to build Outlook solutions. To follow along with each sample, I recommend that you create a new VSTO Outlook add-in by following these steps:

1. Open Visual Studio 2008 and create an Outlook Add-in project, as shown in Figure 2-14. Name the project **OutlookOMSnippets** and click OK.

2. Open ThisAddin.vb, and you're ready to go.

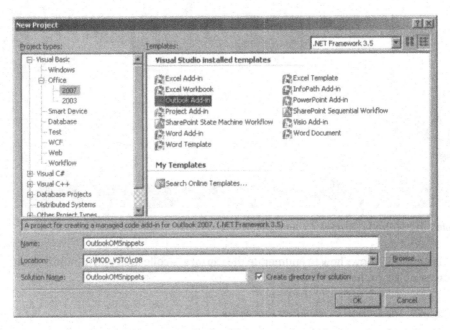

Figure 2-14. *Selecting the VSTO Outlook Add-in project template in Visual Studio*

Using the Explorers Collection Object

The Explorer object represents an Outlook window and the folder it displays. The majority of the time you only need to worry about the existence of a single Explorer object that you can reference with this snippet:

```
Dim objExplorer as Outlook.Explorer
objExplorer = Me.Application.ActiveExplorer
```

Sometimes the user might have more than one Explorer window open, or you might want to open additional Explorer windows (see Figure 2-15).

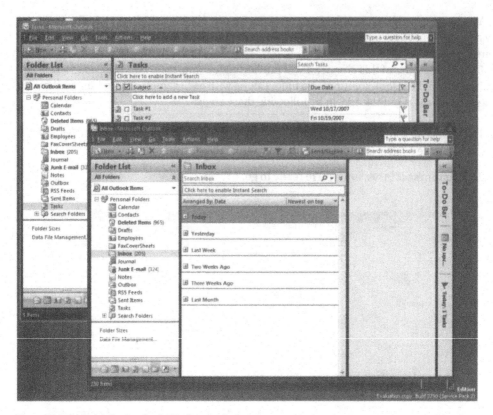

Figure 2-15. *Multiple Outlook Explorer windows*

Listing 2-25 shows how to enumerate the `Explorers` collection and minimize each `Explorer` object in the collection.

Listing 2-25. *The EnumerateExplorers Procedure*

```
Private Sub EnumerateExplorers()
  Dim objExplorers As Outlook.Explorers
  objExplorers = Me.Application.Explorers
  For Each exp As Outlook.Explorer In objExplorers
    exp.WindowState = Outlook.OlWindowState.olMinimized
  Next
End Sub
```

You can open a new Explorer window by adding a new `Explorer` object to the `Explorers` collection. Listing 2-26 shows how to create a new `Explorer` object, set it to display the default tasks folder, and then show the new `Explorer` in the Outlook UI.

Listing 2-26. *The OpenTwoExplorers Procedure*

```
Private Sub OpenTwoExplorers()
  Dim objExplorers As Outlook.Explorers
  Dim objExp1 As Outlook.Explorer
  Dim objExp2 As Outlook.Explorer
  Dim objTaskFolder As Outlook.Folder
  'Grab a reference to the currently active Explorer
  'because it will change to the newly added one later.
  objExp1 = Me.Application.ActiveExplorer
  objExplorers = Me.Application.Explorers
  objTaskFolder = Me.Application.Session. _
    GetDefaultFolder(OlDefaultFolders.olFolderTasks)
  'Add the new Explorer to the Explorers collection
  objExp2 = objExplorers.Add(objTaskFolder, _
    Outlook.OlFolderDisplayMode.olFolderDisplayNoNavigation)

  With objExp2
    .Width = 575
    .Height = 550
    .Display()
  End With
  'Now change the first Explorer to the Calendar folder.
  objExp1.CurrentFolder = Me.Application.Session. _
    GetDefaultFolder(OlDefaultFolders.olFolderCalendar)

End Sub
```

The first thing this procedure does is grab a reference to the current ActiveExplorer object. The reason for grabbing the reference now is that after you add a new Explorer object and display it, the new Explorer object becomes the ActiveExplorer object. Grabbing a reference to the Explorer object now allows you to change its folder to the default Calendar folder at the end of the procedure without affecting the Explorer object that was active prior to the method's execution. Listing 2-26 creates a new Explorer by calling the Explorers collection's Add method, which uses this syntax:

```
ExplorerObject.Add(Folder, [DisplayMode])
```

You are required to pass a valid Outlook Folder object; if you don't, the method will raise an error. The DisplayMode is optional and allows you to fine-tune how the Explorer displays.

■**Note** For the sake of simplifying the code samples, each code listing in this chapter is meant to reside within the ThisAddin class as a member method. If you want to use any of the code listings outside of ThisAddin, just change the Me keyword to Globals.ThisAddin.

Using the Inspectors Collection Object

The Inspectors collection contains all open Inspector objects. If you have multiple items open—for instance, a contact, a task, and an appointment—you can find each in the Inspectors collection. Listing 2-27 loops through all items found in the Inspectors collection and displays each Inspector object's subject.

Listing 2-27. *The EnumerateInspectors Procedure*

```
Private Sub EnumerateInspectors()
  Dim objInspectors As Outlook.Inspectors
  objInspectors = Me.Application.Inspectors
  For Each insp As Outlook.Inspector In objInspectors
    MsgBox(insp.CurrentItem.Subject)
  Next
End Sub
```

Also, you can use the following code to access the active Inspector object whose windows Outlook is displaying on top of all other Inspector windows in the Outlook UI:

```
Dim objInspector as Outlook.Inspector
objInspector = Me.Application.ActiveInspector
```

Figure 2-16 shows two open Inspector windows.

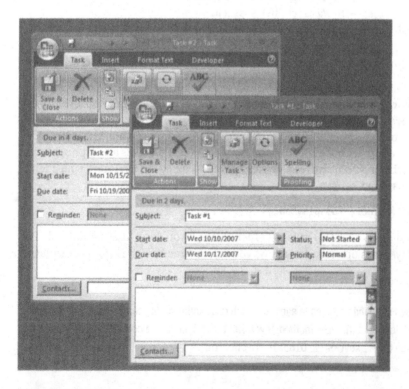

Figure 2-16. *Which Inspector window contains the ActiveInspector object?*

The `ActiveInspector` property does not necessarily return the `Inspector` object that has the user's attention. Because you can view multiple Outlook object windows (from `Explorer` and `Inspector` objects) at the same time, it is possible for the user to actually see two Inspector windows at a time. Only one can be the `ActiveInspector`. The `ActiveInspector` is always the Inspector window that resides at the top of the Outlook UI stack of open windows.

Working with the Namespace Object

The `Namespace` object in Outlook contains the methods, properties, and events for working with MAPI. MAPI provides the messaging infrastructure for Outlook; you need to utilize MAPI anytime you want to work with Outlook data.

In fact, MAPI is the only type supported by the `Namespace` object; this is why in Outlook 2007, you now have the `Session` object that returns the current user's MAPI namespace with a single line of code. The older `GetNamespace` of the `Application` object is still supported. It will return the `Session` object but requires more code, as you can see in Listing 2-28.

Listing 2-28. *The GetNamespaceObject Function*

```
Private Function GetNamespaceObject() As Outlook.Namespace
    Dim objNamespace As Outlook.Namespace
    objNamespace = Me.Application.GetNamespace("MAPI")
    Return objNamespace

    'Or the much simpler version:
    'Return Me.Application.Session
End Function
```

Because the `Session` property returns the current MAPI namespace with a single line of code, I recommend using it in your solutions instead of the `GetNamespace` method.

The `Session` property returns the MAPI `Namespace` object. The `Namespace` object is what you need to gain access to the Outlook data store as well as metadata information related to the current user and Outlook session. The remaining code in this section shows you how to use the `Session` property to work with the current Outlook sessions' `Namespace` object. Each example shows how to read a key data element; this can be useful to know when you build your own solutions.

Reading the Current User's Name

You can discover the information about the current Outlook user by accessing the `Namespace` object's `CurrentUser` property. Listing 2-29 shows how to obtain the user's name.

Listing 2-29. *The GetCurrentUserName Function*

```
Private Function GetCurrentUserName() As String
    Return Me.Application.Session.CurrentUser.Name.ToString
End Function
```

The CurrentUser property returns a Recipient object. The Recipient object is the same object added to an e-mail when the user adds a contact as an addressee in the To:, Cc:, or Bcc: fields.

Reading Outlook's ExchangeConnectionMode Property

Outlook is an e-mail client, and you can use it to work with Post Office Protocol (POP)/Simple Mail Transfer Protocol (SMTP) e-mail systems. However, in a business environment, you will most likely work with users running Outlook with Microsoft Exchange Server. Working with Exchange Server forces you to work around the various connection mode possibilities. Outlook has online and offline scenarios when working with Exchange Server. It can be useful to know the user's connection status when writing code that works with Outlook data.

You can quickly determine if Outlook is online and has a connection with an Exchange Server by reading the session's Offline property, as shown in Listing 2-30.

Listing 2-30. *The GetConnectionStatus Function*

```
Private Function GetConnectionStatus() As Boolean
    Return Me.Application.Session.Offline()
End Function
```

The Offline property returns a Boolean value of true or false. If Outlook has a current connection to an Exchange Server, Offline will return true. Otherwise, the Offline value will return false.

Knowing the offline status is beneficial in and of itself, but the MAPI Namespace object can provide more details related to the Exchange Server connection via its ExchangeConnectionMode property. This property returns the OlExchangeConnectionMode. Table 2-9 lists the more commonly used constant values and their meaning.

Table 2-9. *Common OlExchangeConnectionMode Constant Values*

Constant Name	Description	Offline/Online
olConnected	Outlook is connected to Exchange Server but is not in online mode.	Online
olDisconnected	The connection to Exchange Server has dropped, but Outlook is not in offline mode.	Offline
olOffline	The user is not connected to Exchange Server and is in offline mode. In many cases, the user has taken Outlook offline.	Offline
olOnline	Outlook has an active connection with Exchange Server and is in online mode.	Online

Listing 2-31 shows how to read the ExchangeConnectionMode property.

Listing 2-31. *The GetConnectionMode Function*

```
Private Function GetConnectionMode() As String
  Return Me.Application.Session. _
    ExchangeConnectionMode.ToString()

End Function
```

GetDefaultFolder

When you work with Outlook data, you are typically working with the default items in Outlook, such as contacts, tasks, e-mail, and appointments. Although it is possible to create multiple folders for storing each item type within Outlook, the majority of Outlook users keep their environment simple by storing all items in their related default folder. For example, contact items typically reside in the Contacts folder, appointments reside in the Calendar folder, and tasks reside in the Tasks folder.

However, there is no guarantee of a default folder's location, as the user can modify his location by using Outlook's Tools menu. Luckily, you can grab a reference of a default folder by calling the GetDefaultFolder namespace method. Listing 2-32 shows how to retrieve the default Calendar folder.

Listing 2-32. *The GetDefaultCalendarFolder Function*

```
Private Function GetDefaultCalendarFolder() As Outlook.Folder
  Return Me.Application.Session.GetDefaultFolder( _
    Outlook.OlDefaultFolders.olFolderCalendar)
End Function
```

The GetDefaultFolder requires you to pass your desired folder type as an argument. Table 2-10 describes the supported types that are available in the OlDefaultFolders constant.

Table 2-10. *The Common OlDefaultFolders Constant Values*

Constant Name	Description	Typical Folder Path
olFolderCalendar	The default folder for storing appointments	\\Mailbox\Calendar
olFolderContacts	The default folder for storing contacts	\\Mailbox\Contacts
olFolderInbox	The default folder where received e-mail resides	\\Mailbox\Inbox
olFolderJournal	The default folder for journal items	\\Mailbox\Journal
olFolderJunk	The folder location where e-mail identified as junk mail resides	\\Mailbox\Junk E-mail
olFolderNotes	The default folder for storing notes	\\Mailbox\Notes
olFolderOutbox	The folder where outgoing e-mail items reside	\\Mailbox\Outbox

Constant Name	Description	Typical Folder Path
olFolderRssFeeds	The folder location where items from RSS feeds (typically blogs) reside	\\Mailbox\RSS Subscriptions
olFolderSentMail	The folder where sent e-mails reside	\\Mailbox\Sent Items
olFolderTasks	The default folder for storing tasks	\\Mailbox\Tasks
olFolderToDo	The dynamic search folder for displaying to-do tasks	The To-Do List view is available in the Tasks folder, which you can find at \\Mailbox\Tasks.

SelectFolder

Sometimes it is best to ask the user to specify the folder she wants to execute an action against. For example, if you want to write code that copies items from one folder to another, you will not know at design time which folder is the source or which folder is the target. In situations like these, you can use the PickFolder method of the Namespace object provided, once again, by the Application.Session property. Listing 2-33 shows this method call.

Listing 2-33. *The AskForFolder Function*

```
Private Function AskForFolder() As Outlook.Folder
   Dim objFolder As Outlook.Folder
   objFolder = Me.Application.Session.PickFolder
   Return objFolder
End Function
```

PickFolder displays the Select Folder dialog box to the Outlook user (see Figure 2-17). The user can navigate to his desired folder, select it, and click OK. PickFolder then returns the selected folder as a Folder object.

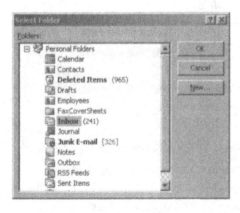

Figure 2-17. *The Select Folder Outlook dialog box*

Working with the Explorer Object

The Explorer object represents an Outlook window. In more common scenarios, only one window is open, and you can reference it by using the ActiveExplorer property of the Application object. As you can see in Figure 2-18, an Explorer window contains several components, each with their own corresponding objects that you can manipulate in code.

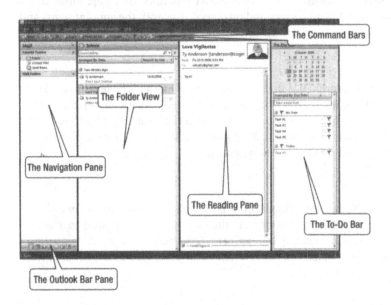

Figure 2-18. *The Outlook Explorer window*

The Explorer Window GUI Components

Each component of the Explorer window provides the user with features and tools that enhance her Outlook experience. The following sections explain each component and name each UI element's corresponding Explorer property (if it has one).

The Navigation Pane

The Navigation pane displays a tree view of the user's Outlook data structure. Using the Navigation pane, you can select any folders within the data store. You can reference the Navigation pane UI by calling an Explorer object's NavigationPane property.

The Folder View

The Folder view of the Explorer UI displays the listing of each item residing in the selected Outlook folder. The CurrentFolder property returns the currently selected folder, and you can access each folder item by using the CurrentFolder.Items collection.

The Reading Pane

The Reading pane of the Explorer UI shows the contents from the currently selected item in the Folder view. This section only provides a read-only preview and does not show every data element available in the item (you will need to open an Inspector window to see everything). The Reading pane does not have a corresponding object. The method for customizing a Reading pane is to create custom form regions that replace the default Reading pane.

The To-Do Bar

The To-Do Bar of the Explorer UI displays a calendar and a list of upcoming appointments and tasks. This section does not have a corresponding object. However, the appointments and tasks that you create, edit, and/or delete are reflected here.

The Outlook Bar Pane

The Outlook Bar pane of the Explorer UI is the shortcut area in Outlook's lower left-hand corner. The Outlook Bar contains links to each of Outlook's default folders for e-mail, calendar, contacts, tasks, and notes. You can increase the bar's height to show full-sized buttons, or you can decrease it to show only icons. The Outlook Bar pane is an Outlook.OutlookBarPane object that you can reference from the Explorer.Panes collection.

The Command Bars

Outlook 2007 continues to utilize the traditional Office menu objects known as *command bars*. Command bars are completely different objects from the Ribbon. You can customize the Explorer UI's menu system by manipulating the Explorer.CommandBars property. Using the returned CommandBars collection object, you can reference and extend Outlook's default menu and toolbars as well as create your own.

Changing Explorer Folders

You can move the user's focus to a different folder and automatically display the new folder's contents by changing the Explorer's CurrentFolder property. This property is an Outlook.Folder type that requires you to create a Folder object and then set it as the value for the CurrentFolder property. Listing 2-34 shows several methods that change the current folder.

Listing 2-34. *The ChangeExplorerFolder Procedures*

```
Private Sub ChangeExplorerFolder1()
  Dim objExplorer As Outlook.Explorer
  objExplorer = Me.Application.ActiveExplorer
  objExplorer.CurrentFolder = _
    Me.Application.Session. _
    GetDefaultFolder(olFolderContacts)

End Sub

Private Sub ChangeExplorerFolder2()
  Dim objExplorer As Outlook.Explorer
  objExplorer = Me.Application.ActiveExplorer
  objExplorer.CurrentFolder = Me.Application.Session.PickFolder

End Sub
```

The first procedure creates a reference to the default Contacts folder and then moves the Explorer to display the folder. The second procedure prompts the user to select a folder and then changes the Explorer to display the selected folder.

Working with Folder Views

Outlook allows the user to create different views for a folder. A user can build views that display a folder's items with custom groups, sorting, and display columns. Using a View object, you can also create filters as well as add custom formatting.

Changing the Explorer View

Listing 2-35 shows how to change the current view of the ActiveExplorer object's current folder.

Listing 2-35. *The ChangeExplorerView Method*

```
Private Sub ChangeExplorerView()
  Dim objExplorer As Outlook.Explorer
  ˋobjExplorer = Me.Application.ActiveExplorer
  'Note the view you specify needs to exist.
  objExplorer.CurrentView = "My Custom View"
End Sub
```

The CurrentView property accepts a string value that represents the name of the view that you want to apply. The view that you specify needs to exist in Outlook; if it doesn't, the code will generate an error.

Creating a New View

You can create a new view by manipulating a Folder object. However, it does make sense to discuss view creation in the context of the Explorer object given you specify a view using an Explorer object. Listing 2-36 creates a new view for the current folder and then applies the view.

Listing 2-36. *The FilterExplorer Procedure*

```
Private Sub CreateExplorerView()
  Dim objFolder As Outlook.Folder
  Dim objExplorer As Outlook.Explorer
  Dim objView As Outlook.View

  objExplorer = Me.Application.ActiveExplorer
  objFolder = objExplorer.CurrentFolder
  objView = objFolder.Views.Add("My New View",_
    Outlook.OlViewType.olTableView, OlViewType.olTableView)

  objFolder.CurrentView = "My New View"
End Sub
```

Listing 2-36 uses the Folder object's (objFolder) CurrentView property to apply the newly created view. You could just as easily use the Explorer object to achieve the same end. However, I wanted to point out that the CurrrentView property is available with the Explorer and Folder objects.

When you call the Add method of the Views collection, you need to follow this syntax:

```
Folder.Views.Add(Name As String, ViewType as Outlook.OlViewType, _
    [SaveOption As Outlook.OlViewSaveOption]
```

The Name argument is the name that you want to give the new view. The view type can be any of the types included by the olViewType constant. Table 2-11 lists each possible view type and its description.

Table 2-11. *Outlook View Types*

View Type Name	Description
olBusinessCardView	This view displays contact items in a format that resembles the digital version of business card.
olCalendarView	This view displays calendar items in a calendar format presented in a day, week, or month view.
olCardView	This view displays all folder items as index cards. This view is typically used with a folder that contains contact items, but it can be applied to any folder.
olDailyTaskListView	This view derives from the olTableView constant, but it is specially suited for the Daily Task List view provided by Outlook 2007's new To-Do Bar feature.
olIconView	This icon-based view is similar to the icon views in Windows Explorer. You can switch between large and small icon views. You also have the option to include icon labels.
olTableView	This table-based view displays a folder's contents as a series of columns and rows. This type is the most common view type in Outlook.
olTimelineView	This view displays folder items in a timeline sequence. The Journal folder defaults to this view, but you can use it with any folder type.

Figure 2-19 shows the contents of the Inbox folder displayed using the Card view. It is an unusual view, but the figure illustrates the display options Outlook provides.

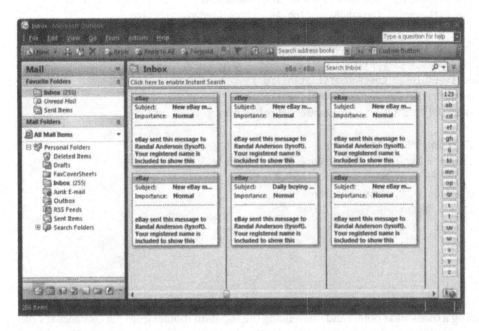

Figure 2-19. *The Inbox folder displaying mail items with a card view*

When you create a view, you can use the optional SaveOption argument to specify which users and folders have permission to see the view. By using this argument, you can specify whether or not the view applies to all folders or only to the reference folder. You can also specify if this view applies only to the current user or if it is available to all users.

Creating Custom Menus

The Outlook menus (also known as command bars) are actually part of the Office library and not exclusive to Outlook. The CommandBar object is shared by all Office applications (even those that no longer utilize it, such as Word and Excel). Within Outlook, you use the CommandBar object to create custom menus and toolbars for your solution. Listing 2-37 contains code for extending Outlook's standard toolbar with an additional button.

Listing 2-37. *The CreateExplorerCommandBar Procedure and Related Code*

```
Private WithEvents _CommandBar As Office.CommandBar
Private WithEvents _CommandBarButton As Office.CommandBarButton

Private Sub CreateExplorerCommandBar()
  _CommandBar = Me.Application. _
    ActiveExplorer.CommandBars("Standard")
  _CommandBarButton = _CommandBar.Controls. _
    Add(Office.MsoControlType.msoControlButton, , , , True)

  With _CommandBarButton
    .Style = Microsoft.Office.Core.MsoButtonStyle. _
      msoButtonIconAndCaption
    .Caption = "My Custom Button"
    .Tag = "MyCustomButton"
    .FaceId = 5817
  End With

End Sub
```

The _CommandBar acts as the container for a CommandBarButton control. Listing 2-37 begins by creating a CommandBar object and referencing the standard toolbar from the CommandBars collection object. With the target command bar in hand, you can create a new button by adding it to the Controls collection of the standard command bar. The syntax for the Add method is as follows:

```
CommandBarControls.Add([Type],[Id],[Parameter],[Before],[Temporary])
```

In most cases, passing only the Type is sufficient, as doing so creates the control and allows you to customize its properties when you see fit. Table 2-12 explains each method argument in detail.

Table 2-12. *The CommandBarControls.Add Method Arguments*

Argument Name	Description	Potential Values
Type	Specifies the type of control to add to the Controls collection.	msoControlButton msoControlEdit msoControlDropDown msoControlComboBox msoControlPopup
Id	Specifies the integer value that represents a built-in CommandBarControl. Retrieving the ID of built-in controls is not a trivial task, as Office does not include features to display them in the UI. For more information on how to retrieve control IDs, see "Programming Office Commandbars—Get the ID of a CommandBarControl" by Guoqiang Wu (http://blogs.msdn.com/guowu/archive/2004/09/06/225963.aspx).	

Argument Name	Description	Potential Values
Parameter	This argument has various purposes depending on context. For a built-in control, it contains information for Outlook (or any other Office application) to execute the command. For custom controls, this argument is available to you to store information that will be sent to the control's attached procedure.	The data type for this argument is a Variant, so you can set the value to almost anything. A common scenario is to add information about the control that could be useful when its events execute.
Before	Specifies the control's position on the command bar. The number you specify should be the control ID of an existing control. The newly created control will reside to the left of the identified control.	Any valid control ID.
Temporary	Specifies if the created control should be destroyed when Outlook shuts down. Specifying True will cause Outlook to destroy the control and prevent it from loading the next time Outlook initializes. You will need to write code to re-create the button each time your add-in starts up.	True False

One important point about command bars and their controls is that you need to write code that responds to their events for them to be useful to your users. Just be sure to declare objects related to your command bar using the WithEvents keyword so that their events are exposed. Listing 2-38 contains the code for the _CommandBarButton control created in Listing 2-37.

Listing 2-38. *The CreateExplorerCommandBar Procedure and Related Code*

```
Private Sub _CommandBarButton_Click(ByVal Ctrl As _
    Microsoft.Office.Core.CommandBarButton, _
    ByRef CancelDefault As Boolean) Handles _CommandBarButton.Click

    MsgBox(Ctrl.Caption)
End Sub
```

Working with the Inspector Object

The Inspector object represents the Outlook window that displays an individual Outlook item, such as an e-mail or an appointment (see Figure 2-20). Unlike with the Explorer object, it is common for a user to have multiple Inspector objects open at any given time. You can reference the Inspector that has the user's focus through the Application.ActiveInspector property.

Outlook 2007 includes several significant changes to the Inspector window, starting with the use of the Ribbon. Outlook is different from other Office applications because it uses a combination of the new Ribbon UI element along with the traditional Office menu system. This situation is confusing, but there is a silver lining, as this mixed usage does not cross objects. Inspector objects always use the Ribbon, and Explorer objects always use the traditional Office command bars.

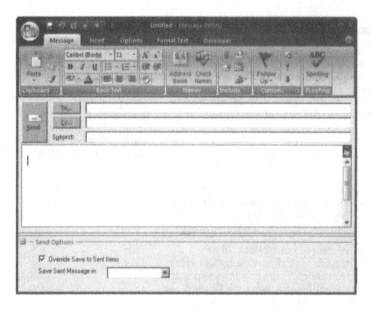

Figure 2-20. *The Outlook Inspector window*

The Inspector Windows Components

The Inspector window includes more new elements than just the Ribbon.

Form Regions

Form regions provide the mechanism for extending the Inspector window. You have the option of building form regions that extend a default Inspector page (pages are equivalent to tabs in previous versions of Outlook), add a new page, replace a default page, or replace all pages.

Custom Task Panes

The Inspector window now supports custom task panes and offers an additional method for extending the Inspector UI. The task panes are different from the action panes that you can build in Word and Excel. Outlook doesn't support the action pane item template. Instead, you build a user control and dock it to the side of the Inspector window. Chapter 6 includes a solution example that explains this technique. Figure 2-21 shows one of the Inspector's two main pages.

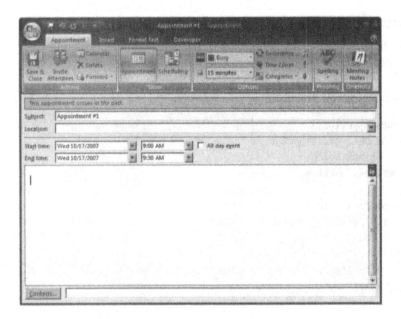

Figure 2-21. *The Appointment page of an Inspector window displaying an appointment*

Inspector Forms

The form is the portion of the Inspector window that displays Outlook item data. The Outlook 2007 forms no longer rely on tabs to separate each section of the Inspector window; instead, they have implemented the concept of pages. Each Inspector form contains pages. Figure 2-22 shows the other of the Inspector's two main pages.

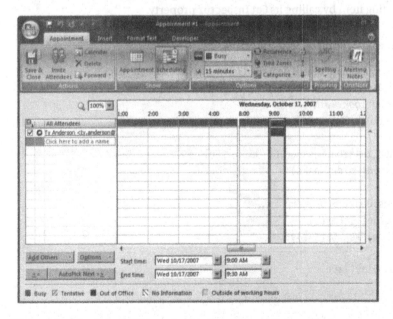

Figure 2-22. *The Scheduling page of an Inspector window displaying an appointment*

Creating a New Inspector

You need an Inspector object to display an Outlook item. The main method for creating a new Inspector is to call the Add method of the Inspectors collection (see Listing 2-39).

Listing 2-39. *The CreateNewInspector Procedure*

```
Private Sub CreateNewInspector()
  Dim objInspector As Outlook.Inspector
  Dim objFolder As Outlook.Folder
  Dim objTask As Outlook.TaskItem

  objFolder = Me.Application.Session. _
    GetDefaultFolder(OlDefaultFolders.olFolderTasks)
  If objFolder.Items.Count > 0 Then
    objTask = objFolder.Items(1)
    objInspector = Me.Application.Inspectors.Add(objTask)
    objInspector.Display(True)

  End If
End Sub
```

Listing 2-39 looks inside the default Tasks folder to determine if any tasks exist. If any are found, the code adds a new Inspector object to the Inspectors collection and passes the referenced task object to the Add method. Passing an Outlook item is required; otherwise, the Add method will raise an error.

There is another method for creating an Inspector. While Listing 2-39 showed how to create a new Inspector by inserting an item object inside it, Listing 2-40 shows how to create an Inspector from an existing item by calling its GetInspector property.

Listing 2-40. *The GetInspectorFromItem Procedure*

```
Private Sub GetInspectorFromItem()
  Dim objInspector As Outlook.Inspector
  Dim objFolder As Outlook.Folder
  Dim objTask As Outlook.TaskItem

  objFolder = Me.Application.Session.GetDefaultFolder( _
    OlDefaultFolders.olFolderTasks)

  If objFolder.Items.Count > 0 Then
    objTask = objFolder.Items(1)
    objInspector = objTask.GetInspector

    objInspector.Display(True)
  End If
End Sub
```

Calling the GetInspector property allows you to reference an item's Inspector object without relying on the ActiveInspector property of the Application object.

Using an Inspector's Item

The Inspector object is the window that displays an Outlook item. It is not the actual item itself, so you will likely work with Inspector objects to gain access to the items that they hold. Listing 2-41 shows how to access an Inspector's CurrentItem property to return its underlying Outlook item.

Listing 2-41. *The GetCurrentItem Procedure*

```
Private Function GetCurrentItem() As Object
  Dim objInspector As Outlook.Inspector
  objInspector = Me.Application.ActiveInspector
  Return objInspector.CurrentItem

End Function
```

The type of item returned can be any Outlook item type, such as e-mail, a task, or an appointment.

Changing an Inspector's Window

You can control how an Outlook item displays to the user by modifying the properties of the item's Inspector object. Listing 2-42 shows how to move the active Inspector's location within Windows.

Listing 2-42. *The ChangeInspectorPosition Procedure*

```
Private Sub ChangeInspectorPosition()
  Dim objInspector As Outlook.Inspector
  objInspector = Me.Application.ActiveInspector
  objInspector.Top = 250
  objInspector.Left = 150
  objInspector.WindowState = _
  Outlook.OlWindowState.olNormalWindow

End Sub
```

Fine-tuning the Inspector window provides you with the ability to completely control the Outlook UI and position Outlook windows according to your solution's needs. For example, you can position Inspector windows side by side and allow a user to craft an e-mail reply while viewing the original.

REAL-WORLD SCENARIO: REPLACING OUTLOOK FORMS

It is possible to replace the design of the Inspector window entirely and display your own custom Windows form in its place. Replacing built-in Outlook forms is much easier now using form regions, but depending on your requirements, knowing how to implement the form *hijacking* technique can be quite useful.

I discovered this technique when building a customer management system for a client. The client wanted to use a Contacts folder to manage existing client relationships. The problem was that he didn't like the standard Contacts form and instead wanted to use a form that better suited his purposes. I explained the options that Microsoft supported, such as adding fields to existing form tabs or creating entirely new tabs. My client rejected these options, insisting he wanted a completely customized form.

I spent some time thinking about how I might meet the requirements, and I developed the theory that if I prevented an Inspector window from opening, I could display my custom form instead. I tested the theory and proved it would work to my client's satisfaction.

The only major negative to this strategy is that I had to implement features normally provided by the contact's form. However, because the client was willing to pay for the effort, I didn't mind making it happen.

To view the code for this technique, read my article, "Outlook the Way You Want It—Build Custom Outlook GUIs with WinForms & VSTO (http://www.devx.com/MicrosoftISV/Article/29261).

Working with Outlook Folders

Outlook stores data inside folders. The Folders collection contains all Folder objects in the user's Outlook data store. You can use the Items collection of the Folders collection to access each Folder in a particular collection. In previous versions of Outlook, the Folder object was the MAPIFolder object. With Outlook 2007, you use the Folder object in favor of the deprecated MAPIFolder.

Creating a New Folder

You create a new folder by calling a Folders collection's Add method and specifying a folder name and folder type. Listing 2-43 shows how to add a new Tasks folder to Outlook's root folder node.

Listing 2-43. *The CreateNewFolder Function*

```
Private Function CreateNewFolder() As Outlook.Folder
    Dim objFolders As Outlook.Folders
    Dim objFolder As Outlook.Folder
    objFolders = Me.Application.Session.Folders
    objFolder = objFolders.Add("MyNewFolder", _
      Outlook.OlDefaultFolders.olFolderTasks)
    Return objFolder
End Function
```

The Add method syntax is as follows:

```
Folders Object.Add(Name as String, Type as Object)
```

The Name argument accepts any valid string that you want to use as the name of your new folder. For the type argument, you can use the Outlook.OlDefaultFolders constant to pass the value of your desired folder type (see Table 2-13 for list of folder types). The type argument is optional, so if you omit it, the new folder will inherit the same type as its parent folder.

Table 2-13. *Folder Type Values*

Folder Type	Constant Value
Calendar	olFolderCalendar
Contacts	olFolderContacts
Drafts	olFolderDrafts
Inbox	olFolderInbox
Journal	olFolderJournal
Notes	olFolderNotes
Tasks	olFolderTasks

Moving a Folder

You can perform the same folder-centric tasks available to the user in Outlook, such as copying, deleting, and moving folders. Listing 2-44 shows how to move a folder to a new location.

Listing 2-44. *The MoveFolder Procedure*

```
Private Sub MoveFolder()
    Dim objFolders As Outlook.Folders
    Dim objFolder As Outlook.Folder
    objFolders = Me.Application.Session.Folders
    objFolder = Me.Application.Session. _
      Folders("Personal Folders").Folders.Item("MyCustomFolder")

    objFolder.MoveTo(Me.Application.Session.GetDefaultFolder( _
      Outlook.OlDefaultFolders.olFolderTasks))
End Sub
```

The first trick in this listing is to grab a reference to the folder that you want to move. This example finds the MyCustomFolder object residing within the Folders collection of the Personal Folders folder within the Outlook data store. The Personal Folders folder serves as the root folder in a non-Exchange Outlook configuration. After the code has a reference to the desired folder, it calls the MoveTo method, passing the default Tasks folder as the DestinationFolder parameter.

Retrieving a Folder

You have three options for retrieving Outlook Folder objects. The first option is to identify a folder and then retrieve a folder by name. Listing 2-45 illustrates this method. Finding a folder by name certainly works, but I would not call it a best practice, as it requires you to know not only the name of your desired folder, but also its parent folder(s) names. You'll then need to traverse each folder until you reach the target folder.

The second and third options provide better strategies. You can retrieve a folder directly by using the `Application.Session.GetFolderFromID` method. This method navigates the Outlook folder structure and returns the `Folder` object that you request. It does not matter how many levels down the folder is in the data store. Listing 2-45 illustrates the `GetFolderID` method call.

Listing 2-45. *Calling the GetFolderFromID Method*

```
Private Function FindFolder(ByVal FolderID As String) _
  As Outlook.Folder

    Dim objFolder As Outlook.Folder
    objFolder = Me.Application.Session.GetFolderFromID(FolderID)
    Return objFolder
End Function
```

The `GetFolderFromID` method is useful for retrieving folders that are important to your solution. You can save the folder IDs of these folders to a settings file, a database, an XML application, or another data source as part of your solution's settings. Then when your add-in initializes, you can use the saved folder IDs to create folder references when needed.

The third method for retrieving folders is to use a known folder path. Unfortunately, Outlook does not provide a method that accepts a folder path and then returns a `Folder` object. However, with a little custom code, you can easily implement this function. Listing 2-46 contains a function that accepts a path string, finds the specified folder, and returns a reference to the folder as an `Outlook.Folder` object.

Listing 2-46. *The FindFolderFromPath Function*

```
Private Function FindFolderFromPath(ByVal FolderPath As String) _
    As Outlook.Folder

    Dim objFolder As Outlook.Folder
    objFolder = Nothing
    Dim objArray As Array
    Dim i As Integer
    'The path will include leading "\\", remove them.
    Dim path As String = Right(FolderPath.ToString, _
      Len(FolderPath.ToString) - 2)
    'Extract each folder name
    objArray = path.Split("\")
```

```
Dim objRootFolder As Outlook.Folder
'Grab the folder, which will be the first item in the array.
objRootFolder = Globals.ThisAddIn.Application.Session. _
  Folders.Item(objArray(0))

Dim fldrsSub As Outlook.Folders
'Now loop through the remaining array values
'Return the last folder found.
fldrsSub = objRootFolder.Folders

For i = 1 To objArray.Length - 1
  objFolder = fldrsSub.Item(objArray(i))
Next
Return objFolder

End Function
```

This method looks tricky, but all it does is take the FolderPath argument value and split each folder name in the path into an array. The first folder in the array is the root folder. The last folder name in the array is the folder that you want to retrieve. The easiest way to retrieve the desired folder is to loop through the remaining array items until you reach the last item and return the referenced Folder object.

This method relies on the FolderPath argument following the \\\FolderName\ FolderName\FolderName syntax. You can pass any number of nested folders in the path as long as the syntax is correct. The following code snippet shows how to call the FindFolderFromPath function:

```
FindFolderFromPath("\\Personal Folders\Contacts\Mkt Campaign")
```

Adding a Folder to the Favorites List

One of the Outlook features that I use the most is the Favorite Folders list found in the upper left-hand corner of the Outlook UI (see Figure 2-23). This element provides a convenient location to place the folders that you use most often. You can drag and drop folders from the Navigation pane, but you have the ability to perform the same action in code.

Figure 2-23. *The Favorites Folder UI element in Outlook*

Adding a folder to the Favorite Folders list requires you to manipulate the Navigation Folders collection. This collection is part of an Outlook Pane object and requires you to reference a few objects to get the job done, as Listing 2-47 shows.

Listing 2-47. *The AddSelectedFolderToFavorites Procedure*

```
Private Sub AddSelectedFolderToFavorites()
    Dim objSelectedFolder As Outlook.Folder
    Dim objPane As Outlook.NavigationPane
    Dim objMailModule As Outlook.MailModule
    Dim objGroup As Outlook.NavigationGroup
    Dim objNewFolder As Outlook.NavigationFolder

    objSelectedFolder = Me.Application.ActiveExplorer.CurrentFolder
    objPane = Me.Application.ActiveExplorer.NavigationPane
    objMailModule = objPane.Modules.GetNavigationModule( _
        OlNavigationModuleType.olModuleMail)

    objGroup = objMailModule.NavigationGroups. _
        GetDefaultNavigationGroup(OlGroupType.olFavoriteFoldersGroup)

    objNewFolder = objGroup.NavigationFolders.Add(objSelectedFolder)
End Sub
```

The first object that you need is the NavigationPane associated with the ActiveExplorer. With a reference to this pane, you can then call the pane's GetNavigationModule method and specify that you want the MailModule.

The MailModule holds the navigation elements that Outlooks displays in the Navigation pane anytime the current folder is a folder whose default item type is a mail item. Modules exist for each type of Outlook item and have names that represent their type (CalendarModule, TasksModule, ContactsModule, and so forth). The module object (objMailModule, in this example) contains the NavigationGroups collection where the Favorite Folders group resides.

You call the GetDefaultNavigationGroup and specify the group type that you want, which in this case is the Favorite Folders group (olFavoriteFoldersGroup). After you have the group referenced, its Add method accepts a Folder object and adds it to the Folders collection within the Group object.

Working with Outlook Items

Outlook's data store is a flexible data system that can handle the various default Outlook data types, such as the contacts, e-mail, tasks, and appointment items, as well as custom types that a user or developer creates. Each item type shares many common methods, properties, and events, but differences do exist among them. Table 2-14 explains each of the creatable item types.

Table 2-14. *Outlook Items You May Create Using Code*

Outlook Item Name	Object Model Name	Description
Appointment	AppointmentItem	A calendar item in an appointment folder.
Contact	ContactItem	A contact item that typically resides in a contacts folder.
Distribution List	DistListItem	A distribution list that resides in a contacts folder.
Document	DocumentItem	A document or executable that resides in any folder.
Email (or Mail)	MailItem	An e-mail item in an inbox folder.
Meeting	MeetingItem	A special e-mail item that contains updated meeting details for an appointment. A meeting item normally resides in the inbox.
Note	NoteItem	A note that resides in a notes folder.
Post	PostItem	A post that resides in an inbox folder.
Storage Post Item	StorageItem	A hidden item that resides in a folder. This item is new to Outlook 2007 and is meant to store setting or configuration data for your solution.
Task	TaskItem	A task that resides in a tasks folder.

For a full listing of all Outlook item objects, see http://msdn2.microsoft.com/library/bb147566.aspx.

Mostly likely you will need to add, edit, and delete Outlook items. The examples in the following sections explain how to perform each of these tasks using contact items. The following procedures could just as well work with other item types.

Creating a New Contact Item

The Outlook Application object provides the shortest path to creating a new item through the usage of its CreateItem method. You can call this method to create a new item of the type that you specify in the ItemType argument. Listing 2-48 shows how to create a new contact item.

Listing 2-48. *The CreateMailItem Procedure*

```
Private Sub CreateOutlook()
  Dim objMail As Outlook.MailItem
  objMail = Me.Application. _
    CreateItem(Outlook.OlItemType.olMailItem)

  objMail.Subject = "Email created using code"
  objMail.Body = "This is the body of the email"
  objMail.To = "someone@anywhere.com"
  objMail.DeleteAfterSubmit = True
  objMail.Send()
End Sub
```

After creating the mail item, you set a few properties required to send an e-mail and then call the mail item's Send method to send the e-mail.

Opening and Editing a Contact Item

Opening an Outlook item requires you to first reference the folder where it resides. With the appropriate folder reference in hand, you retrieve the desired item from the folder's Items collection, as Listing 2-49 shows.

Listing 2-49. *The GetAndEditContact Procedure*

```
Private Sub GetAndEditContact()
  Dim objFolder As Outlook.Folder
  Dim objContact As Outlook.ContactItem
  objFolder = Me.Application.Session.GetDefaultFolder(Outlook.OlDefaultFolders)
  objContact = objFolder.Items("Doe, John")
  With ObjContact
    .CompanyName = "Beta Corp"
    .AssistantName = "Jane Doe"
    .Close(Outlook.OlInspectorClose.olSave)
  End With
End Sub
```

Once again, you need to reference the folder that contains the item that you want. In this case, you want the default Contacts folder. You retrieve your desired contact by passing the name of the item to the folder's Items collection.

To edit an item, you update the item's properties as needed to meet your requirements. In this example, I only edited two properties and then closed the item. The Close method allows you to specify if the changes should be saved or discarded, or if the user should be prompted to decide for himself. In this example, you save the object to complete the procedure.

Using Custom Item Properties

In every Outlook solution that I build, I end up needing to add fields to the Outlook items. Outlook items include the UserProperties collection that contains every custom field (UserProperty objects) created either by the user in the Outlook UI or by you, the developer, using code. Listing 2-50 includes a method for saving or updating a UserProperty value for a task item.

Listing 2-50. *The SaveCustomProperty Procedure*

```
Private Sub SaveCustomProperty(ByVal UserPropName As String, _
    ByVal UserPropValue As String, ByVal Task As Outlook.TaskItem)
  Dim objProp As Outlook.UserProperty
  objProp = Task.UserProperties.Find(UserPropName)
```

```
If objProp Is Nothing Then
  objProp = Task.UserProperties.Add(UserPropName, _
        OlUserPropertyType.olText, True)
  objProp.Value = UserPropValue
Else
  objProp.Value = UserPropValue
End If

End Sub
```

This method includes code for both creating a new UserProperty as well as for updating an existing one. It's a good strategy because if the property does not exist, the code will create it. If the property does exist, then the code will update it. In either case, you don't really care, as the end result will be that the property exists with the value that you specify.

In the SaveCustomProperty procedure, you use the Find method of the UserProperties collection. Using Find instead of the collection's Item method avoids raising an error if the property does not exist. If the property exists, Find will return it as a UserProperty object.

By testing whether or not your desired property exists, you can determine how to branch the code to take the appropriate steps of either creating the property and setting its value or just setting its value.

Outlook Summary

This section explained the two main Outlook objects (Explorer and Inspector) and how to use VSTO to automate actions in Outlook. VSTO doesn't provide host controls for Outlook, but it does provide easy access to Outlook's Namespace object, which is key for working with the current Outlook session.

Summary

As promised, this is a long chapter filled with useful information and code listings for working with Excel, Word, and Outlook. It is well worth the effort required to understand these topics, as these three applications run on the majority of business users' desktops.

CHAPTER 3

■■■

Understanding the Office Fluent User Interface and Action and Task Panes

The Office user interface (UI) has remained largely static in its appearance over the last several versions. Sure, changes have been made, but you could stand confident that the Office menu and toolbar system would always be there with minor improvements here and there. Besides, the Office UI is mature and has proven itself to be incredibly useful, release after release.

With Office 2007, Microsoft believed it could greatly enhance the Office menu system by addressing findings discovered in its user testing and research. The result of this desire to improve the UI is the Office Fluent User Interface. The Fluent UI refers to the new, completely revamped Office UI, and it includes all menu elements, such as the Ribbon, context menus, action panes, and so forth.

The new UI is a dramatic change for Office users everywhere, but the changes are dramatic for developers as well, because the Fluent UI exposes a new application programming interface (API) known as the RibbonX API. RibbonX is an XML-based API, which means that all you need to do to customize the Fluent UI is create a RibbonX-compliant XML file and load it with your add-in.

THE FLUENT UI AND RIBBONX

Microsoft sometimes uses the terms *Fluent UI* and *Ribbon* to define the menu system included in Office 2007. The menu system refers to all the menus, toolbars, and task panes found in the various Office applications. As a result, some amount of confusion surrounds the term *RibbonX*.

In this book, I use *Fluent UI* to refer to the graphical representation of the menu elements as the Office applications render them. I use *RibbonX* to refer to the underlying XML description of the graphical Fluent UI.

This chapter discusses the basics of manipulating two of the newer Office UI elements: the Fluent UI and the action and task panes. After reading this chapter, you will know how to

- Customize the Fluent UI Ribbon

- Attach a method to the Ribbon control

- Differentiate between an action pane and a task pane

The Office Fluent User Interface

Office 2007 includes a menu and toolbar system known as the Fluent UI. With previous versions of Office, the menu system remained largely the same and included changes only for new features and commands available to the user. The Office menu was solid, well known, and an industry standard that was mimicked throughout the software industry. The menu system also had a knack for hiding powerful features like pivot tables in Excel.

The Fluent UI seeks to change this situation by dramatically overhauling Office menus and toolbars to change depending on the task the user is performing. Microsoft's studies have shown the *context-enabled* Fluent UI to provide significant improvements to users for finding the tools that they need for the job at hand.

Fluent UI Components

The Fluent UI includes several UI components beyond the Ribbon component, which receives most of the press attention. Let's take a look at each UI element in detail. Figure 3-1 shows how each element displays within Office.

Figure 3-1. *The Fluent UI displaying within Word 2007*

The Ribbon

The Ribbon is the UI element that replaces the traditional Office menu and toolbar system. Instead of top-level menus, the Ribbon contains tabs. These tabs contain commands organized by the task areas for the host application. For example, Word contains tabs with commands specific to authoring documents, such as Page Layout, References, Mailings, and Review. Excel's Ribbon tabs, on the other hand, are suited for building spreadsheets; they include Formulas and Data. Each tab contains numerous command buttons grouped according to type.

Note The Fluent UI is only available completely within Word 2007, Excel 2007, PowerPoint 2007, and Access 2007. Outlook 2007 only utilizes the Fluent UI within individual Inspector items (for example, Mail, Appointment, Tasks, and so forth) while continuing to use the traditional Office menu system with the Outlook application window. All other Office applications, such as Visio, Groove, InfoPath, and Publisher, continue to use the traditional Office menus as well.

Contextual Tabs

Contextual tabs are special Ribbon tabs that display commands relevant to the current object, such as Tables, Images, and so forth. The Ribbon includes these commands within additional Ribbon tabs that vary depending on the task that the user attempts. Contextual tabs are an attempt to take the pain out of finding commands tucked away deep down in the traditional Office menu system.

The Quick Access Toolbar

The Quick Access Toolbar (QAT) is the customizable portion of the Fluent UI. It is the only area of the Fluent UI that provides user customization. You can add any button within the Ribbon to the QAT by right-clicking the desired button and clicking "Add to Quick Access Toolbar." This toolbar is a user-centric feature and not something developers should manipulate. Resist the urge to do so, no matter how awesome you think your add-in is.

ARE THE OTHER OFFICE APPLICATIONS UNWORTHY?

It is frustrating that not all Office applications use the new Fluent UI. In fact, my hunch is that this lack of consistency confuses the daylights out of users everywhere. However, Microsoft's stated reason for the dual UIs is that the traditional menus in the less mature (in terms of the object model and the number of features) Office applications are not overly complex or prone to hiding features from their users. That's the official answer anyway.

Galleries

A gallery provides a set of predefined results for the user to select. Think of a gallery as providing a set of predefined dialog-box results. These selections simplify the document-creation process and dramatically reduce the time required to create a document according to your standards. The traditional dialog boxes still exist and are available should you need them. You can use Gallery controls in your solution to provide users with quick configuration sets related to options that you provide in your add-ins (see Figure 3-2).

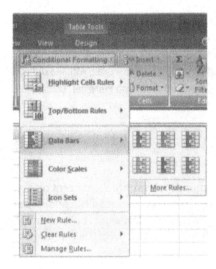

Figure 3-2. *The Excel Conditional Formatting gallery*

The Microsoft Office Button

The Microsoft Office Button ![icon] consolidates all application-level commands and configuration settings into a single location. In previous versions of Office, file and application commands resided in the same set of menus, mixed in a way that made it difficult for users to discern a command's context. With the implementation of the Microsoft Office Button, true separation exists between commands that execute against the file or the document, and commands that execute against the application.

> **MICROSOFT OFFICE BUTTON AND RIBBON CUSTOMIZATION BEST PRACTICE**
>
> Knowing the purpose of both the Microsoft Office Button and the Ribbon helps when you determine where to place the commands in your Visual Studio Tools for the Microsoft Office System (VSTO) customizations. For example, it is best to place all commands that work with document content in the Ribbon or context menu. It is best to place commands that affect the host application or your add-in within the Microsoft Office Button menu.

Customizing the Ribbon

If you know how to follow an XML schema to build an XML file, you have the skills required to create your own Ribbon customizations. VSTO 2008 provides a visual designer that allows you to draw the Ribbon controls on a Ribbon form canvas just as you would with a Windows Forms canvas. If you desire more granular editing capabilities, you also have the option of using a Ribbon (XML) item template.

Creating a Ribbon with the Ribbon Designer

Let's take a look at the basics of creating a Ribbon using the Ribbon Designer item template. With Visual Studio open, perform the following steps:

1. Click File ➤ New Project from the Visual Studio main menu, and navigate to Visual Basic ➤ Office ➤ 2007 in the "Project types" section of the dialog box. Select Word Document from the available project templates (see Figure 3-3), and click OK to accept the project default values.

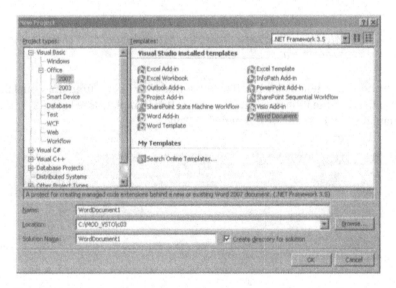

Figure 3-3. *The Word Document project template in Visual Studio*

2. In the "Select a Document for Your Application" dialog box (shown in Figure 3-4), accept the defaults and click OK.

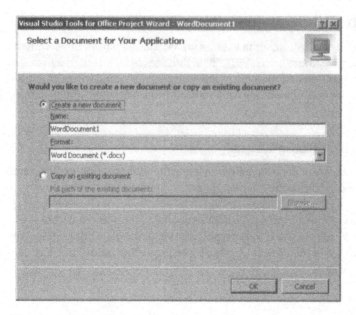

Figure 3-4. *VSTO allows you to choose an existing Word document or choose to base the solution on a new document.*

3. Open the Add New Item dialog box (Project ➤ Add New Item… from the Visual Studio menu), and select the Ribbon (Visual Designer) item template (see Figure 3-5). Accept the default values in the dialog box and click Add.

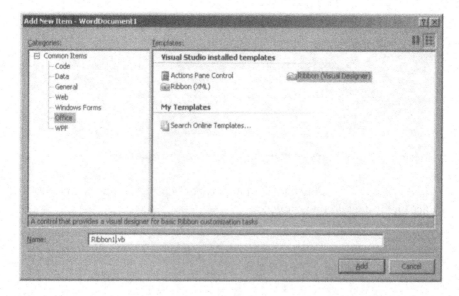

Figure 3-5. *The Ribbon (Visual Designer) in the common item templates available to a Word document project*

4. Visual Studio adds a file named Ribbon1.vb. In the Solution Explorer, double-click this file to open its designer. By default, the Ribbon contains a single tab named Tab1. This tab also contains a group control named Group1, as shown in Figure 3-6.

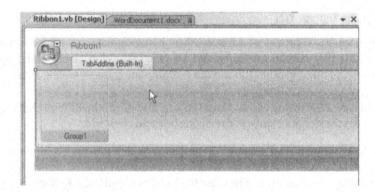

Figure 3-6. *A blank Ribbon waiting to be customized*

5. Make sure that the Visual Studio toolbox is visible. Expand the Office Ribbon Controls section and draw ComboBox and Button controls within the Group1 control so that the Ribbon resembles Figure 3-7.

Figure 3-7. *The Ribbon Designer allows you to draw controls to a canvas as you would with a Windows form.*

6. Press F5 to execute the Word document add-in. You should see a new Ribbon tab labeled Add-Ins. Click this tab to view the controls you added in step 5 (see Figure 3-8).

Figure 3-8. *Your first Ribbon customization using the Ribbon Designer*

Creating Ribbon customizations can be a simple and quick process with the Ribbon Designer. After you build the visual design to contain the controls that you need, you can add code to the controls' events to support your business rules.

Creating a Ribbon Using Ribbon XML

Like the Ribbon Designer, VSTO provides a Ribbon (XML) item template that provides the impetus for creating XML that extends the Ribbon UI. Use the same Word document project that you used previously to build another Ribbon tab by completing the following steps:

1. Open the Add New Item dialog within Visual Studio, and select the Ribbon (XML) item template. Accept the default values in the dialog box and click Add.

   When you add a Ribbon XML file to a VSTO project, Visual Studio adds a Ribbon XML file and a Ribbon class file. The XML file is where you add your desired customizations, such as tabs, groups, and controls. The class file handles the plumbing of loading your XML into the Ribbon. The host application calls this class at runtime.

2. Open the Ribbon2.xml file so that the XML it contains displays in Visual Studio. Add the XML chunk shown in Listing 3-1 below the `<Tabs>` element.

Listing 3-1. *The RibbonX Definition for the Ribbon XML File*

```xml
<tab idMso="TabAddIns">
  <group id="MyGroup" label="My Group">
    <checkBox label="My Custom Checkbox" id="Checkbox1"/>
    <button label="My Custom Button" id="Button1"/>
  </group>
</tab>
```

This XML chunk creates a new tab named MyCustomTab. This tab contains a single group that includes a check box and a button.

3. Attach an event to the Button1 control by adding the OnAction attribute to the Button1 element. Edit the Button1 element as shown:

```xml
<button label="My Custom Button" id="Button1"
 onAction="HelloWorld"/>
```

Each Ribbon control has an OnAction attribute for attaching a method. These methods are called *callback methods.* You define callback methods within the Ribbon class and then assign them as a button's event using the OnAction attribute. Properly configured, this architecture works similar to Windows Forms.

4. Button1 calls the HelloWorld method. Create this method by opening the Ribbon2.vb class and adding the code shown in Listing 3-2 within the Ribbon CallBacks region.

Listing 3-2. *The HelloWorld Method*

```
Public Sub HelloWorld(ByVal control as Office.IRibbonControl)
    MsgBox "Hello World"
End Sub
```

Creating a callback method properly requires that the method be declared as public and that the method name match the name specified in the calling control's OnAction attribute. You must pass the Ribbon control as a parameter (Office.IRibbonControl). If this parameter is missing, your callback method will not execute.

5. In order for the Ribbon XML to load at runtime, you need to add a single method to the ThisDocument class (or ThisWorkbook for Excel, or ThisAddin for application-level add-ins). Open the code view for ThisDocument and insert the code shown in Listing 3-3.

Listing 3-3. *The CreateRibbonExtensibilityObject Function*

```
Protected Overrides Function CreateRibbonExtensibilityObject()
    As Microsoft.Office.Core.IRibbonExtensibility
    Return New Ribbon2()
End Function
```

This method overrides the Microsoft.Office.Core.IRibbonExtensibility method to return your custom ribbon.

6. Press F5 to test the customization. After it loads, click the Add-Ins tab and click My Custom Button to see the Hello World message (see Figure 3-9).

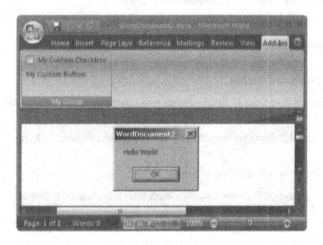

Figure 3-9. *A successful Hello World Ribbon XML customization*

Understanding Ribbon Controls

Eight controls are available to you when developing Ribbon customizations. Microsoft made these controls part of the `Microsoft.Office.Tools.Ribbon` namespace to avoid naming collisions with their Windows Forms brethren. Still, they function as you would expect and should be largely familiar to you with the exception of one or two. Table 3-1 lists each of the Office Ribbon controls and describes their purpose

Table 3-1. *The Office Ribbon Controls Available in VSTO*

Ribbon Control	Description
Box	A container for other controls that allows you to group controls horizontally or vertically.
Button	The same standard button everyone knows and loves. It raises an event that allows you to respond to a user's action.
ButtonGroup	A container control that groups Button controls horizontally.
CheckBox	A standard control that enables or disables selections.
ComboBox	A standard control that displays a list of values. It also enables direct entry via the control's text field.
DropDown	A standard control that displays a list of values. It doesn't allow entry for values not included in the list.
EditBox	The equivalent of a Windows Forms TextBox control. It provides the ability to enter text.
Gallery	A standard control that displays a list of visual choices. It provides the ability to include icons and detailed tool tips known as SuperTips.
Group	A container control that frames a group of controls with a caption.
Label	A standard control that provides descriptive text to a control.
Menu	A drop-down control that is a container for other controls. It is a more powerful version of traditional menus.
Separator	A standard control that draws a line between two controls to provide a visual separation between them, either vertically or horizontally.
SplitButton	A container control that might contain Button, ToggleButton, and/or Menu controls.
Tab	A container for one or more Group controls.
ToggleButton	A standard on/off toggle. It raises an event each time it is clicked, which allows you to respond to a user's action.

Figure 3-10 shows a Ribbon tab that contains each of the different Ribbon controls.

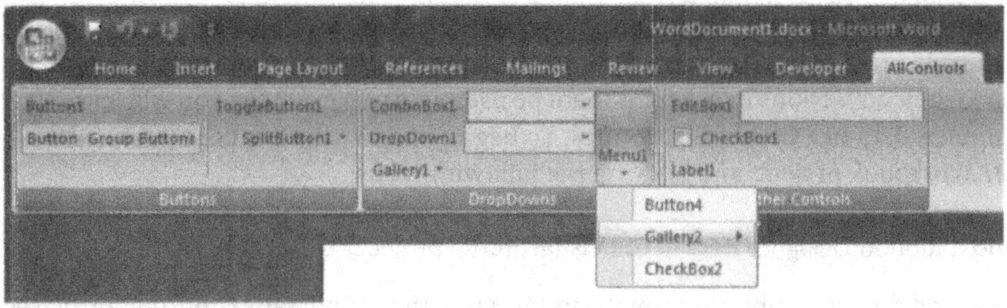

Figure 3-10. *Each and every Ribbon control type on a single tab*

THE OFFICE RIBBON REQUIRES USERS TO ADJUST

Many companies are struggling with the decision of whether or not to deploy Office 2007. Prior to Office 2007, the applications were more or less the same as far as the UI was concerned, and they required little training. Office 2007's Fluent UI changed this situation, and while users eventually grow to appreciate the new UI, the initial response of many long-time Office users is one of disdain.

When conducting Office user research, Microsoft found users were frustrated with the previous Office UI. For example, in previous Office versions, the image-editing toolbar appeared when pictures were inserted into a Word document. Microsoft discovered that most people closed the toolbar to get it out of the way. Minutes later, they would become frustrated when they couldn't figure out how to edit the image. Microsoft also discovered that users would often repeatedly insert and remove pictures in an attempt to correct the placement inside a document. Users inserted and removed pictures over and over, like hamsters running on a wheel.

When Microsoft first created the new Fluent UI, it gave early Office 2007 software to a handful of testers from Fortune 500 companies in the Seattle area. At the time, Office 2007 had the basic framework and concepts in place. Although users found the changes overwhelming at first, they grew to prefer them over the traditional interface after completing five months of testing.

The results at my company have been similar except for the fact that the Ribbon received a positive reception initially. The majority of our staff welcomed the new UI but experienced varying degrees of frustration for a week or two. Almost all of the frustration was due to not knowing where a favorite button was located in the Ribbon, for instance. The user would spend 15–20 minutes hunting for the lost command button. However, after this initial time investment, the frustration levels withered away, and the Ribbon made our staff more productive.

Some Common Customization Examples

With the extensibility of the Fluent UI and the low customization barrier it provides, you will no doubt want to add UI customizations in your projects. Let's build three sample projects that show how to perform some common customization tasks.

Populating a Ribbon Control with Data

Several controls, such as the DropDown control and the ComboBox control, require you to add items to their collections in order for them be useful. In this example, you will learn how to add database data to a ComboBox control. To begin, open Visual Studio, create a new Excel 2007 Workbook project, and perform the following steps:

1. Add a Ribbon Designer item to the Visual Studio project.

2. Drag and drop a ComboBox from the toolbox into the default tab's Group1 control (see Figure 3-11).

Figure 3-11. *A Ribbon ComboBox control just waiting for data*

3. Open the Ribbon's code window and add the code shown in Listing 3-4 to the Ribbon's Load event.

Listing 3-4. *The Ribbon1_Load Event*

```
Private Sub Ribbon1_Load(ByVal sender As System.Object, _
  ByVal e As RibbonUIEventArgs) Handles MyBase.Load
    Dim cnn As New OleDbConnection
    'Set the connection string to the Access DB.
    cnn.ConnectionString = "Provider=Microsoft.ACE.OLEDB.12.0;" & _
      "Data Source=C:\MOD_VSTO\CommonFiles\Northwind2007.accdb"
    cnn.Open()
    'Specify a custom query for Top 10 customers
    Dim cmd As New OleDbCommand("Select Top 10 Company from Customers;", cnn)
    Dim dr As OleDbDataReader = cmd.ExecuteReader()
    'read all returned records and add items
    'to the combo box using the Company field as the label
    While dr.Read()
      Dim ddItm As New RibbonDropDownItem
      ddItm.Label = dr.Item("Company")
      ComboBox1.Items.Add(ddItm)
    End While

    dr.Close()
    cnn.Close()
  End Sub
```

This method opens a connection to the Northwind 2007 database and reads the top ten Company values from the Customers table. The database location on your system might not be the same, so be sure to change the database path if needed.

INSTANT NORTHWIND 2007 DATABASES

A copy of the Northwind 2007 sample database is included in the Source Code/Download area of the Apress web site (http://www.apress.com). You can also download the source code from Microsoft at http://office. microsoft.com/en-us/templates/TC012289971033.aspx?CategoryID=CT102115771033.

You can create a copy of the Northwind 2007 anytime you like, provided you have a copy of Access 2007 lying around. Microsoft solved one of my biggest development problems by including the Northwind database as an Access database template. I no longer need to remember where Northwind resides on my system; I can create a copy anytime I need it. If you have Access 2007 and want to create a Northwind database of your own, just open Access and click Microsoft Office Button ➤ New from the Ribbon. The Northwind template is located in the Samples category.

The code then reads the table row by row and creates a `RibbonDropDownItem`. The `RibbonDropDownItem` object is what populates the ComboBox control. Once created, the code adds the `RibbonDropDownItem` to the ComboBox's `Items` collection.

4. Press F5 to view the ComboBox populated with company names (see Figure 3-12).

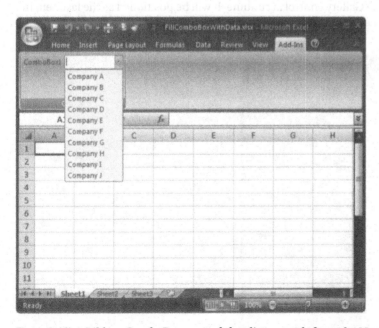

Figure 3-12. *A Ribbon ComboBox control that lists records from the Northwind database*

Customizing the Microsoft Office Button Menu

In this example, you will customize the Microsoft Office Button menu by adding a Gallery control. Let's create a new Word 2007 document project in Visual Studio and add a Ribbon Designer to the project. After you create the project, open the Ribbon1.vb file in the Ribbon Designer, and perform the following steps:

1. Click the Microsoft Office Button to display its menu canvas in Visual Studio (see Figure 3-13).

Figure 3-13. *The Microsoft Office Button canvas at design time*

2. Select the Gallery control from the toolbox and drag it to the Microsoft Office Button's menu canvas.

3. Select a Separator control from the toolbox and drag it above the Gallery control.

4. Press F5 to view the Gallery control at runtime. It will be positioned as the last item in the Microsoft Office Button menu, as shown in Figure 3-14.

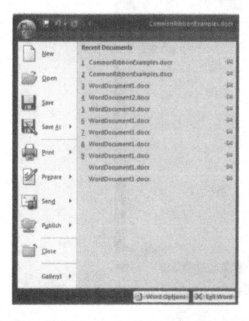

Figure 3-14. *A customized Microsoft Office Button at runtime*

The Microsoft Office Button only supports the Button, CheckBox, Gallery, Menu, Separator, SplitButton, and ToggleButton controls.

Customizing a Built-In Ribbon Tab

Most likely you will want to integrate your add-in's custom commands within the existing Ribbon tab structure of your add-in's host applications. You can incorporate your customizations easily within a built-in Ribbon tab by modifying your custom Ribbon's properties. Let's build a new Word 2007 document project in Visual Studio to build this example. After you create the new project, add a Ribbon Designer item to the project, and perform the following steps:

1. Select Tab1 in the Visual Studio Properties window.

2. Expand the `ControlID` property to display its child properties.

3. Change the `OfficeID` property to **TabHome**. This edit causes any groups that are contained in your custom Ribbon to display on the host application's home tab.

4. Select the Group1 group control. Expand the control's `Position` property to display the `PositionType` property.

5. Change the `PositionType` value to **BeforeOfficeID**. The `OfficeID` property should now be visible.

6. Change the `OfficeID` property value to **GroupStyles**. This value positions Group1 to the left of the Styles group.

7. Press F5 to see the custom Ribbon at runtime (see Figure 3-15).

Figure 3-15. *A custom Ribbon's Group control integrated with the standard Ribbon Home tab*

For a full listing of all the Ribbon control IDs, you can download the reference documents available from Microsoft at `http://www.microsoft.com/downloads/details.aspx?familyid=4329d9e9-4d11-46a5-898d-23e4f331e9ae`.

Creating Action Panes and Task Panes

Office includes the ability to create a special type of form known as a pane. If you're familiar with Office, then you already use panes today, as they typically display on the right side of the screen when you perform a specific task. Action panes are solely implemented within document-level VSTO add-ins. This limitation means that you can only build them when you target Word or Excel. VSTO provides a template for creating action panes (which inherit the Windows

Forms User control). After you build your action pane, follow the familiar Windows Forms development model to display it within the host application and interact with the host document.

Task panes are implemented with application-level VSTO add-ins. A good example of a task pane is the one that Office applications display when you insert clip art (see Figure 3-16). VSTO provides you with the ability to quickly and easily build two types of Office panes: action panes and task panes.

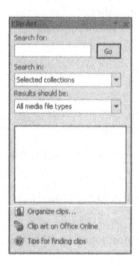

Figure 3-16. *The Clip Art task pane*

With VSTO 2008, only Word, Excel, Outlook, and PowerPoint support task panes. VSTO does not provide a task pane template; instead, you start with a Windows Forms User control.

Task and action panes provide a powerful way to provide your users with context-sensitive tools to help them author documents and perform tasks within an application.

Creating an Action Pane

In this example, you will build an action pane for an Excel workbook add-in. Start by creating an Excel 2007 workbook VSTO add-in and then perform the following steps:

1. Add an ActionPane control to the project in Visual Studio. Leave the name of the control as ActionPaneControl1.

2. Add a Button control to the ActionPaneControl1 ActionPane control.

3. Select ThisWorkbook.vb in the Solution Explorer and open its code view.

4. Add the code shown here to the ThisWorkbook_Startup event:

```
Dim apc As New ActionsPaneControl1
Globals.ThisWorkbook.ActionsPane.Controls.Add(apc)
```

5. Press F5 to run the add-in and see your action pane during runtime (see Figure 3-17).

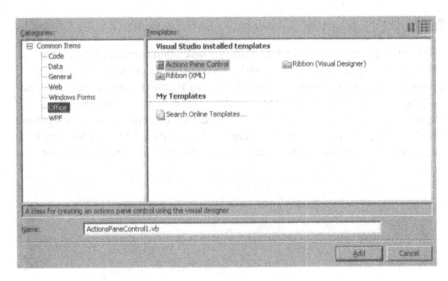

Figure 3-17. *An action pane attached to an Excel workbook*

Creating a Task Pane

In this example, you will build an application-level task pane for Excel. Begin by creating an Excel 2007 add-in VSTO project and then perform the following steps:

1. Add a User control to the project in Visual Studio. Leave the name of the control as UserControl1.

2. Add a Button control to the User control.

3. Select `ThisAdddin.vb` in the Solution Explorer and open its code view.

4. Add the following statement to the Declarations section of the class:

   `Dim tp As Microsoft.Office.Tools.CustomTaskPane`

5. To make the task pane display at startup, add the code shown in Listing 3-5 to the `ThisAddin_Startup` event.

Listing 3-5. *The ThisAddin_Startup Event*

```
Dim uc As New UserControl1
tp = Me.CustomTaskPanes.Add(uc, "Custom Task Pane")
tp.Visible = True
```

6. Press F5 to run the add-in and see your task pane during runtime.

Summary

Using VSTO, customizing the Office UI is a much simpler task when compared with other/older methods of performing UI customization tasks. VSTO provides the Ribbon Designer template and the Ribbon (XML) template for quickly building Ribbon customizations. In addition, VSTO allows you to build two types of panel controls that display within the host application, similar to the Clip Art task pane common to all Office applications. Action panes are intended for document-level solutions and utilize the Actions Pane Control item template. Task panes are intended for application-level add-ins and utilize a User control item template.

■ ■ ■

CHAPTER 4

Building VSTO Excel Add-Ins

Excel is the powerhouse of data modeling. It is revered the world over by users of all types, from hedge-fund managers building highly complex financial models, to hospital administrators managing capital expenditures budgets, to mothers managing their schedules and to-do lists. Excel takes all comers and doesn't even blink.

Visual Studio Tools for the Microsoft Office System (VSTO) gives you the ability to quickly build solutions against the Excel application as well as its file types (.xlsx for workbooks and .xltx for workbook templates). The objects that users typically build, such as tables and named ranges, are full-featured .NET objects inside VSTO. You can identify tables (called ListObject controls in VSTO) and named ranges by name and respond to them. This is a major limitation in Visual Basic for Applications (VBA). VSTO gives you the ability to code directly against the most common Excel objects.

After building the add-ins discussed in this chapter, you will know and understand the following strategies:

- How to navigate to named ranges and list objects in Excel workbooks

- How to synchronize two list objects without using any code

- How to dynamically populate list objects with data

Building the Workbook Explorer

If you've had the pleasure of working with accountants or other financial types, you have most likely encountered more than one ridiculously enormous Excel spreadsheet. Larger and complicated spreadsheets often have 10, 20, 30, or more worksheets, and their related tabs become obscured by Excel's horizontal scrollbar (see Figure 4-1).

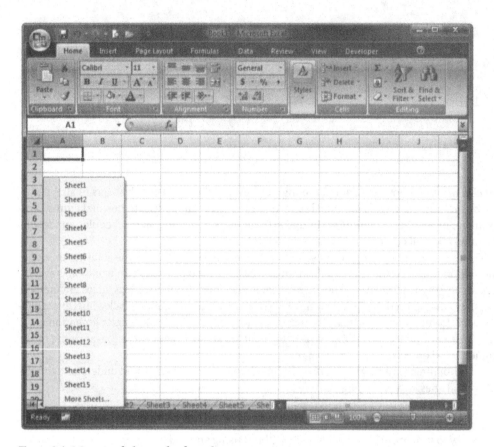

Figure 4-1. *More worksheet tabs than the eye can see*

When you work with an Excel workbook like this, the easiest way to navigate between worksheet tabs is to use the sheet navigator or the name-selection box. The name-selection box is perhaps the quickest and easiest method for navigating within an Excel workbook. This box lists all named objects (ranges and tables) in the workbook and allows you to move instantly to the desired location from anywhere in the spreadsheet.

The combination of the worksheet tabs and the name-selection box works for an individual file. But what about when you have multiple files open? Excel does not provide a user interface (UI) element that displays worksheets and named objects residing in all open files. As a result, working with multiple Excel files at once can require a lot of mouse-clicking just to locate and display data, copy it, move to another workbook, and paste it.

The Workbook Explorer (WEX) provides the ability to view an Excel file's worksheets, named ranges, and tables within a custom action pane (see Figure 4-2). The action pane contains a TreeView control that displays each of these objects in a hierarchical fashion.

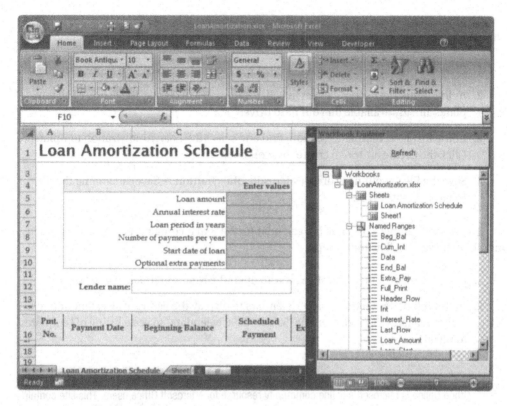

Figure 4-2. *The Workbook Explorer displayed in Excel*

When you open a workbook, the add-in scans the opened file and adds nodes to the Tree-View control for the workbook's worksheets and all named ranges and tables contained in the workbook. You can expand and collapse nodes to find the object you want to see. To move to an object displayed in the tree view, double-click a node; the WEX moves you to and displays the object represented in the node.

The WEX add-in is an Excel application-level add-in and only requires Excel and VSTO. I'll show you how to build the WEX add-in, but first let's build a couple of sample Excel workbooks that contain the objects we want to manipulate.

Building the Sample Excel Workbooks

To highlight the features of the WEX, you need two sample workbooks that each contain a few named ranges and tables. In addition, you need to add several additional worksheets to showcase how the WEX simplifies navigation within a workbook through increased visibility within the TreeView control. You'll use Excel templates files as the basis for the sample workbooks, as they provide ready-made, structured documents that closely resemble workbooks used in organizations everywhere.

The first sample workbook is a loan-amortization schedule that contains a single worksheet and several named ranges. To build it, open Excel and follow these steps:

1. Click Microsoft Office Button and select New to open the New Workbook dialog box.

2. In the Templates section, select Installed Templates to display the listing of all templates already available on your hard drive.

3. In the Installed Templates section, find and select the Loan Amortization template. Click the Create button to create the workbook.

4. Save the file to your hard drive (Microsoft Office Button ➤ Save) and name the file LoanAmortization.xlsx.

The second sample workbook is a calendar for 2008 that contains a worksheet for each month of the year. Follow these steps:

1. Click Microsoft Office Button ➤ New to open the New Workbook dialog box.

2. In the Templates section, select Calendars to display the listing of all calendar templates available via Office Online. Select "2008 calendars" to see a listing of templates for 2008.

■**Tip**   Office Online is Microsoft's online community resource for Microsoft Office users. This site contains tons of great content, including how-to articles, add-ins, and templates. You can find the Office Online template gallery at http://office.microsoft.com/en-us/templates/default.aspx.

---

3. In the "2008 calendars" section, find and select the "2008 calendar on multiple worksheets (12-pp)" template. Click the Download button to download the template from Office Online and create the workbook.

4. Save the file to your hard drive (Microsoft Office Button ➤ Save) and name the file Calendar.xlsx.

Both of these samples include the objects needed to showcase the features of the WEX add-in. Now let's build the add-in project.

Designing the Workbook Explorer Task-Pane Control

The add-in's UI is a custom task pane that displays a visual representation of the supported objects residing in all open workbook files. The UI is a WinForm user control that resides in the right-hand portion of all Excel windows.

The task pane for this add-in is different from the action-pane project templates that VSTO provides in Visual Studio (VS). The action-pane control only works with document-level add-ins and is intended to provide actions related to a specific document. Task panes resemble action panes but are global to the application. The features provided by a task pane should be built to work against all open files in the Office application.

The custom task pane in the WEX add-in does work with all open Excel files. To build the task pane, follow these steps:

1. Create a new VS project using the Excel 2007 Add-in project item template. Name the project **WorkbookExplorer** and click OK.

2. Once VS creates the project, add a WinForm user control by selecting Project ➤ Add New Item from the VS menu.

3. In the Add New Item dialog box, select the User Control item template (see Figure 4-3). Name the new user control **WBExplorer** and click Add.

Figure 4-3. *Adding the WBExplorer WinForm user control to the WEX add-in*

4. With the WBExplorer user control displaying in the designer, add an ImageList control and name it **ImageList**. You need four images to use for the nodes that will populate the control's tree view added in the next step. Select four images from Visual Studio's image library (typically residing in [Boot Drive]:\Program Files\Microsoft Visual Studio 9.0\Common7\VS2005ImageLibrary). Choose any four images; it doesn't matter which ones you choose, since this is a sample. You can see the files I chose in Figure 4-4.

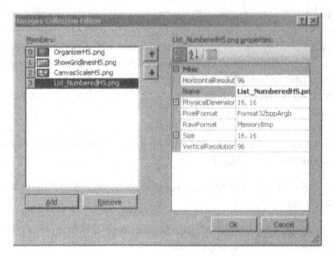

Figure 4-4. *The Images Collection Editor of the ImageList control*

5. Add a TreeView control and set its properties according to Table 4-1.

Table 4-1. *Properties for the WBExplorer TreeView Control*

Property Name	Value
Dock	**Top**
FullRowSelect	**True**
ImageList	**ImageList**
Location	**3,53**
Modifiers	**Friend**
Name	**tvWorkbooks**
SelectedImageIndex	**0**
Size	**186,299**
TabIndex	**2**

6. Add a Button control and name it **btnRefresh**. Table 4-2 lists the properties for this button.

Table 4-2. *Properties for the WBExplorer Button Control*

Property Name	Value
Dock	**Top**
Location	**3,3**
Modifiers	**Friend**
Name	**btnRefresh**

Property Name	Value
Size	186,44
TabIndex	1
Text	&Refresh

Once you complete all the steps, the WBExplorer user control should resemble the one shown in Figure 4-5.

Figure 4-5. *The completed WBExplorer user control in design time*

The control's design is simple, but its simplicity hides the power of its functionality. The code for the WEX add-in illustrates how to trap events at both the Excel application level and the Excel workbook level. The following section explains these strategies in detail.

Writing the Add-In Code

All code for the WEX add-in resides in the project's user control and the ThisAddin class. The actual business rule logic is encapsulated in the user control, while the methods in ThisAddin respond to Excel application and workbook events to call the appropriate user-control methods. Let's build the user control first and then complete the project by writing the event code in ThisAddin.

Coding the WBExplorer User Control

The WBExplorer user control utilizes three class-level objects:

```
Public ndWorkbooks As Windows.Forms.TreeNode
Public SelectedNode As Windows.Forms.TreeNode
Public KeepSelectedNode As Boolean
```

The ndWorkbooks and SelectedNode objects are TreeView node objects. The first node object represents the root node of the tree view and provides access to all nodes in the Tree-View control. The second node object represents the current node selected by the user. The KeepSelectedNode object is a Boolean type that specifies if the code should reselect the currently selected node after performing actions against the tree view.

The WBExplorer_Load Event Method

When the WEX add-in loads, it displays a single node by default. This node is the ndWorkbooks object declared in the previous section as a class-level object. The WBExplorer does not perform any actions automatically. For example, it does not automatically read the contents of Excel's workbooks collection and load their supported objects (i.e., sheets, named ranges, and tables) into the TreeView control. Instead, it provides methods that allow you to add nodes as you require. Listing 4-1 contains the code for the Load event.

Listing 4-1. *The WBExplorer_Load Event*

```
Private Sub WBExplorer_Load(ByVal sender As System.Object, _
  ByVal e As System.EventArgs) Handles MyBase.Load

  ndWorkbooks = tvWorkbooks.Nodes. _
    Add("WEX.Workbooks", "Workbooks", 0, 0)

End Sub
```

The Load event adds a single node to the ndWorkbooks object. The key and text arguments are not important for the proper execution of the add-in, but their names are descriptive and tell the user exactly what the node contains. The last two arguments are imageIndex and selectedImageIndex. Both arguments expect an integer value that represents an image ID of an image in the TreeView control's ImageList control. We're not looking to be fancy in this sample, so let's use one image for both the selected and unselected node states.

The AddWorkbook Procedure

The AddWorkbook procedure takes care of adding an entire workbook to the TreeView control. You should have the Application_WorkbookOpen event call this procedure anytime the user opens or creates a new Excel workbook. Using the workbook passed as a procedure argument, the code sets up all the parent nodes required for a workbook. The code then scans the workbook and adds child nodes representing the worksheets, named ranges, and tables residing in the workbook (see Listing 4-2).

First, the procedure creates a parent node that contains all child nodes for the workbook. Using this parent node, the code then adds three child nodes for the worksheets, named ranges, and tables.

Listing 4-2. *The AddWorkbook Procedure*

```
Friend Sub AddWorkbook(ByVal workbook As Excel.Workbook)
    Dim nodeWb As Windows.Forms.TreeNode

    nodeWb = ndWorkbooks.Nodes.Add(workbook.Name, _
                                    workbook.Name, 0, 0)
    Dim nodeS As Windows.Forms.TreeNode = _
      nodeWb.Nodes.Add("Sheets", "Sheets", 1, 1)
    Dim nodeR As Windows.Forms.TreeNode = _
      nodeWb.Nodes.Add("Ranges", "Named Ranges", 2, 2)
    Dim nodeLst As Windows.Forms.TreeNode = _
      nodeWb.Nodes.Add("TableObjects", "Tables", 3, 3)

    'Loop through all sheets in the wb
    'add a node for each sheet
    'add nodes for each list in each sheet.
    For Each ws As Excel.Worksheet In workbook.Sheets
      Dim SheetNode As Windows.Forms.TreeNode = _
        nodeS.Nodes.Add(workbook.Name & "!" & _
          ws.Name, ws.Name, 1, 1)

      SheetNode.Tag = "Sheets"

      AddListObjectNodes(nodeLst, ws, workbook)

    Next

    'Loop through all named ranges and add nodes
    For Each n As Excel.Name In workbook.Names
      Dim RangeNode2 As Windows.Forms.TreeNode = _
        nodeR.Nodes.Add(workbook.Name & "!" & _
          n.Name, n.Name, 3, 3)

      RangeNode2.Tag = "Ranges"
    Next

End Sub
```

Second, the procedure scans the workbook and adds a new node to the nodes object for each worksheet in the workbook. Third, the code calls the AddListObjectNodes procedure to add nodes for each table object found in the workbook. Fourth (and last), the code reads the workbook's Names collection and adds a node to the nodeR node object for each named range in the file.

Each node you create receives a combination of the workbook's name and the sheet's name as its Key value. This value is strategic, as other code can parse the combined string to quickly identify the workbook and worksheet where the node's represented object resides. In addition, the node's Tag property specifies the type of object the node represents. Again, this value is strategic, as it allows you to branch your code logic based on the type of node you encounter.

The AddListObjectNodes Procedure

The AddListObjectNodes procedure scans a worksheet and adds nodes to a node object. It accepts a tree-node object, a worksheet object, and a workbook object as required arguments (see Listing 4-3).

Listing 4-3. *The AddListObjectNodes Procedure*

```
Private Sub AddListObjectNodes(ByVal node As _
  Windows.Forms.TreeNode, ByVal sheet As Excel.Worksheet, _
  ByVal workbook As Excel.Workbook)

  For Each l As Excel.ListObject In sheet.ListObjects

    Dim newNode As Windows.Forms.TreeNode = _
      node.Nodes.Add(workbook.Name & "!" & l.Name, l.Name, 3, 3)
    newNode.Tag = "Lists"
  Next
End Sub
```

The code reads the contents of the sheet object's ListObjects collection. This collection contains all the tables residing in an Excel worksheet. As the code moves through the ListObjects collection, it adds a new node to the node object passed as an argument. Each node follows the same strategy for the Key and Tag properties implemented in the AddWorkbook procedure.

The AddWorksheet Procedure

The AddWorksheet procedure adds a new node to a workbook's set of nodes. The new node represents a worksheet. This procedure allows you to add new nodes to the TreeView control when a user adds new worksheets in an Excel file (see Listing 4-4).

Listing 4-4. *The AddWorksheet Procedure*

```
Friend Sub AddWorksheet(ByVal workbook As Excel.Workbook, _
                        ByVal sheet As Excel.Worksheet)

  Dim nodeWB As Windows.Forms.TreeNode = _
    ndWorkbooks.Nodes(workbook.Name)
  Dim nodeS As Windows.Forms.TreeNode = nodeWB.Nodes("Sheets")
```

```
    Dim SheetNode As Windows.Forms.TreeNode = _
        nodeS.Nodes.Add(workbook.Name & "!" & _
                          sheet.Name, sheet.Name, 1, 1)
    SheetNode.Tag = "Sheets"
End Sub
```

The procedure uses the Name property of the Workbook argument to find the parent node that will receive the new node. Once found, the procedure adds a new node. Just as is done in the AddWorkbook procedure, the workbook name and the sheet name combine as the value for the node's Key property. You set the node's Tag property to Sheets to identify the node as one representing worksheet objects.

The DeleteWorkbook Procedure

When the user closes a workbook in Excel, you need to remove the workbook node and all its related child nodes from the TreeView control. The DeleteWorkbook procedure performs this task nicely (see Listing 4-5).

Listing 4-5. *The DeleteWorkbook Procedure*

```
Friend Sub DeleteWorkbook(ByVal workbook As Excel.Workbook)
  Dim node As Windows.Forms.TreeNode = _
    ndWorkbooks.Nodes(workbook.Name)

  ndWorkbooks.Nodes.Remove(node)
End Sub
```

The code removes the workbook node and its children in one swoop by calling the Remove method of the user control's TreeView Nodes collection. There is no need to first remove all child nodes.

The tvWorkbooks_NodeMouseDoubleClick Method

The TreeView control waits for you to double-click a node before attempting to navigate to the object that the node represents. The code reads the node's Tag property to determine the type of object the node represents and branches the logic to make the appropriate method call for moving Excel's focus to the selected object (see Listing 4-6).

Listing 4-6. *The tvWorkbooks_NodeMouseDoubleClick Method*

```
Private Sub tvWorkbooks_NodeMouseDoubleClick_1(ByVal sender _
  As System.Object, ByVal e As System.Windows.Forms. _
  TreeNodeMouseClickEventArgs) Handles _
  tvWorkbooks.NodeMouseDoubleClick

  Dim str() As String = e.Node.Name.Split("!")
  Dim wb As Excel.Workbook = _
  Globals.ThisAddIn.Application.Workbooks(str(0))
```

```
    If Not e.Node.Tag Is Nothing Then
      Select Case e.Node.Tag.ToString
        Case "Sheets"
          Dim s As Excel.Worksheet = wb.Sheets(str(1))
          s.Activate()
        Case "Ranges"

          Globals.ThisAddIn.Application.Goto(str(1))
        Case "Tables"

          wb.Activate()
          Globals.ThisAddIn.Application.Goto(str(1))
        Case Else
      End Select
    End If
End Sub
```

The code begins by splitting the node's Tag property into a string array. The array has two items: the first contains the name of the workbook file, and the second contains the name of the worksheet where the node's object resides. Using the first value in the string array, you create a reference to the workbook.

For worksheets, the code creates a reference to the worksheet by finding it in the workbook's Sheets collection and then activating it. This causes Excel to display the sheet in the Excel window. This action also sets the sheet as the Excel Application object's ActiveSheet property.

For ranges and tables, you call the application object's Goto method. This method accepts the string that represents an Excel named reference. Using Goto, you can navigate to named ranges, tables, cells, and even Visual Basic procedures contained in the file.

The btnRefresh_Click Event

The WBExplorer provides the user with the ability to rebuild the tree view at any time. Although not anticipated (because of the solid nature of this example's code), it is possible for the tree view and the open workbooks to lose their synchronization with each other. Even if they are in sync, a user might have reason to believe they are not. The Refresh button solves this situation by calling a method (RefreshAll) that resides in the ThisAddin class (see Listing 4-7).

Listing 4-7. *The Refresh Button's Click Event*

```
Private Sub btnRefresh_Click(ByVal sender As System.Object, _
  ByVal e As System.EventArgs) Handles btnRefresh.Click

  Globals.ThisAddIn.RefreshAll()
End Sub
```

The method resides in ThisAddin in order to make it globally available to the entire project. I'll cover the RefreshAll method in the "The RefreshAll Procedure" section.

Coding the ThisAddin Class

The ThisAddin class provides access to a VSTO application-level add-in and all of its objects. It is the top-level class of the add-in, and it implements the methods required for add-ins to run in Office. The class contains the add-in's Startup and Shutdown methods that allow you to initialize and clean up an add-in's environment.

You can access the host application object in ThisAddin's Application property. This fact makes ThisAddin the best location for responding to events raised by host application objects.

Declarations and References

The WEX add-in needs to respond to user events that add new workbooks, worksheets, named ranges, and tables. You can respond to all these events using the ThisAddin.Application object. Each of these events need to call methods from the WBExplorer control, so you need a class-level object to store this reference. To create the reference, add the following code to the Declarations section:

```
Private _uc As WBExplorer
```

The ThisAddin_Startup Event

When the WEX add-in initializes and loads into memory, you need to display the WBExplorer user control in the Excel window. Listing 4-8 contains the code to create a reference to the user control and add it to the add-in's CustomTaskPanes collection.

Listing 4-8. *The ThisAddin_Startup Event*

```
Private Sub ThisAddIn_Startup(ByVal sender As Object, _
    ByVal e As System.EventArgs) Handles Me.Startup
    Dim tp As Microsoft.Office.Tools.CustomTaskPane

    _uc = New WBExplorer
    tp = Me.CustomTaskPanes.Add(_uc, "Workbook Explorer")
    tp.Visible = True

End Sub
```

You specify "Workbook Explorer" as the task pane's title. This is the string Excel displays at the top of the task pane; it provides the user with a hint as to its purpose. The last step is to make sure the task pane is visible.

The RefreshAll Procedure

You only need one procedure to handle calls to the WBExplorer user control. Each workbook and worksheet event you respond to will call the RefreshAll procedure (see Listing 4-9) and trust it to make the necessary updates to WBExplorer.

Listing 4-9. *The RefreshAll Procedure*

```
Friend Sub RefreshAll()
  _uc.KeepSelectedNode = True
  For Each wb As Excel.Workbook In _
    Globals.ThisAddIn.Application.Workbooks

    _uc.DeleteWorkbook(wb)
    _uc.AddWorkbook(wb)
  Next
  _uc.tvWorkbooks.Nodes(0).ExpandAll()
  _uc.KeepSelectedNode = False
End Sub
```

The code begins by setting the control's KeepSelectedMode property to true to tell the control to maintain the currently selected TreeView node after you finish updating the control. The code updates the WBExplorer control by looping through all open workbooks and deleting them from the control's TreeView control. Once deleted, the code adds the work back into the TreeView control. The effect is a full update of all nodes related to the workbook. The TreeView control properly reflects any edits affecting worksheets, named ranges, and tables.

You need to call RefreshAll for the events listed in Table 4-3. For the add-in to function properly, you need to add code to the events listed.

Table 4-3. *Application Events in ThisAddin That Call RefreshAll*

Event Name

NewWorkbook

SheetCalculate

SheetDeactivate

WorkbookActivate

WorkbookBeforeClose

This strategy might seem overly simplistic and rough around the edges, but it's the simplest approach and serves our purposes for this sample. For an Excel application-level add-in, you can only respond to workbook- and worksheet-related events. The application object does not provide events for the Names and ListObjects (tables) collections. As a result, you can't tell if the user makes changes to these collections directly. You could respond to the Application.SheetChange event and scan the affected sheet to determine the nature of the change, but we don't need to do that here.

The Application_WorkbookOpen Event

Anytime you open a new Excel workbook, you need to update the WBExplorer control to include nodes for the workbook and its related worksheets, named ranges, and tables. The WorkbookOpen event, shown in Listing 4-10, performs tasks with a call to the control's AddWorkbook method.

Listing 4-10. *The Application_WorkbookOpen Event*

```
Private Sub Application_WorkbookOpen(ByVal Wb As  _
    Microsoft.Office.Interop.Excel.Workbook) _
    Handles Application.WorkbookOpen

    _uc.AddWorkbook(Wb)

End Sub
```

The Application_WorkbookNewSheet Event

When you create a workbook, you often add additional worksheets as needed to meet your spreadsheet requirements. The WorkbookNewSheet event executes anytime you add a new worksheet to a workbook. This event is the logical location to call the WBExplorer's AddWorksheet method (see Listing 4-11).

Listing 4-11. *The Application_WorkbookNewSheet Event*

```
Private Sub Application_WorkbookNewSheet(ByVal _
    Wb As Microsoft.Office.Interop.Excel.Workbook, _
    ByVal Sh As Object) Handles Application.WorkbookNewSheet

    _uc.AddWorksheet(Wb, Sh)
End Sub
```

The code passes the affected workbook (Wb) and its new worksheet (Sh) as method arguments.

Running the Workbook Explorer Add-In

Let's take the WEX add-in for a test drive by pressing F6. Once VS compiles the add-in and opens Excel, perform the following steps to test the supported scenarios:

1. Open the LoanAmortization.xlsx sample workbook. The Workbook Explorer task pane creates a set of nodes in the TreeView control. Expand the Sheets node and the Named Ranges node.

2. Add a new sheet to the workbook. The Sheets node updates to include the new sheet (see Figure 4-2).

3. Add a table to the new sheet you created in step 2. The data is not important. Add several columns and rows and add some data, then format the data as a table by clicking the "Format as Table" Ribbon button (this button resides on the Home Ribbon tab in the Styles group). After Excel creates the table, the tree view updates to the workbook's Tables node to include a node for the table.

4. Open the Calendar.xlsx sample workbook. The TreeView control updates to include a node for this workbook and its related objects.

5. Test the add-in's navigation capabilities by double-clicking nodes in the tree view. The add-in instantly changes Excel's focus and displays the object represented by the node you double-click.

Building the Customer Dashboard Workbook

Microsoft has long touted the benefits of using Office applications as a development platform for custom business solutions. And though Office has arguably been a solid platform since Microsoft released Office 95, thanks in large part to VBA, it has struggled to reach the popularity with developers that Microsoft seeks.

A key obstacle preventing many developers from adopting Office was the lack of integration with VS. Sure, you could have used the Shared Add-in project template to build an application-level add-in. But if you wanted to customize the Office user interface, you had to write lots of code. No tools existed to draw the menus or add controls directly to an Office document.

With VSTO, Microsoft just might have hit a home run, as you can now design and build not only application add-ins, but document add-ins as well. Document add-ins allow you to target a single document (Word or Excel only). The development model mimics the Windows Forms model. VSTO provides a designer for the Office document, which allows you to add controls and add code behind them in a manner already familiar to you.

In this sample, you will see how quickly you can build an Excel workbook that reads data from a database to provide you with a dashboard-type summary. The Customer Dashboard (CDASH) is a VSTO Excel workbook add-in that presents the user with several data elements related to a customer record. The following workflow shows how the user uses this add-in:

1. The user opens the Customer Dashboard workbook file. The main worksheet in the file contains a list box filled with customer records from an external data source.

2. Once the user selects a customer from the list box, that customer's order history fills the Order History table. Each time the user makes a new selection in the customer list box, the add-in updates the Order History table (see Figure 4-6).

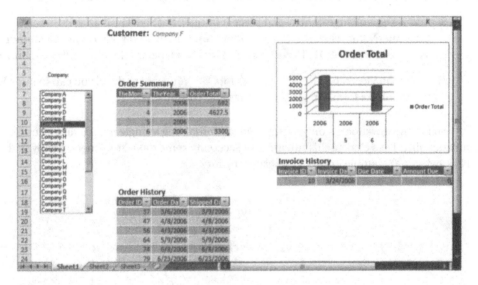

Figure 4-6. *The Customer Dashboard in Excel*

3. Each time the user selects a new customer, the Order Summary table and related chart update to show the customer's order history by month.

4. The user can see the invoice history for an order. If the user selects a row in the Order History table, the Invoice History table will populate with any related invoice records. The Invoice History table updates as the user selects new rows in the Order History table.

Designing the Customer Dashboard Workbook

The Customer Dashboard is a document-level VSTO add-in; it works against a single Excel workbook file. Excel functions as the front-end UI for data from a Northwind 2007 sample Access application.

To begin creating the CDASH add-in, open VS and follow these steps:

1. Create a new VS project using the Excel 2007 Workbook project item template. Name the project **CustomerDashboard** and click OK.

2. In the "Select a Document for Your Application" dialog box, select the "Create a new document" option. Accept the default values for the other fields and click OK.

3. Add a NamedRange control and place it in cell E1 of Sheet1. Change its name to **CustomerName** using the Visual Studio Properties window. Also, enter **Customer:** as the value for cell D1. This string will serve as a label for the NamedRange control.

4. Select the View tab in the workbook's Ribbon. You want to do all you can to force Excel to resemble a form. Uncheck Gridlines and Formula Bar.

So far, the workbook is only a blank canvas containing a single named range and zero functionality. Let's change this situation by accessing some data. You'll need a copy of the Northwind 2007 sample Access database going forward.

INSTANT NORTHWIND 2007 DATABASES

A copy of the Northwind 2007 sample database is included in the book's source code package, which you can find in the Source Code/Download area of the Apress web site (http://www.apress.com). You can download the Northwind 2007 source code from Microsoft at http://office.microsoft.com/en-us/templates/TC012289971033.aspx?CategoryID=CT102115771033.

Also, you can create a copy of Northwind 2007 anytime you like, provided you have a copy of Access 2007 lying around. Microsoft solved one of my biggest development problems by including the Northwind database as an Access database template. I no longer need to remember where Northwind resides on my system; I can now create a copy anytime I need it. If you have Access 2007 and want to create a Northwind database of your own, just open Access and click Microsoft Office Button ➤ New from the Ribbon. The Northwind template is located in the Samples category.

Configuring the Data Objects

One of the great features of VSTO is the simplicity it provides when working with data. Using VSTO, you can attach a data source to your project and bind it to controls without writing any code. This scenario works well for building more simple solutions with a quick turnaround time. However, given the fact that VSTO utilizes the standard data classes in the .NET Framework, you have full control over data sources. If your business rules require you to create data sources and/or SQL statements dynamically, you can make it happen.

In the CDASH sample, I'll show you how to make use of the drag-and-drop data features in VSTO as well as dynamic SQL statements for binding data to list objects in the workbook. However, before you can do any of this, you need to create the project's data source. You can add the Northwind 2007 database to the project by performing the following steps:

1. From the Visual Studio menu, click Project ➤ Add Existing Item. Navigate to the location where the Northwind database resides on your system. Select the Northwind database and click Add to add it to the project and open the Data Source Configuration Wizard (see Figure 4-7).

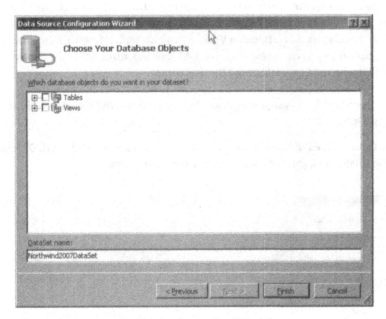

Figure 4-7. *The Data Source Configuration Wizard*

2. In the Data Source Configuration Wizard, expand Tables and select the Customers, Invoices, and Orders tables.

3. Name the dataset **Northwind2007DataSet**, and click the Finish button to add the data source to the project.

The Data Source Configuration Wizard adds two objects to the project. The first is a local copy of the Northwind database. This is a copy of the file you selected and will be the data source the project uses to read data.

The second object is an XML schema file that details the data schema of the objects you selected while adding the database to the project. If you open the file in Visual Studio (see Figure 4-8), you will see each of the tables mapped in the schema. Their table names, columns, data types, and relationships are part of the schema. This schema is vital to VSTO's drag-and-drop functionality. For example, if you add a list object control to a worksheet and then bind the Customers table as its data source, the list object will grow automatically to accommodate all the fields in the table. It is the data within the dataset's schema that the list object reads to build its own set of related columns.

Now that you have the dataset as part of your project, you can continue building out the user interface by adding more controls and binding data to them.

Adding the Company List Box and Filling It with Data

The add-in provides you with the ability to select a customer from a list-box control filled with customer names. The list box is a standard WinForm list box. The unique aspect of this list box is that resides in an Excel worksheet. It isn't a VBA control; instead, it is a .NET control, and it provides all the capabilities you would expect from a WinForm control. Add the list-box control to the form and fill it with data by performing these actions:

1. Open the Sheet1.vb file's designer in Visual Studio (you can right-click the file and select View Designer).

2. Open the Data Sources window (see Figure 4-8) and expand the Northwind2007DataSet so that the Customers, Invoices, and Orders nodes are visible.

Figure 4-8. *The Data Sources window displaying the Northwind2007DataSet*

3. Expand the Customers node, and select the Company node. This node represents the Company data column contained in the Customers table. Look again at Figure 4-8, where you can see a drop-down arrow next to the Company node. This drop-down arrow allows you to specify what type of control VSTO will use when you drag and drop the Company node onto the worksheet.

4. Click the drop-down arrow, and change the Company node's control type to ListBox. The data source window updates to show the ListBox icon next to the Company node (see Figure 4-9).

Figure 4-9. *The Company node displaying a ListBox as its control type*

5. Table 4-4 lists the control types available in an Excel workbook project. The default control type is NamedRange.

Table 4-4. *Control Types Available for Data Fields*

Control	Type	Description
NamedRange	VSTO control	A host-control wrapper for an Excel named range. Use this control to display a single data element.
ListObject	VSTO control	A host-control wrapper for an Excel table. Use this control to display a list of data within Excel columns and rows.
TextBox	WinForm control	A standard WinForm text box. Use this control to capture data input in a manner typical to WinForm applications.
ComboBox	WinForm control	A standard WinForm combo-box control. Use this control to select a value from a list of values in a manner typical to WinForm applications.

Table 4-4. *Control Types Available for Data Fields (Continued)*

Control	Type	Description
Label	WinForm control	A standard WinForm label control. Use this control to label a control or to provide additional information related to a form.
LinkLabel	WinForm control	A standard WinForm link-label control. Use this control to provide a link to additional data not displayed in the current form.
ListBox	WinForm control	A standard WinForm list-box control. Use this control to display a list of values that you can select in a manner typical to WinForm applications.

6. Drag the Company node to Sheet1.vb's design surface and place it near cell A5. VS adds a new ListBox control to the worksheet and binds its data source automatically to the Company field of the Customers table.

7. Move the list box's position to be just under the Company label, and change the control's settings to those listed in Table 4-5. The Company list box is now complete.

Table 4-5. *The Property Settings for the Customers ListBox Control*

Property Name	Value
Name	CompanyListBox
Width	120
Height	210
DataSource	CustomersBindingSource
DataMember	Customers
ValueMember	ID

Once you add the Company field to Sheet1, you may notice several new objects added to the bottom of Sheet1's designer (see Figure 4-10).

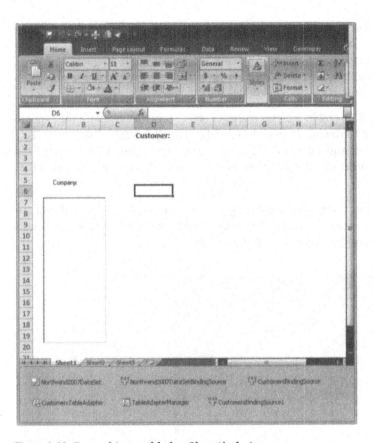

Figure 4-10. *Data objects added to Sheet1's designer*

VSTO requires the following objects to perform data binding:

- `Northwind2007DataSet`: The dataset contains a reference to the data source utilized within the designer. This object provides schema type information for the dataset.

- `Northwind2007DataSetBindingSource` *and* `CustomersBindingSource`: A binding source acts as a proxy for the underlying data source. VSTO utilizes a proxy because it can't be sure if the underlying data source will contain data when the add-in initially loads. The use of a proxy binding source allows the project's controls to bind to the data source even if it is empty. Once the data source fills with data, the bound controls will update via the binding source proxy.

- `CustomersTableAdapter`: Table adapters open a connection to the data source, query it for the specified table or query, and fill the dataset with the returned data. The data returned is a local copy disconnected for the source data. The table adapter provides methods for updating the source data with any updates performed on the local copy (i.e., any data that's been added, edited, or deleted).

- `TableAdapterManager`: The table-adapter manager object provides you with the capability to save data in the `TableAdapter` objects. This object performs SQL `INSERT`, `UPDATE`, and `DELETE` actions that affect the tables represented by each table-adapter object. This object manages the order of the SQL actions to maintain relational integrity across the affected tables.

At this point, you can test the add-in by pressing F5. The project opens Excel and displays the `CustomerDashboard.xlsx` workbook. Shortly after loading the workbook, Sheet1 becomes visible, and CompanyListBox fills with data (see Figure 4-11).

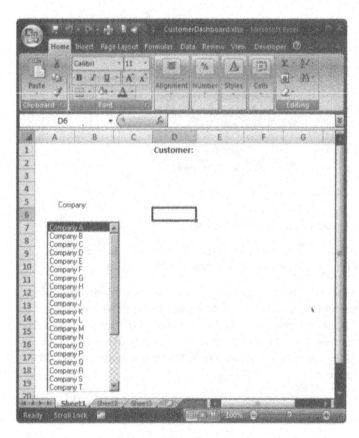

Figure 4-11. *The CompanyListBox filled with customer records*

You need only a few more objects before you're ready to code the project. The following sections detail how to add the remaining UI controls.

Configuring the OrderHistory ListObject

The OrderHistory ListObject control automatically synchronizes with the value you select in the CompanyListBox control. You don't need to write any code, as VSTO handles this synchronization automatically, provided you set up the controls correctly. To create a ListObject control to contain a company's order history, complete the following steps:

1. With the Data Sources window visible, expand the Customers node.

2. The Orders node resides at the bottom of the Customers node. Drag and drop this Orders node to cell A15.

3. VS adds a new list-box object that is bound to the CustomersBindingSource object. The list-box object also expands to include all fields in the Orders table.

4. You don't want to display all columns in the list box, so you need to remove those that you don't need. Select the EmployeeID cell inside the order list box and right-click to display the context menu. Click Delete ➤ Table Columns from the context menu to delete the EmployeeID column.

5. Repeat step 4 until only the Order ID, Order Date, and Shipped Date columns remain.

Configuring the InvoiceHistory ListObject

The InvoiceHistory ListObject control automatically synchronizes with the order record selected in the OrderHistory ListObject control. The InvoiceHistory ListObject control displays invoices that exist related to the selected order. Once again, VSTO handles synchronization automatically. To create the InvoiceHistory ListObject control, perform the following steps:

1. In the visible Data Sources window, expand the Customers node.

2. At the bottom the Customers node, expand the Orders node.

3. Select the Invoices node (visible as the last node of the Orders node) and drag it to cell H15 in Sheet1.

4. Following the same method for deleting columns described in step 4, delete all columns until only the columns for Invoice ID, Invoice Date, Due Date, and Amount Due remain.

Configuring the OrderSummary ListObject

The OrderSummary ListObject control contains order summary data for the record selected in the CompanyListBox. This list object does not automatically fill with data for the Northwind2007DataSet. Instead, you fill the list dynamically with a custom query.

You fill a list object dynamically with data using a dynamic SQL statement and a call to the project's data source. I explain the code to perform this action in the "Writing the Add-In Code" section. For now, you only need to build a bland list object to act as a shell. Follow these steps:

1. Add the ListObject control to Sheet1 by dragging the ListObject control from the VS toolbox to cell D7. Click OK in the Add ListBox Control dialog box.

2. A new list object now resides in Sheet1 with a single column labeled Column1. Change the name of this column to **TheMonth**. This column contains an integer value that represents a month of the year.

3. Select cell E7 and enter **TheYear** as the cell's value. This column contains an integer value that represents the year.

4. Select cell F7 and enter **OrderTotal** as the cell's value. This column contains a summation of all order amounts for the month and year represented in columns E7 and F7.

For now, the list remains blank. That said, this list provides the schema you need to build the dashboard's chart.

Configuring the Order Summary Chart

The Order Summary chart displays a bar chart that visually represents the data in the OrderSummary ListObject control. This chart updates automatically when the OrderSummary ListObject control updates. To create the pie chart and bind it to the OrderSummary ListObject control, complete the following steps:

1. Make Sheet1 visible in Designer view, and select cell D7.

2. From the Excel Ribbon, select the Insert tab.

3. In the Charts group, click Column ➤ Clustered Cylinder to insert the chart into Sheet1.

4. Resize the chart and position it to the right of the OrderSummary ListObject control and just above the InvoiceHistory ListObject control (see Figure 4-12).

5. Right-click the chart, and click Select Data from the context menu.

6. In the Select Data Source dialog box, click Add in the Legend Entries section.

7. In the Edit Series dialog box, enter **OrderTotal** in the Series Name field. In the Series Values field, enter =Sheet1!$F$8. Click OK to return to the Select Data Source dialog box.

8. In the Horizontal (Category) Axis Labels section, click Edit. The Axis Labels dialog box displays. Enter =Sheet1!$D$8:$E$8 as the value for the Axis label range field. Click OK twice to close all the dialog boxes and complete the chart configuration.

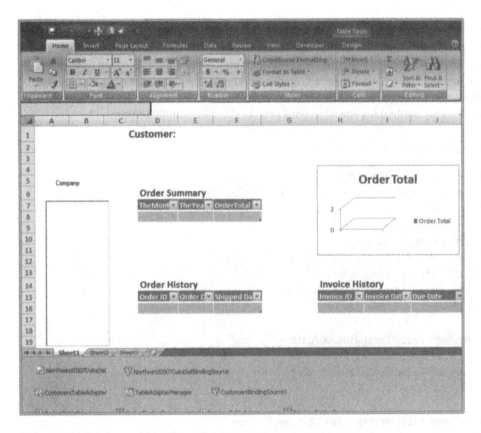

Figure 4-12. *The chart object in its rightful position*

Your version of the workbook should closely resemble the one shown in Figure 4-12. Some of the features already function as needed (i.e., the CompanyListBox control, the OrderHistory List-Object control, and the InvoiceHistory ListObject control). However, the OrderSummary ListObject control and the CustomerName named range require some code to function properly. The remainder of this chapter explains how to write the code required to complete the CDASH project.

Writing the Add-In Code

The code for the CDASH add-in resides behind the Sheet1 worksheet (Sheet1.vb). All workbook add-ins have Startup and Shutdown events in the ThisWorkbook.vb class. This class is the location for initializing and cleaning up any objects that the entire project requires at runtime. For the CDASH add-in, you'll leave those methods in their stubbed-out form, as you don't need use them in this project.

Each worksheet also implements the Startup and Shutdown methods. The Sheet1.vb class contains all the code needed to dynamically populate the worksheet with data, starting with the Sheet1_Startup method.

The Sheet1_Startup Method

When a VSTO add-in attaches to an Excel workbook, the VSTO runtime fires a series of Startup events. The process begins with the workbook's Startup event and proceeds to execute the Startup method for each worksheet within the workbook. The order of the process follows the index order of the workbook's Worksheets collection.

The Startup method for Sheet1 in your project should resemble Listing 4-12.

Listing 4-12. *The Sheet1_Startup Method*

```
Private Sub Sheet1_Startup(ByVal sender As Object _
, ByVal e As System.EventArgs) Handles Me.Startup
  'TODO: Delete this line of code to
  'remove the default AutoFill for
  'Northwind2007DataSet.Invoices'.
  If Me.NeedsFill("Northwind2007DataSet") Then
    Me.InvoicesTableAdapter.Fill( _
      Me.Northwind2007DataSet.Invoices)
  End If


  If Me.NeedsFill("Northwind2007DataSet") Then
    Me.OrdersTableAdapter.Fill( _
      Me.Northwind2007DataSet.Orders)
  End If


  If Me.NeedsFill("Northwind2007DataSet") Then
    Me.CustomersTableAdapter.Fill( _
      Me.Northwind2007DataSet.Customers)
  End If


  GetOrderData(True)
End Sub
```

The code for the Startup method is generated 100% by VSTO when you set up the controls using Sheet1's visual designer. Notice the comment at the beginning of the method. VSTO defaults to automatically filling each table adapter with data at startup.

You can change this behavior by editing the code and choosing to fill the table adapter somewhere else. For example, you might have an extremely large dataset that you want to populate a worksheet. In this case, you might not want to load the data during the add-in's initialization, as it will slow down its performance. Instead, you could wait and fill the dataset when the user chooses to by providing a button and placing the code for filling the dataset in the button's Click event.

You only need to add a call to the GetOrderData method. This method populates the OrderSummary ListObject control and the OrderSummary chart control using the entire order history as its data source.

The CompanyComboBox_SelectedIndexChanged Method

When you select a company using the CompanyComboBox, you want to take a couple of actions. First, you want to update the NamedRange control in the worksheet to display the value you selected. Second, you want to call a custom procedure that queries the Northwind database and updates the OrderSummary ListObject control. Listing 4-13 shows you how to do this.

Listing 4-13. *The CompanyComboBox_SelectedIndexChange Method*

```
Private Sub CompanyComboBox_SelectedIndexChanged(ByVal sender _
  As System.Object, ByVal e As System.EventArgs) _
  Handles CompanyComboBox.SelectedIndexChanged


  GetOrderData(False)
End Sub
```

The event method reads the Text property of the CompanyListBox control and inserts it as the value of the CustomerName NamedRange control. Then the procedure calls the GetOrderData method.

GetOrderData Procedure

The GetOrderData procedure (see Listing 4-14) reads order data from the project's Northwind database. It has a single Boolean argument (IncludeAll) that specifies if the procedure should return a summary for all orders in the database or if it should only return a summary for the company selected in the CompanyListBox control.

Listing 4-14. *The GetOrderData Procedure*

```
  Private Sub GetOrderData(ByVal IncludeAll As Boolean)
    Dim sql As String
    sql = "SELECT Month([Order Summary].[Order Date])"
    sql = sql & " AS TheMonth, Year([Order Summary].[Order Date]) "
    sql = sql & " AS TheYear, Sum([Order Summary].[Order Total]) "
    sql = sql & " AS [SumOfOrder Total] FROM [Order Summary] "
    If Not IncludeAll Then
      sql = sql & " WHERE [Order Summary].[Customer ID]=" & _
        CompanyComboBox.SelectedValue
    End If
    sql = sql & " GROUP BY Month([Order Summary].[Order Date]), "
    sql = sql & " Year([Order Summary].[Order Date]); "

    'Set up the connection and the query
    Dim cnn As OleDb.OleDbConnection = _
      Globals.Sheet1.OrdersTableAdapter.Connection
    Dim cmd As New OleDb.OleDbCommand(sql, cnn)
```

```
'Reset the data for the list.
Dim adpProducts As New OleDb.OleDbDataAdapter
adpProducts.TableMappings.Add("Table", "Products")
adpProducts.SelectCommand = cmd

Dim ds = New DataSet("Products")
adpProducts.Fill(ds)
Dim dt As DataTable = ds.Tables(0)

Me.List1.DataSource = dt
End Sub
```

The procedure dynamically creates a SQL statement to summarize the results from the
OrderSummary query residing in the Northwind database. If the IncludeAll argument is true, the
SQL statement will return all records. If IncludeAll is false, the procedure will add a WHERE
clause to the SQL statement and use the Customer ID selected in the CompanyListBox control.

In either case, the procedure executes the custom query against the project's connection
to the Northwind database. The data returned by the query fills the OrderSummary list object
(List1).

Testing the Customer Dashboard Workbook Add-In

Now is the time to put the Customer Dashboard add-in to the test. Compile and run the
project, and test the features you've implemented. Once Excel opens, follow these steps to
test each feature:

1. When Excel opens, check the CompanyListBox control to ensure it populates with company names from the Northwind Customers table.

2. In the CompanyListBox control, select Company F. The worksheet updates to display
   data related to Company F.

3. Select a row in the OrderHistory ListObject control. The InvoiceHistory updates to display invoices attached to the order.

Summary

Named ranges and list objects define regions of rows and columns in an Excel workbook. They
allow users to provide a meaningful name to the region and return to the region more easily as
they work with the workbook.

ListObject controls are actually wrappers of tables within Excel. Using VSTO, you can populate list objects with data external to Excel without writing any code. In addition, you can keep
list objects synchronized, provided they contain related data.

VSTO provides powerful tools that allow you to quickly incorporate external data in you
Excel add-ins without requiring you to write any code. These tools work in a lot of situations,
but you can take control and populate a list object with data using dynamic data objects.

You can create a connection to the external data source using a .NET connection object. You can then execute a query against the data source and return a dataset. You can then assign the dataset as the data source of the ListObject and configure the ListObject as needed to display the appropriate text.

CHAPTER 5

■ ■ ■

Building VSTO Word Add-Ins

Word is perhaps the most appropriately named Office application. Word is, well, about putting words on paper. Whether you're crafting a status report, building a proposal, or writing a book, Word is there for you to help you shape and format your content.

Visual Studio Tools for the Microsoft Office System (VSTO) provides you with the ability to create both document-level and application-level add-ins. These add-in types allow you to target solutions that support a single Word document (.docx and .docm files) or Word template (.dotx and .dotm files) file. In addition, you can build solutions that target the Word application itself and are available anytime Word executes.

As it does for Excel, VSTO provides .NET controls for Word that correspond to the most common objects utilized when creating Word solutions. All the controls minus one (the Bookmark control) fall under the category of *content controls*. Content controls serve as named placeholders within a document. They provide a familiar WinForm-type method for accessing content directly in a document without requiring you to scan the document, as VBA would require.

This chapter will explain how to build two sample VSTO Word add-ins. The first is a document-level add-in that demonstrates how to use objects in Word to automate document creation. The second is an application-level add-in that shows how to enhance a user's experience in Word by extending Word's functionality.

After building the add-ins in this chapter, you will know and understand the following strategies:

- How to add content controls to documents and insert data within them

- How to use code to create new document building blocks

- How to build an action pane that allows a user to select reusable content from a database and insert it into the document

- How to build a custom Ribbon that works with the user's file system and places a library of document templates at the user's fingertips.

Building the ReportBuilder Document Add-In

If you use Word, you've probably created the same document (or at least very similar documents) more than once. When creating a similar document, you'll most likely execute one of the following strategies:

- Create a document from one of the standard document templates included in a typical Word installation. The templates provide nice structure but lack 100% of the content.

- Find a similar document created for a different audience (a client, a professor, the PTA, etc.), copy it, and edit it. This strategy has the advantage of including content, but it requires a disciplined eye to tailor it to the new audience and remove references to the previous audience.

- Find a talented programmer to build a tool that lets you build documents quickly while effectively reusing existing content and tailoring content to your audience.

The last option is exactly what the first sample add-in does. The ReportBuilder add-in provides the user with an action pane filled with existing content (see Figure 5-1). With only a few clicks, the user can select content and insert it into the desired location within the document.

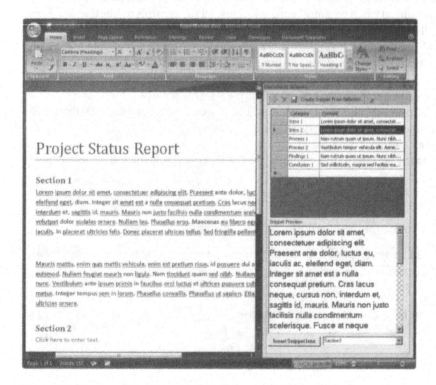

Figure 5-1. *The ReportBuilder add-in helps a user build a report.*

Designing the Sample Report Document

The ReportBuilder add-in targets a single Word document named ReportBuilder.docx. This document contains three content controls that serve as placeholders for inserting content later. You can build this document in Word and then import it into a new Word VSTO document add-in, or you can build it using Visual Studio. I'll show you how to use the latter option, as the Visual Studio Word designer provides the capabilities you need.

To build the ReportBuilder.docx document, follow these steps:

1. Create a new Visual Studio project using the Word 2007 "Document project" template. Name the project **ReportBuilder** and click OK.

2. In the Select a Document for Your Application dialog box, select the "Create a new document" option and accept the default values for the remaining fields. Click OK.

3. Open the ReportBuilder.docx object in its designer. Use Figure 5-2 as a guide and add three RichTextContentControl controls to the document's design canvas.

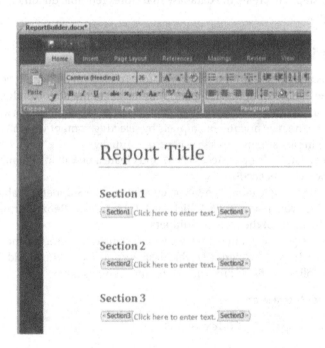

Figure 5-2. *The ReportBuilder.docx document displayed in its Visual Studio designer*

4. Select the first content control, and set the Tag and Title property values to **Section1**.

5. Follow step 4 for the two remaining controls by setting their property values to correspond with their content control's number (i.e., **Section2** or **Section3**).

6. Add a report title at the top of the document and format it with the Title format. Also, add section headers for Section 1, Section 2, and Section 3. Format each as Heading 1.

MORE ABOUT CONTENT CONTROLS

Word provides several types of content controls that you can use to host different types of content. Most of the controls will be familiar to you and will function as you would expect. For example, the ComboBoxContentControl contains a list of values the user can select. The PlainTextContentControl and RichTextContentControl each support text entry and formatted text entry, respectively.

The building block gallery is unique in its concept. This control displays a listing of formatted content choices called a *gallery*. The user can select from this listing, and the chosen text is inserted into the content control along with its specified formatting.

To learn more about content controls, visit the Office Online web site at `http://office.microsoft.com/word/HA100307501033.aspx`.

Although simple, this design provides a solid document structure that you can utilize for the sample add-in. The next step is to create the database that stores reusable document snippets that this add-in can utilize.

Creating the DocSnippets Database

The DocSnippets database is an Access 2007 database that stores chunks of content. It contains a single table with three fields. When DocSnippets is connected to the ReportBuilder add-in, the user will be able to insert existing document snippets from the database. In addition, the user will be able to create new document snippets by selecting content within Word and clicking a button or by entering snippets in a grid control manually.

To build the DocSnippets database, open Access 2007 and create a new blank database (see Figure 5-3). Name it **DocSnippets.accdb**.

The database contains only a single table. When you created the DocSnippets database, Access created a default table for you named Table1. Rick-click Table1, select Rename from the context menu, and change the name of the table to **Snippets**.

To complete the table's design, open it in Design view by clicking the Home tab and then selecting View ➤ Design View. This action opens the table designer and allows you to add fields and set their properties. The following fields are required for the Snippets table:

- `FieldName=ID; DataType=AutoNumber`

- `FieldName=Category; DataType=Text; FieldSize=255`

- `FieldName=Content; DataType=Memo`

Be sure to set the ID column as the table's primary key by clicking the Primary Key button (see Figure 5-4), which is available in the Design tab (be sure the ID field is the current field).

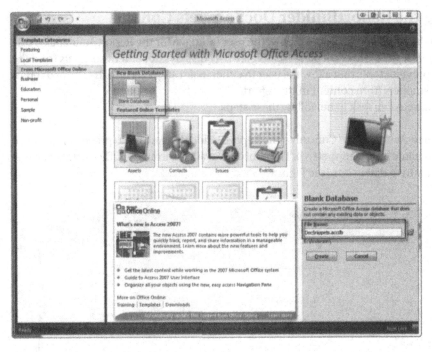

Figure 5-3. *Creating a blank database in Access 2007*

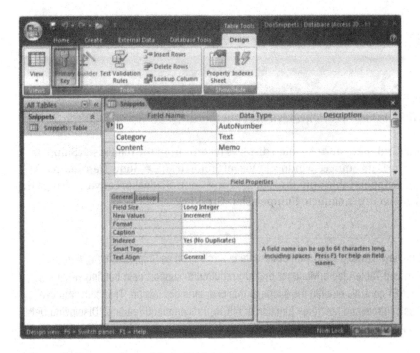

Figure 5-4. *The Snippets table in Design view*

Designing the ReportBuilder DocSnippets Control

In addition to the Word application window, the user interface for the ReportBuilder also utilizes a custom task pane. This task pane (see Figure 5-1) displays document snippets from the database and provides tools that allow the user to either insert snippets into the opened report or create new snippets from content in the report.

To build the custom task pane, follow these steps:

1. Add a new Actions Pane Control to the ReportBuilder Visual Studio project created earlier and name it **DocSnippets.vb**. The control is available from the Office category in the Add New Item dialog box (see Figure 5-5).

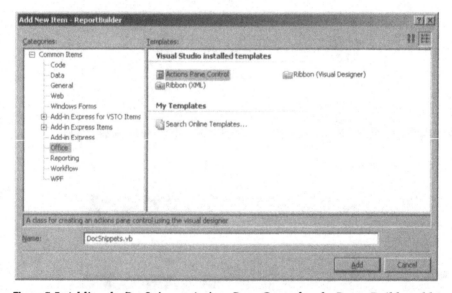

Figure 5-5. *Adding the DocSnippets Actions Pane Control to the ReportBuilder add-in*

2. Add the DataGridView control, which displays records from the database's Snippets table. Open the Data Sources window in Visual Studio (Data ➤ Show Data Sources) and drag the Snippets table onto the Actions Pane Control's design canvas. Change the DataGridView control's name to **SnippetsDataGridView**.

■**Note** The DataGridView control, along with other data controls such as SnippetsBindingSource, SnippetsTableAdapter, and TableAdapterManager that are required to support data binding within the control, are standard .NET controls outside the scope of this chapter's discussion. That said, you can read more about these controls and how they function at MSDN. I recommend reading "Displaying Data on Forms in Windows Applications" (http://msdn.microsoft.com/ms171923(VS.80).aspx) to get you started.

---

3. You don't want to display the ID column in the grid. To hide this column, open the DataGridView control's Columns property in the Properties window. In the Edit Columns dialog box, select the ID column and change its Visible property to False (see Figure 5-6). Click OK.

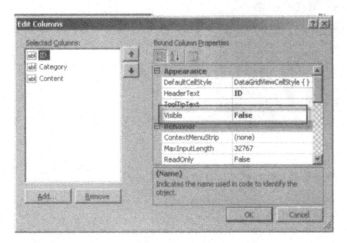

Figure 5-6. *Setting the ID column's Visibile property to False*

4. Add the Label control below the DataGridView control and set its Text property to Snippet Preview.

5. Add a RichTextBox control below the Label control and name it **PreviewBox**. This control will display text from the record selected in the DataGridView control, so it needs to be large enough so you can see several lines of text. Set the Font to Ariel, 12pt. This will make the preview easier on the eyes.

6. Add a Button control below the TextBox control and name it **btnInsert**. When you click this button, it will execute the code that inserts the selected text into the document. Set the Text property to Insert Snippet Into:. If needed, resize the button so that the button text displays on a single line.

7. Add a ComboBox control next to the Button control and name it **cboContentControlList**. This control will contain the names of all content controls residing in the ReportBuilder.docx document. Combined with the Button control you created in step 6, this control will determine where text should be inserted.

8. Customize the SnippetsBindingNavigator control that Visual Studio added along with the DataGridView control in step 2. This control is the toolbar residing at the top of the DocSnippets control (see Figure 5-7). Delete all buttons except for the AddNewItem, DeleteItem, and SaveItem buttons. You can delete the buttons by right-clicking them and selecting Delete from the context menu.

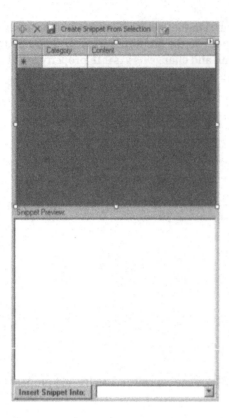

Figure 5-7. *The DocSnippets Actions Pane Control in the designer*

9. Add a new button to the SnippetsBindingNavigator control by clicking the
   AddToolStripButton button at the end of the toolstrip. A drop-down menu shows
   the different types of controls you can add to the control's toolstrip. Select Button
   to add a new button. Be sure the new button is the active selection, and change
   its name to **InsertSelection**. Set the button's Text property to **Create Snippet From
   Selection**. The DisplayStyle is Text.

10. Add an additional button to the SnippetsBindingNavigator control and name it
    CreateBlock. Leave all other properties at their default values. If you'd like, you can
    customize the image icon by editing the Image property and browsing for an image
    of your choosing.

After you complete these steps, the DocSnippets control should somewhat resemble
Figure 5-7. The control follows a logical sequence from top to bottom. The user selects his
desired snippet from the grid control, causing the selected content to display in the preview
control. The user can select the desired location for the selected content from the combo box
at the bottom of the control. By clicking the Insert Snippet Into button, the add-in will insert
the selected text into the selected location.

Writing the Add-In Code

With the exception of the code required to actually display the DocSnippets action pane, all of the add-in code resides in the DocSnippets control. The business rules logic resides within the control itself, while the ThisDocument class performs the task of loading the action pane into the Word application window. Let's add the code for the control before moving on to the ThisDocument class.

The DocSnippets control manipulates several Word objects. To make referencing these objects easier, the control declares the Word namespace as follows:

```
Imports Microsoft.Office.Interop.Word
```

There are no class-level variables, so let's build out the code behind this control, beginning with the Load event.

The DocSnippets_Load Event Method

Before the DocSnippets action pane loads into the Word window, you want to fill its controls with their expected data. This includes scanning the ReportBuilder.docx file for any existing content controls and placing their names in the form's ComboBox control. It also includes connecting to the DocSnippets Access database and filling the DataGridView control with available document snippets. Listing 5-1 contains the action pane's Load event.

Listing 5-1. *The DocSnippets_Load Event Method*

```
Public Class DocSnippets
  Private Sub DocSnippets_Load(ByVal sender As System.Object, _
  ByVal e As System.EventArgs) Handles MyBase.Load

    Dim controls As ContentControls
    controls = Globals.ThisDocument.ContentControls

    For Each ctl As ContentControl In controls

      Me.cboContentControlList.Items.Add(ctl.Tag)
    Next

    Me.SnippetsTableAdapter1.Fill(Me.DocSnippetsDataSet1.Snippets)

  End Sub
```

The code creates a reference to the document's ContentControls collection and loops though each content control in the collection, adding the value of the current content control's Tag property as an item in the ComboBox control. Because the DataGridView control is bound to the Snippets table, all that is required is to call the Fill method of the SnippetsTableAdapter control to populate the DataGridView control with data.

The SnippetsDataGridView_SelectionChanged Event Method

When the user of the add-in selects a record in the DataGridView control, you want to provide a preview of the selected snippet by displaying its value in the control's RichTextBox control, as shown in Listing 5-2.

Listing 5-2. *The SelectionChanged Event of the SnippetsDataGridView Control*

```
Private Sub SnippetsDataGridView_SelectionChanged(ByVal sender As _
    System.Object, ByVal e As System.EventArgs) Handles _
    SnippetsDataGridView.SelectionChanged

    Me.PreviewBox.Text = SnippetsDataGridView.CurrentRow.Cells(2).Value.ToString()

End Sub
```

Anytime the selected record in the grid changes, the SelectionChanged event grabs the value from the Content column, which is column 2 in a 0-based index. The result is a nice preview (see Figure 5-8).

Figure 5-8. *A selected document snippet displayed in the Preview control*

The BindingNavigatorAddNewItem_Click Event Method

The BindingNavigator control is the toolstrip residing at the top of the DocSnippets action pane control. This control is directly linked to the SnippetsDataGridView control and provides the methods for editing the data displayed in the grid. The BindingNavigatorAddNewItem_Click event, shown in Listing 5-3, adds a new line to the grid control.

Listing 5-3. *The BindingNavigatorAddNewItem_Click Event*

```
Private Sub BindingNavigatorAddNewItem_Click(ByVal sender As _
    System.Object, ByVal e As System.EventArgs)

    Me.SnippetsBindingSource.AddNew()
End Sub
```

Once executed, the grid will display a new line at the bottom of the existing records. The user can then create a new record by inputting values into the grid.

The SnippetsBindingNavigatorSaveItem_Click Event Method

After the user adds, deletes, and/or edits items, it makes sense to let the user save any changes back to the database. Listing 5-4 contains the code for the SnippetsBindingNavigatorSaveItem_Click event.

Listing 5-4. *The SnippetsBindingNavigatorSaveItem_Click Event*

```
Private Sub SnippetsBindingNavigatorSaveItem_Click(ByVal sender As _
    System.Object, ByVal e As System.EventArgs)

    Me.Validate()
    Me.SnippetsBindingSource.EndEdit()
    Me.TableAdapterManager1.UpdateAll(Me.DocSnippetsDataSet1)
End Sub
```

Writing changes to the database is a three-step process of validating the data in the DataGridView control, exiting edit mode, and calling the TableAdapterManager control's UpdateAll method. The UpdateAll method uses any changed values to generate the SQL statements required to update the database.

The InsertSelection_Click Event Method

ReportBuilder users not only have the ability to reuse existing document snippets, but they can also create document snippets from content they create within the ReportBuilder.docx document. The strategy is to allow a user to select text within the document and insert it into the SnippetsDataGridView control (see Listing 5-5). Once inserted, you can rely on the grid's binding source and table adapter controls to handle updating the database.

Listing 5-5. *The InsertSelection_Click Event*

```
Private Sub InsertSelection_Click(ByVal sender As System.Object, _
    ByVal e As System.EventArgs) Handles InsertSelection.Click

    'Get the current selection
    Dim r As Range = Globals.ThisDocument.Application.Selection.Range
    Me.SnippetsBindingSource.AddNew()
    Me.SnippetsDataGridView.CurrentRow.Cells(2).Value = r.Text

End Sub
```

The first step is to reference the text selected in the document. The Word Range object provides you with this ability. With the selected text at your magical coding fingertips, you can call the AddNew method of the binding source control. Clicking the AddNewItem button in the toolstrip has the same effect as adding a new row to the DataGridView control. Once you have a new blank row, you can insert the Content column with the text from the referenced Range object.

The CreateBlock_Click Event Method

Building blocks are new objects introduced in Word 2007. They're globally reusable content snippets, similar to the document snippets in the ReportBuilder sample add-in. Building blocks allow you to create rich, reusable content and categorize it with custom categories. Word even provides a Building Blocks Organizer, shown in Figure 5-9.

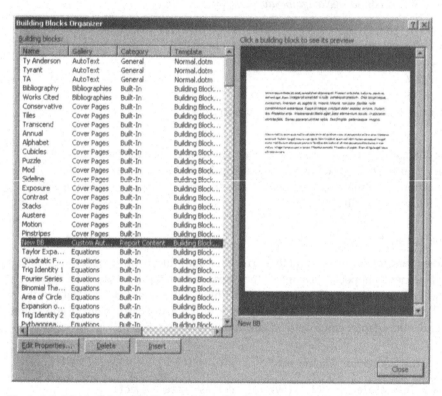

Figure 5-9. *The Building Blocks Organizer displaying a newly created custom building block*

The CreateBlock_Click event (see Listing 5-6) works like the InsertSelection_Click event shown in Listing 5-5. The difference is that the content is added to the Building Blocks library instead of the DocSnippets database.

Listing 5-6. *The CreateBlock_Click Event*

```
Private Sub CreateBlock_Click(ByVal sender As System.Object, _
  ByVal e As System.EventArgs) Handles CreateBlock.Click

    Dim r As Range = Globals.ThisDocument.Application.Selection.Range

  Globals.ThisDocument.Application.Templates.LoadBuildingBlocks()
  Dim BBs As Template = Globals.ThisDocument.Application.Templates(1)
  BBs.BuildingBlockEntries.Add("[Insert Custom BB Name Here]", _
    WdBuildingBlockTypes.wdTypeCustomAutoText, "Report Content", r)
  BBs.Save()
End Sub
```

Here again you reference the text the user has selected in the document by utilizing the Range object. Next, you need to ensure the Building Blocks library is loaded into Word's Templates collection. You do this by calling the LoadBuildingBlocks method. This is a best practice, because Word waits to load building blocks until they are needed. There is a risk that they may not already exist in the Templates collection.

Once loaded, create a Template object and set its value to reference the building blocks' Template objects. You add a new building block by calling the Add method of the template's BuildingBlocks collection and saving it.

■**Note** You can read more about building blocks and how to utilize them in your solutions in MSDN's article, "Working with Building Blocks" (http://msdn.microsoft.com/en-us/library/bb258119.aspx).

The btnInsert_Click Event Method

After selecting the desired document snippet and specifying where to insert it into the document, the btnInsert_Click event executes the actual insertion task (see Listing 5-7).

Listing 5-7. *The btnInsert_Click Event*

```
Private Sub btnInsert_Click(ByVal sender As System.Object, _
  ByVal e As System.EventArgs) Handles btnInsert.Click
  For Each ctl As ContentControl In Globals.ThisDocument.ContentControls
    If ctl.Tag = cboContentControlList.SelectedItem Then
      ctl.Range.Text = SnippetsDataGridView.CurrentRow.Cells(2).Value.ToString()
    End If
  Next
End Sub
```

The method loops through all existing content controls in the document. To identify the desired target, it checks the Tag property looking for the content control that matches the value selected in the action pane's ComboBox control. Once found, the content control's Range object fills with the text in the data grid's Content column.

Coding the ThisDocument Class

Before testing the add-in, you need to edit the add-in's Startup method to display the DocSnippets Actions Pane Control. The good news is that this task requires only two lines of code.

The ThisDocument_Startup Event Method

The Startup event of the ThisDocument class is the entry point of the add-in. Word calls the ThisDocument_Startup event after loading the add-in. Listing 5-8 contains the code for displaying the add-in's Actions Pane Control.

Listing 5-8. *The ThisDocument_Startup Event*

```
Private Sub ThisDocument_Startup(ByVal sender As Object, _
   ByVal e As System.EventArgs) Handles Me.Startup
   Dim ap As New DocSnippets
   Me.ActionsPane.Controls.Add(ap)


End Sub
```

First, the method instantiates an instance of the DocSnippets action pane. Once properly instantiated, the method adds the action pane to the Controls collection of ThisDocument's ActionsPane collection. Adding the control causes it to display within Word.

Running the ReportBuilder Add-In

You're now ready to test the ReportBuilder add-in. Go ahead and press F5 to build and run the add-in. After Word displays and loads the ReportBuilder.docx document, perform the following the steps to give the add-in a good test drive:

1. Insert a new record in the DataGridView control and click the Save button. Close the document and rerun the add-in. Did the record save properly? Try editing the new record too.

2. When you select a record in the grid, does the PreviewBox control display the selected content? Try selecting other records in the grid to see the PreviewBox control display different content.

3. Select a target section in the combo box and click the Insert Snippet Info: button. Did the text insert into the targeted content control?

Building the Templates Library Application Add-In

If you're anything like me, you probably tend to create the same documents over and over again. And even if the only thing we have in common is an interest in VSTO and Office development topics, I still bet that when you use Word, you need to create documents that have a similar look or design.

The Templates Library application-level add-in provides users with quick access to a library of document templates. You can achieve this convenience with a custom Ribbon control. When combined with a collection of Word template files, the result is both simple and powerful. With the click of a button, the user can create documents instantly from a set of defined templates.

The benefit to this solution is that an organization can use a library like this one to improve document standardization, including the document structure as well as the document design or branding. When combined with VSTO document-level add-ins like the ReportBuilder from the previous section, users begin to spend less time *creating* a document and more time *authoring* a document. By authoring, I mean writing content that is meaningful to the intended audience and not needlessly worrying about how to format it or structure it correctly.

DOCUMENTS VS.TEMPLATES

When should you use documents in a VSTO solution, and when should you use templates? This can be difficult to discern, given that a VSTO solution attached to either file type will execute similarly. You need to determine how the ultimate solution will be utilized. If you need a solution that functions as a GUI to present data from external systems, a document-based solution will be a good fit. If you need a cookie-cutter template for multiple documents that are more or less the same except for slight data differences (i.e., customer names and contact info), a template-based solution will be a good fit. Having said this, you could pull off either scenario with either solution type. However, you can publish templates to the Word Templates folder to make them available via the New Document dialog box.

Building the Sample Templates Library Documents

Before you build the Templates Library, you need some sample documents that can serve as suitable templates. Fortunately, you can use the ones provided by Word: Fax Cover Sheet, Blank Letterhead, and Blank Report.

To build the document templates, open Word and click Microsoft Office Button ➤ New to open the New Document dialog box (see Figure 5-10). Choose the Installed Templates option from the Templates section of the dialog box.

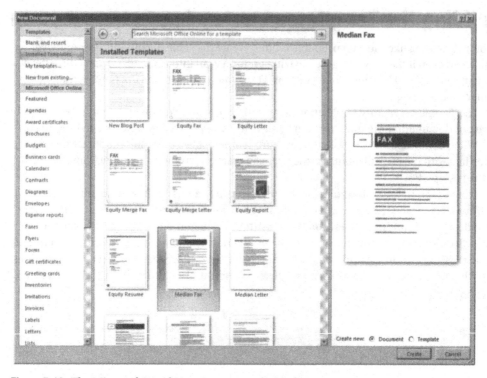

Figure 5-10. *The Microsoft Word New Document dialog box*

For this sample add-in, you'll base your templates off the Median style. In the Installed Templates section of the dialog, select the Median Fax template. You want to create another template, so choose the Template in the "Create new" section just above the Create button. Click Create to open the new template in Word. Once opened, save the document to a path of your choosing and name it **Fax Cover Sheet.dotx**.

Note For my purposes, the template path is C:\Projects\ProVSTO\c05\Templates. Your path may vary, so remember the path, as you'll need it later.

Perform these same steps again to create two more documents according to Table 5-1.

Table 5-1. *Additional Document Templates for the Templates Library Add-In*

Installed Template Name	Document Name for Templates Library
Median Letter	Letterhead.dotx
Median Report	Report.dotx

You'll use these template files to fill a RibbonGallery control and allow the user to select an available template as the basis of her document.

Designing the Templates Library Ribbon Control

The custom Ribbon for this add-in provides features for selecting and opening a template document from the Templates Library. The library in this sample is a file folder in the Windows file system (i.e., the path where you saved the templates earlier). The add-in allows the user to specify the location of the templates. When loaded, the add-in will read the path and go to Select a Template ➤ Templates to load the control with items for each document found.

All the code for the Templates Library add-in resides within this Ribbon control. In fact, the VSTO add-in's main class, ThisAdd-In, will remain a stubbed-out skeleton. Nothing is required of you to display the Ribbon control, as VSTO handles this step for you.

To build the add-in, open Visual Studio and create a new Word 2007 add-in. Name the project **TemplateLibrary**. After Visual Studio creates the project, follow these steps to design the project's Ribbon layout.

1. Add a new Ribbon control to the project (Project ➤ Add New Item ➤ Office ➤ Ribbon (Visual Designer)) and name it **LibraryRibbon** (see Figure 5-11).

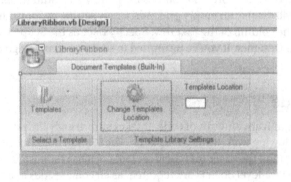

Figure 5-11. *The LibraryRibbon control in its designer*

2. Select the Ribbon's tab and change its Label property to **Document Templates**.

3. Add the RibbonGroup control to the Ribbon's design canvas. Name the control **TemplateGroup** and set its Label property to **Select a Template**.

4. Add a RibbonGallery control inside the TemplateGroup control. Name the RibbonGallery control **TemplateGallery** and select RibbonControlSizeLarge as the value for the ControlSize property. Change the Label property to **Templates**.

■**Note** For the images in these controls, I use standard PNG icons provided with Visual Studio. You can add custom icons to a control by changing the Image property.

---

5. Add another RibbonGroup control to the right of the TemplateGroup control. Specify **SettingsGroup** as its Name property and **Template Library Settings** as the Label property value.

6. Add a RibbonButton control inside the SettingsGroup control and name it **btnChangeTemplatesFolder**. Specify **Change Templates Location** as the Label property. Set the ControlSize property to RibbonControlSizeLarge.

7. Add a Label control next to the RibbonButton. Set its Label property to **Templates Location**.

8. Add a RibbonEditBox control under the Label property and name it **TemplatesPath**. In the SizeString property, input 50 1s (i.e., **11111111111111111111111** ...). This string specifies the length of the control. Why Microsoft didn't just allow developers to input an integer value here I'll never know. This situation is simply how it is.

After completing these steps, the Ribbon design is complete. Now you need to add a custom setting required by the add-in's code.

The add-in stores the file path where the templates reside within a custom application setting. This setting is a user-level string named TemplatesFolderPath. To add this setting to the application, select Project ➤ TemplateLibrary Properties from the Visual Studio menu. The project's Settings Designer will display an empty grid. Add a new setting by inputting **TemplatesFolderPath** in the Name column of the first row. Specify **User** as the Scope type for the setting, and close the Settings Designer. If you're prompted to save any changes, go ahead and save them.

Writing the Add-In Code

The Ribbon does not require a significant amount of code. It takes surprisingly little code to build this functionality, as the following walk-through explains. The Ribbon does not require any namespace declaration other than the Microsoft.Office.Tools.Ribbon namespace provided by default. In addition, no class-level objects are required, as all code resides in event or custom methods.

The LibraryRibbon_Load Event Method

The Load event sets up the Ribbon UI by reading the TemplatesFolderPath setting and displaying it in the Ribbon's TemplatePath control (see Listing 5-9).

Listing 5-9. *The LibraryRibbon_Load Event*

```
Private Sub LibraryRibbon_Load(ByVal sender As System.Object, _
    ByVal e As RibbonUIEventArgs) Handles MyBase.Load

    Me.TemplatesPath.Text = My.Settings.TemplatesFolderPath
    LoadTemplates()
End Sub
```

In addition to displaying the current path where the templates reside, the Load event also calls the LoadTemplates method to initiate an update to the template's RibbonGallery control.

The btnChangeTemplatesFolder_Click Event Method

You can't rely on the hope that the user will never change the location for the templates. Change is a fact of life, and you can't ignore the need for it in your code. The Click event of the btnChangeTemplatesFolder control, shown in Listing 5-10, prompts the user to specify a folder location. This prompting is done through a separate method named PickTemplatesFolder.

Listing 5-10. *The btnChangeTemplatesFolder_Click Event*

```
Private Sub btnChangeTemplatesFolder_Click(ByVal sender As System.Object, _
  ByVal e As Microsoft.Office.Tools.Ribbon.RibbonControlEventArgs) _
    Handles btnChangeTemplatesFolder.Click

    Me.TemplatesPath.Text = PickTemplatesFolder()
  My.Settings.TemplatesFolderPath = Me.TemplatesPath.Text
  My.Settings.Save()
  LoadTemplates()
End Sub
```

After the user selects a folder location, the PickTemplatesFolder function returns the folder path as a string. This method stores the path in the add-in's TemplatesFolderPath setting and saves the project's settings. To make sure that the UI reflects the change in location, the Click event calls LoadTemplates to reload the TemplateGallery control.

The LoadTemplates Method

LoadTemplates scans the contents of the Templates folder (the file path in the TemplatesFolderPath property) and adds them as items to the TemplateGallery control (see Listing 5-11). These items then act like menu items, allowing the user to see a drop-down of available options and click the desired one.

Listing 5-11. *The LoadTemplates Method*

```
Private Sub LoadTemplates()
  Dim fld As New System.IO.DirectoryInfo(My.Settings.TemplatesFolderPath)
  For Each f As System.IO.FileInfo In fld.GetFiles("*.do*")
    Dim ddi As New RibbonDropDownItem
    ddi.Label = f.Name
    ddi.Tag = f.Name
    ddi.Image = My.Resources.Generic_Document
    TemplateGallery.Items.Add(ddi)

  Next
End Sub
```

The method begins by specifying a filter for the type of files to scan. In this case, you only want Word template or document types, so the filter is set to look for any file name with a file extension beginning with .do. For each file that matches this pattern, the method creates a new RibbonDropDownItem control, sets its properties, and adds it to the TemplateGallery control's Items collection.

The PickTemplatesFolder Method

The PickTemplatesFolder method displays a browser dialog box to prompt the user to select a folder for where the templates reside (see Listing 5-12).

Listing 5-12. *The PickTemplatesFolder Method*

```
Private Function PickTemplatesFolder() As String
  Dim path As String = ""
  Me.FolderBrowserDialog1.SelectedPath = My.Settings.TemplatesFolderPath
  If FolderBrowserDialog1.ShowDialog() = Windows.Forms.DialogResult.OK Then
    path = FolderBrowserDialog1.SelectedPath
  End If

  Return path
End Function
```

If the user selects a folder path, the method will return the path as a string to the calling method. In this add-in, the calling method is the btnChangeTemplatesFolder_Click event.

The TemplateGallery_Click Event Method

To select the desired template, the user clicks an item the TemplateGallery control. Each item in this control corresponds to a template residing in the template folder path. Listing 5-13 contains the code for the TemplateGallery_Click event.

Listing 5-13. *The TemplateGallery_Click Event*

```
Private Sub TemplateGallery_Click(ByVal sender As System.Object, _
  ByVal e As Microsoft.Office.Tools.Ribbon.RibbonControlEventArgs) _
    Handles TemplateGallery.Click

    Dim s As RibbonGallery = sender

  Globals.ThisAddIn.Application.Documents.Add( _
      My.Settings.TemplatesFolderPath & "\" & s.SelectedItem.Tag)
End Sub
```

This event references the TemplateGallery control passed via the Sender parameter. You can identify the template to open via the RibbonGallery control's SelectedItem.Tag property. The Tag property was set to the file template file name in the LoadTemplates method. By combining the file name with the file path, you can open the template by calling the Add method of the Word Application object.

Running the Templates Library Add-In

You're now ready to test the Templates Library. Press F5 to build and run the add-in. To test the add-in's features, try out the following actions:

1. Click the Change Templates Location button and select the folder where you saved the document templates earlier in this section. Is the selected path reflected in the Templates Location control?

2. Click the Templates control. Does the control display the drop-down items that represent the document templates?

3. Select an available template listed in the Templates control. Does the template open within Word?

Summary

Word is the home for document creation. Thanks to VSTO, you can build .NET add-ins that automate Word at the document and application levels. These solutions can greatly enhance the user's ability to author documents and focus on the quality of the content. You could combine the solutions in this chapter so that the Templates Library add-in opens the ReportBuilder add-in. This combo would give users quick access to an organization's standard documents while providing features that let them build a document quickly using preexisting document content.

■ ■ ■

CHAPTER 6

Building VSTO Outlook Add-Ins

Due to the key role e-mail plays in the modern business workday, Outlook is the Office application many Office users use most. Given that Outlook also tracks appointments and schedules, manages contacts, provides to-do lists, and much more, it is understandable why users want Outlook to be the starting point for all of their work-related processes.

Visual Studio Tools for the Microsoft Office System (VSTO) allows you to build solutions that extend Outlook and incorporate processes specific to your user base. These processes can be specific to a single user and customize how that user works with Outlook, or they can be complex, multiuser and multiapplication solutions that automate workflows and use Outlook to display information from separate systems.

You are only limited by your imagination and what's possible using the .NET Framework. In this chapter, I will show you how to build VSTO Outlook add-ins from start to finish. Not only will I explain each solution, but I'll also talk about additional Outlook objects and discuss development techniques particular to Outlook.

Specifically, this chapter will teach you the following strategies:

- How to use the StorageItem object to store add-in settings

- How to use a form region to build a custom reading pane

- How to perform fast searches using Outlook's search features

Building the Fax Cover Sheet Wizard

In this first add-in walkthrough, I will explain how to build an add-in that automates creating a fax cover sheet using the information provided by a selected Outlook contact item. When some people go to fax a document and then realize they need to fill out a cover sheet, they often resort to writing (often illegibly) the required information by hand on a blank sheet of paper instead of using a professional-looking, corporate-approved cover sheet. The Fax Cover Sheet Wizard (FCSW) is here to help.

The FCSW does what its name implies. It creates a document to be used as the first page of a fax. The user follows these steps:

1. Build a fax cover sheet template within Microsoft Word using content controls that act as content placeholders. The FCSW will insert the appropriate values into these placeholders.

2. Save the template in a folder within Outlook named **FaxCoverSheets**.

3. Search for the targeted recipient's contact record within Outlook. The user could use the "Search address books" button, shown in Figure 6-1, or the user could navigate to the Contacts folder and open the contact record directly. Either way, the user needs to find and open the contact in an Inspector window.

Figure 6-1. *The Outlook "Search address books" button residing in the Outlook toolbar*

4. With the contact open, click the Fax Add-in tab in the Ribbon. The user can change any of the available settings as needed.

5. Click the Create Cover Sheet button. The FCSW opens the chosen cover sheet template, inserts the data, and displays the finalized cover sheet within Word.

6. Print the cover sheet and head to the fax machine.

These steps cover the main process. A secondary process exists that allows the user to choose the Outlook folder that serves as the location for the templates. These features are also made available within the add-in's custom Ribbon.

The FCSW executes within Outlook and manipulates a Word document. All the code for the add-in resides behind the custom Ribbon.

Along with Outlook, the add-in includes the following components:

- *Word documents*: The fax cover sheets are Word documents. The add-in only requires the existence of one cover sheet document. The user can build as many as she likes, and if the user installs them correctly, the add-in will make them available automatically.

- *Custom Ribbon*: The custom Ribbon for this add-in contains all the user interface (UI) elements that enable the user to initiate actions. All code for the add-in resides here as well.

- `ThisAddin`: This VSTO add-in class exists in its default, stubbed-out state with no changes. This class loads the add-in when Outlook executes.

Before I explain how to build the FCSW add-in using VSTO, let's build a fax cover sheet and install it to an Outlook folder that will store all fax cover sheets used by the add-in.

Creating the Fax Cover Sheet Templates in Word

The fax cover sheet templates that Word provides are more than suitable for these purposes, as they are prebuilt with structure and formatting. Using a provided template allows you to focus on the development tasks and not have to worry about creating and formatting a document. Therefore, you'll use one of the available templates as the foundation to build the document required by the FCSW add-in.

Building the Cover Sheet Templates

Each cover sheet requires the existence of 13 Word content controls. New to Word 2007, content controls act as text placeholders within a document. You can access a document's content controls directly in your code by name. Given that Word documents are unstructured, you can add content controls to provide structure and allow for coding against named areas within the document.

Follow these steps to build a fax cover sheet template for the add-in:

1. Open Word 2007 and create a new document by clicking Microsoft Office Button ➤ New.

2. In the New Document dialog box, shown in Figure 6-2, select the Installed Templates option in the Templates section. In the listing of Installed Templates, select the Median Fax template and click Create.

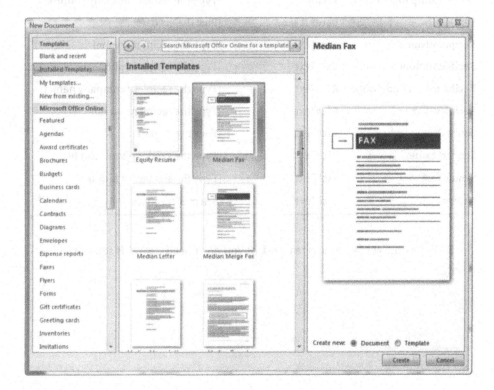

Figure 6-2. *The New Document dialog box*

3. Click the Developer tab in the Word Ribbon, and place the document in design mode by clicking the Design Mode button (see Figure 6-3).

Figure 6-3. *The Developer tab visible in the Word Ribbon*

4. Each content control needs a name that you can reference in the FCSW add-in. Make sure the document has the content controls listed in Table 6-1. The content control names are the names you'll reference later to insert values into the document. The content control types are the types of content that you should use. The surrounding text is the document text that the content control surrounds.

Table 6-1. *The Required Content Controls*

Content Control Name	Content Control Type	Surrounding Text
SenderCompanyName	RichText	[Type the sender company name]
SenderCompanyAddress	RichText	[Type the sender company address]
FaxDate	DatePicker	[Pick the fax date]
RecipientName	RichText	[Type the recipient name]
RecipientPhone	RichText	[Type the recipient phone number]
RecipientCompanyName	RichText	[Type the recipient company name]
RecipientFax	RichText	[Type the recipient fax number]
SenderName	RichText	[Your username]
SenderPhone	RichText	[Type the sender phone number]
SenderFax	RichText	[Type the sender fax number]
Urgent	RichText	[Select the option]

5. Delete the Action Requested field, as you don't need it for this solution.

6. The default version of the Urgent content control is a combo box, and you want your version to be a text box. Delete the existing Urgent content control, and replace it with RichText control as listed in Table 6-1.

7. Save the document to your file system, and name it **Median Fax.docx**. Exit Microsoft Word. Be sure to note the location, as you'll need this file in the next section.

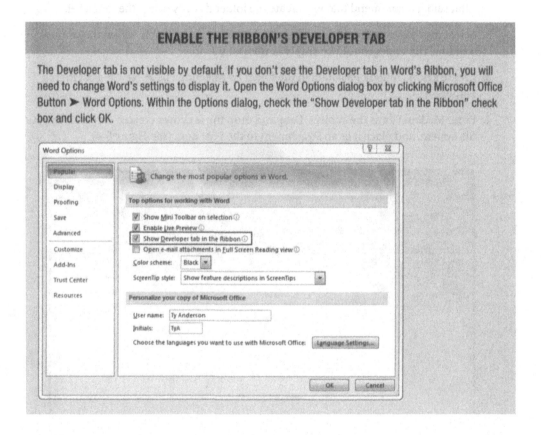

ENABLE THE RIBBON'S DEVELOPER TAB

The Developer tab is not visible by default. If you don't see the Developer tab in Word's Ribbon, you will need to change Word's settings to display it. Open the Word Options dialog box by clicking Microsoft Office Button ➤ Word Options. Within the Options dialog, check the "Show Developer tab in the Ribbon" check box and click OK.

Installing the Templates in Outlook

The FCSW add-in's templates actually reside in a folder within the Outlook data store. This strategy helps the add-in be fully functional even if the user operates in Exchange Server mode and installs the add-in on multiple machines. Since the documents are stored in the Outlook file structure, each template is available to the user as part of the normal Outlook and Exchange Server synchronization.

You can store the templates in any Outlook folder. For these purposes, store them in a folder immediately below the Outlook root folder. Complete the following steps to install the cover sheet template that you created in the previous section:

1. Open Outlook 2007 and create a new folder named **FaxCoverSheets**. It really does not matter where you create this folder, as you'll use the Outlook interface to select it later. That said, I recommend that you create the folder directly below the root level.

2. Select the FaxCoverSheet folder so that its contents are viewable within the Outlook window. The folder should be empty at this point.

3. Create a new Outlook Post item in the folder by selecting File ➤ New ➤ Post in this Folder.

4. Enter **Median Fax** as the subject. Drag and drop the fax cover created earlier from your file system, and place it as an attachment to the Post item (see Figure 6-4).

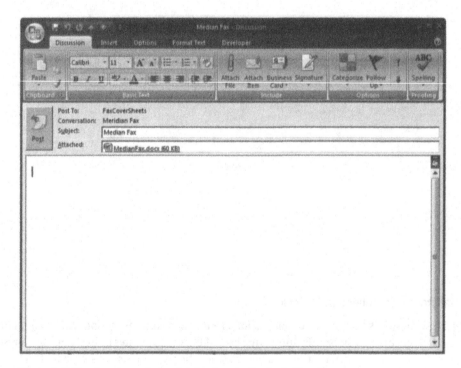

Figure 6-4. *The fax cover sheet attached to an Outlook Post item*

5. Click the Post button to save the item to the FaxCoverSheets folder and complete the cover sheet's installation.

You created only a single template for this solution. If you'd like, you can create and install additional templates. Just follow the steps described in this section; the templates will be fully functional and available to the FCSW add-in.

Designing the Fax Ribbon

The add-in utilizes a custom Ribbon to group the add-in's features and provide the user with the ability to trigger them. The custom Ribbon contains a single tab with three groups (see Figure 6-5). The goal is to use the Ribbon to organize the controls in an intuitive way that guides the user through the process of creating a fax cover sheet. Creating an add-in is a two-step process. In the first step, the user enters values required by the cover sheet. In the second step, the user initiates the cover sheet creation process by clicking a button.

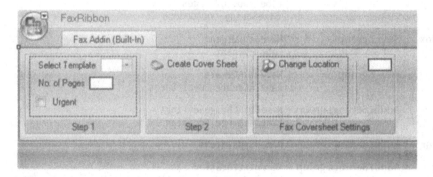

Figure 6-5. *The FaxRibbon custom Ribbon*

The add-in's settings are not part of the cover sheet creation process and are separated accordingly. To build the add-in's custom Ribbon, follow these steps:

1. Create a new Visual Studio project using the Outlook 2007 project template. Name the project **FaxCoverSheetWizard** and click OK.

2. Once Visual Studio creates the project, add a new Ribbon by selecting Project ➤ Add New Item from the Visual Studio menu.

3. In the Add New Item dialog box, select the Ribbon (Visual Designer) item template. Name the new ribbon **FaxRibbon** and click Add.

4. Chang the Label property of the built-in tab to **Fax Add-in**. This is the label that the user will see at runtime.

5. Using Table 6-2 as a reference, add the controls listed and change their properties accordingly.

Table 6-2. *The FaxRibbon Controls and Properties*

Control Type	Location	Property=Value
Group	Fax Add-in tab	Name=Step1 Label=Step 1
Group	Fax Add-in tab	Name=Step2 Label=Step 2
Group	Fax Add-in tab	Name=AddinSettings Label=Fax Coversheet Settings
RibbonComboBox	Step1 group	Name=cboTemplate Label=Select Template
RibbonEditBox	Step 1 group	Name=txtNumberOfPages Label=No. of Pages SizeString=0000000000
RibbonCheckBox	Step 1 group	Name=chkUrgent Label=Urgent
RibbonButton	Step 2 group	Name=btnCreate Label=Create Cover Sheet
RibbonButton	Addin Settings group	Name=btnChangeSettings Label=Change Location
RibbonSeparator	Addin Settings group	Name=Separator1
RibbonEditBox	Addin Settings group	Name=txtLocation Label=Templates Location SizeString=0000000000000000000000000000
OutlookRibbon		Name=FaxRibbon RibbonType=Microsoft.Outlook.Contact

The Name and Label properties are mostly likely familiar to you, but the SizeString properties require some explaining. Ribbon controls do not have a Width property. Instead of specifying the width of the field using an integer, Ribbon controls like the RibbonEditBox provide the SizeString property. This property accepts any string value. The length of the string you enter in this property determines the size of the control at runtime. For the FCSW, you're using a string of 10 and 25 0s to specify the width of the txtNumberOfPages and txtLocation controls, respectively. With the Ribbon designed, you're now ready to add code to the solution.

Writing the Add-In Code

The add-in makes use of four methods and three events to implement its required features. All code resides in the FaxRibbon object, so go ahead and open it in Visual Studio and change the view to the code view window. This project works with both Word and Outlook, so you need to add a reference to the Word object model. Perform the following steps to add the reference:

1. Select Project ➤ Add Reference from the Visual Studio menu.

2. In the Add Reference dialog box, select the COM tab.

3. Scroll down and select the Microsoft Word 12.0 Object Library component (see Figure 6-6).

4. Click OK to add the reference to the project.

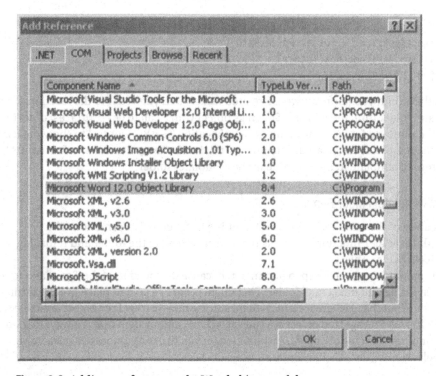

Figure 6-6. *Adding a reference to the Word object model*

Declarations

The FaxRibbon class utilizes three namespace declarations. Make sure the following lines of code are at the top of the FaxRibbon class:

```
Imports Microsoft.Office.Tools.Ribbon
Imports W = Microsoft.Office.Interop.Word
Imports OL = Microsoft.Office.Interop.Outlook
```

With the user process in mind, write the code in the same order starting with the Ribbon's Load event.

The FaxRibbon_Load Event

The Ribbon's Load event works like a Windows form's Load event. The event provides the Ribbon object via the sender argument. In addition, the Load event provides a RibbonUIEventArgs object, which inherits from System.EventArgs and provides state information related to the Ribbon object. The Load event is the location for code that initializes the objects required by the add-in.

Listing 6-1 contains the code for the FaxRibbon's Load event.

Listing 6-1. *The FaxRibbon_Load Event*

```
Private Sub FaxRibbon_Load(ByVal sender As System.Object, _
  ByVal e As RibbonUIEventArgs) Handles MyBase.Load

  Dim folder As OL.Folder = GetTemplatesFolder()
  txtLocation.Text = folder.FolderPath
  FillTemplatesComboBox(folder)
End Sub
```

In this event, you perform two UI-related tasks. First, you retrieve the location of the Templates folder from the add-in's Settings object with a call to GetTemplatesFolder(). You insert the retrieved folder location into the txtLocation TextBox control to show the user where the templates are located. Second, you fill the cboTemplates ComboBox control with the names of template items available in the Templates folder.

The GetTemplatesFolder Function

The location of the add-in's Templates folder is a key piece of information. The GetTemplatesFolder function performs the task of retrieving the folder and returning an Outlook.Folder object.

The method does not accept a parameter, because the location of the Templates folder resides in the default inbox mail folder. That might seem like an odd place to store settings information, but that's where it resides, thanks to the new StorageItem object available with Outlook 2007. A StorageItem object is a special type of Outlook item that is always hidden. The user cannot see this type of object. It is intended for you to use as a storage device for your Outlook projects.

> **OUTLOOK ADD-IN SETTINGS PRIOR TO OUTLOOK 2007 AND THE STORAGEITEM OBJECT**
>
> Prior to the existence of the StorageItem object, I would store my settings in an XML file. Most of the time, I would store the XML settings file in the Windows file system, as I wanted to reduce the risk of the user discovering the file and editing it. For several applications, however, I would risk the user discovering the settings file by storing it within the body of an Outlook PostItem object. I did this to take advantage of Outlook's synchronization features. I wanted the users of my add-in to have access to the same set of add-in settings on multiple machines.
>
> The strategy typically worked well, and the users tended to leave the settings alone if they discovered them. However, the risk always existed, and sometimes issues occurred. Some users would delete the PostItem object containing the settings file, not realizing its significance.
>
> The StorageItem object resolves these issues. You can implement the same strategy but hide the settings in a default Outlook folder. Since the item is invisible, the risk of the user deleting it is almost zero (although the user could delete its parent folder, which would delete the folder's content, including any StorageItem objects).

To retrieve the storage item, you need call the GetStorage method of a Folder object. If the requested storage item exists, the method will return it and all the data it contains. If the storage item does not exist, the method will return a new, blank storage item. You need to check the item's size to determine if you're dealing with a new or existing item. If the size is 0, then the item is a new item, and the add-in does not yet know the location of the Templates folder.

If the storage item does exist, GetTemplatesFolder reads the TemplatesFolder property of the item. This property contains the path to the Templates folder, and the function parses the path and loops through Outlook's folder structure to return the Templates folder as an Outlook.Folder object. Listing 6-2 shows the code for GetTemplatesFolder.

Listing 6-2. *The GetTemplatesFolder Function*

```
Private Function GetTemplatesFolder() As OL.Folder
    'Set a reference to the default inbox folder
    Dim fldStorage As OL.Folder
    Dim fld As OL.Folder = Nothing
    'The session object provides GetDefaultFolder method
    'specify the olFolderInbox to retrieve the default mail folder
    fldStorage = .ThisAddIn.Application. _
      Session.GetDefaultFolder( _
      Outlook.OlDefaultFolders.olFolderInbox)

    'Create and store the item.
    Dim si As OL.StorageItem
    Dim up As OL.UserProperty
    'attempt to grab a reference the Settings
    'StorageItem by calling GetStorage
    si = fldStorage.GetStorage("FaxCoverSheetAddin.Settings", _
      Outlook.OlStorageIdentifierType.olIdentifyBySubject)

    'The way to know if the item is new is to check its size.
    If si.Size = 0 Then
      'No setting exists.
      fld = Nothing
      Return fld
    Else
      'We have a reference to an existing Settings StorageItem
      'so now we will use the values in it.
      up = si.UserProperties("TemplatesFolder")
      'Now retrieve the folder Path
      Dim arry As Array
      Dim i As Integer
      'we need to traverse the Path of the folder
      'to find the actual destiniation folder.
      'First remove the "\\" chars from the folder path.
      Dim path As String = Right(up.Value, Len(up.Value) - 2)
      'Split the path string into an array using "\"
```

```
      'as the split character
      arry = path.Split("\")
      'grab a reference to the first item in the array -
      'it is the root Outlook folder and we need to
      'use its Folders collection to reach the target Folder
      Dim fldRoot As OL.Folder
      fldRoot = Globals.ThisAddIn.Application.Session. _
        Folders.Item(arry(0))

      Dim fldrsSub As OL.Folders
      fldrsSub = fldRoot.Folders
      'Loop through the Folders collection and
      'return the last folder as it is the target folder.
      For i = 1 To arry.Length - 1
        fld = fldrsSub.Item(arry(i))

      Next
      Return fld

    End If
End Function
```

Keep in mind these key points when working with the StorageItem object in your solutions:

- StorageItem objects are hidden from the user, but the data they contain is not encrypted.

- StorageItem objects reside within the Outlook data store and can roam with the user (assuming Outlook is running in Exchange mode).

- The StorageItem object does not have a StorageItems collection object. You cannot access a listing of storage items in a folder with a call to Folder.StorageItems. However, it is possible to use the Folder.GetTable method to search a folder for hidden objects. (I talk more about the Table object later in the "Building the Quick Search Add-In" section of this chapter).

- The StorageItem object is an Outlook item type. You can manipulate it to the same way you can manipulate other Outlook items. For example, you can create custom properties, add attachments, insert values to default properties (such as Subject and Body), and retrieve the object using its EntryID property.

- The size of a new StorageItem object is 0. Checking the size property is the best method to determine if the item is new. After you call the item's Save method, the size property changes to the actual size value.

- You can retrieve a StorageItem object by Subject, by MessageClass, or by EntryID. You do this when calling the Folder.GetStorage method and passing the appropriate olStorageIdentifierType constant value: olIdentifyBySubject, olIdentifyByMessageClass, or olIdentifyByEntryID, respectively.

The FillTemplatesComboBox Function

The FCSW add-in adds items to the cboTemplate drop-down control (see Listing 6-3). The FillTemplatesComboBox function loops through all items in the folder object that you pass as a function parameter. For each item found in the passed folder object, the function creates a new RibbonDropDownItem object to the cboTemplate control's Items collection.

Listing 6-3. *The FillTemplatesComboBox Function*

```
Private Function FillTemplatesComboBox( _
    ByVal folder As OL.Folder) As Boolean

  Try
    For Each itm As OL.PostItem In folder.Items
      Dim dditm As New RibbonDropDownItem
      dditm.Label = itm.Subject
      cboTemplate.Items.Add(dditm)
    Next
    Return True
  Catch ex As Exception
    Return False
  End Try

End Function
```

Each drop-down item uses the subject of the Post item as the label. Using the subject of a Post item allows the user to change the cover sheet's template name without actually changing the file name of the cover sheet document.

The btnCreate_Click Event

The user initiates the cover sheet creation process by clicking the Create Cover Sheet button (btnCreate). The user must first open an Outlook contact, as this is the only type of item that displays the FaxRibbon control.

The button's Click event, shown in Listing 6-4, creates a reference to Word, finds the item containing the cover sheet selected in the Select Template combo box (cboTemplates), and inserts values into the cover sheet's content controls using the selected contact. In addition, the event inserts the user's contact information by retrieving the related contact item (via the GetUserContact function) and inserting the appropriate values into the cover sheet.

Listing 6-4. *The btnCreate_Click Event*

```
Private Sub btnCreate_Click(ByVal sender As System.Object, _
    ByVal e As Microsoft.Office.Tools.Ribbon. _
    RibbonControlEventArgs) Handles btnCreate.Click
```

```vbnet
Dim w As New W.Application
Dim doc As W.Document
Dim fldTemplates As OL.Folder = GetTemplatesFolder()
Dim pi As OL.PostItem = fldTemplates. _
  Items(cboTemplate.Text)

Dim at As OL.Attachment = pi.Attachments(1)
Dim strPath As String = My.Computer.FileSystem. _
  SpecialDirectories.MyDocuments & "\faxcoversheet.docx"

at.SaveAsFile(strPath)
w.Documents.Open(strPath)
doc = w.Application.ActiveDocument

Dim ciRec As OL.ContactItem = _
  Globals.ThisAddIn.Application.ActiveInspector.CurrentItem

Dim ciSender As OL.ContactItem = _
  GetUserContact(Globals.ThisAddIn.Application. _
               Session.CurrentUser.Name)

For Each ctl As W.ContentControl In doc.ContentControls
  Select Case ctl.Title
    Case "RecipientName"
      ctl.Range.Text = ciRec.FullName
    Case "RecipientPhone"
      ctl.Range.Text = ciRec.BusinessTelephoneNumber
    Case "RecipientCompanyName"
      ctl.Range.Text = ciRec.CompanyName
    Case "RecipientFax"
      ctl.Range.Text = ciRec.BusinessFaxNumber
    Case "SenderName"
      ctl.Range.Text = ciSender.FullName
    Case "SenderPhone"
      ctl.Range.Text = ciSender.BusinessTelephoneNumber
    Case "SenderCompanyName"
      ctl.Range.Text = ciSender.CompanyName
    Case "SenderFax"
      ctl.Range.Text = ciSender.BusinessFaxNumber
    Case "FaxDate"
      ctl.Range.Text = Format(Today(), "Short Date")
    Case "NumberOfPages"
      ctl.Range.Text = Me.txtNumberOfPages.Text.ToString
    Case "Urgent"
      ctl.Range.Text = chkUrgent.Enabled.ToString
```

```
    Case Else

    End Select
Next

'Now that we are done, show the user the completed
'file within Word.
w.Visible = True

End Sub
```

The btnCreate_Click method stores a copy of the cover sheet to the user's My Documents folder in Windows. This strategy leaves the template version in Outlook unchanged.

To insert text into the cover sheet's content controls, the function iterates through the document's ContentControls collection. This collection does not provide a method for identifying an item by name or index. Instead, you must loop through all controls in the collection and branch your code with a Select statement to insert values to the appropriate control. The code completes by displaying the completed cover sheet to the user.

The GetUserContact Function

The GetUserContact function, shown in Listing 6-5, searches the contact items contained in the default Contacts folder to return a contact item that corresponds to the name of the current Outlook user. If the function finds the contact, it will return the item as the function value.

In order for the FCSW to insert the user's data in the cover sheet's Sender fields, the user must have a contact record that contains the user's contact information (name, address, phone, fax, and so on). If the record does not exist, then the Sender fields will ultimately be blank in the cover sheet.

Listing 6-5. *The GetUserContact Function*

```
Private Function GetUserContact(ByVal name As String) As _
    Outlook.ContactItem

  Dim folder As Outlook.Folder
  Dim contact As Outlook.ContactItem
  folder = Globals.ThisAddIn.Application.Session. _
     GetDefaultFolder(Outlook.OlDefaultFolders. _
     olFolderContacts)

  contact = folder.Items.Find("[FullName] = '" & name & "'")

  Return contact

End Function
```

After retrieving a reference to the default Contacts folder, the function calls the Items collection's Find method. This method uses SQL-like syntax to filter the Items collection to contain only the items that meet the parameters of the search string. In this case, you want to filter on the FullName field of a contact item.

The SelectTemplatesFolder Function

When the user clicks the Change Location button (btnChangeSettings), its Click event calls the SelectTemplatesFolder function (see Listing 6-6). The purpose of this function is to prompt the user for the location of the folder containing the cover sheet templates.

Once the user provides the location of the templates, you can store the path of this folder as a storage item in the default inbox folder.

Listing 6-6. *The SelectTemplatesFolder Function*

```
Private Function SelectTemplatesFolder() As String
    Dim strPath As String = ""
    Dim fldSelect As OL.Folder
    fldSelect = Globals.ThisAddIn.Application _
      .Session.PickFolder

    'Now store the name of the selected foler as a hidden
    'StorageItem in the default Notes folder.
    Dim fldStorage As OL.Folder
    fldStorage = ns.GetDefaultFolder(Outlook. _
      OlDefaultFolders.olFolderInbox)

    'Create and store the item.
    Dim si As OL.StorageItem
    Dim up As OL.UserProperty
    si = fldStorage.GetStorage("FaxCoverSheetAddin.Settings",_
      Outlook.OlStorageIdentifierType.olIdentifyBySubject)

   'The way to know if the item is new is to check its size.
    If si.Size = 0 Then
      up = si.UserProperties.Add("TemplatesFolder", _
        Outlook.OlUserPropertyType.olText)
    Else
      up = si.UserProperties("TemplatesFolder")
    End If
    up.Value = fldSelect.FolderPath.ToString
    si.Subject = "FaxCoverSheetAddin.Settings"
    si.Save()
    strPath = up.Value
    Return strPath

End Function
```

Creating a new storage item and editing an existing one both require calling the GetStorage folder method. The trick is to check the size of the returned StorageItem object. In this case, if the item is a new one, you'll create a new user property and store the path of the Templates folder as a string. If the storage item exists, you'll update the already existing user property.

The method completes by saving the storage item and returning the folder path as the function value.

The btnChangeSettings_Click Event

The user can initiate changing the location of the Templates folder by clicking the Change Location (btnChange) button (see Listing 6-7). This button's Click event calls the SelectTemplatesFolder function and stores the returned value inside the Location (txtLocation) text box.

Listing 6-7. *The btnChangeSettings_Click Event*

```
Private Sub btnChangeSettings_Click( _
  ByVal sender As System.Object, _
  ByVal e As Microsoft.Office.Tools. _
  Ribbon.RibbonControlEventArgs)

  txtLocation.Text = SelectTemplatesFolder()
End Sub
```

Running the FCSW Add-In

All the components are in place to test the add-in. Let's test it in debug mode and see how the FCSW works in runtime. Go ahead and press F5 to compile and run the solutions. Once Outlook opens, take the following actions to test each feature:

1. Navigate to the default Contacts folder and open a contact that will serve as the intended fax recipient. Click the FaxAddin Ribbon tab (see Figure 6-7).

2. Specify the location for the Templates folder by clicking the Change Location button. In the Select Folder dialog box (see Figure 6-8), select the FaxCoverSheets folder. The text box next to the Change Location button should display the selected folder's path.

3. Select the Median Fax from the Select Template drop-down control. Enter a number for the No. Of Pages text box, and check the Urgent check box.

4. Click the Create Cover Sheet button to create the new fax cover sheet (see Figure 6-9), and view the fruits of your labor.

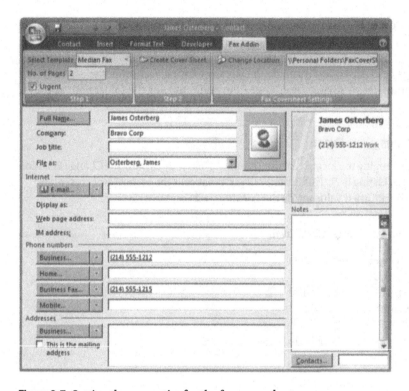

Figure 6-7. *Setting the properties for the fax cover sheet*

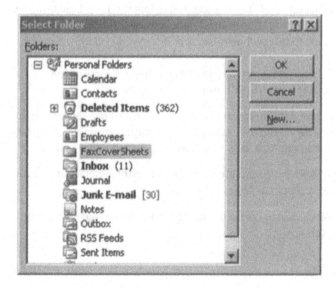

Figure 6-8. *Selecting the Templates folder's location in Outlook*

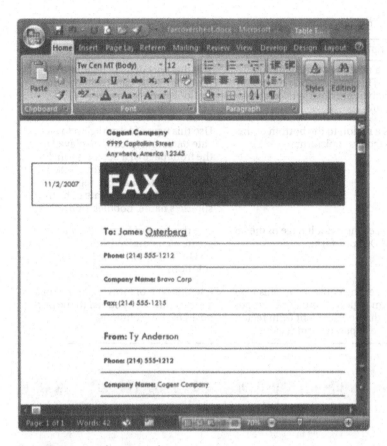

Figure 6-9. *A new fax cover sheet*

Creating a Custom Reading Pane

Outlook form regions provide developers with a method for extending default Outlook forms. Prior to the existence of form regions, you could only extend an Outlook form by creating additional tabs. You were also limited to the types of customizations you could create, because some default forms did not support customizations in the default tab (the Contact form is a prime example).

Form regions bring freedom and (potential) excess to the Outlook developer. Freedom, because you're no longer limited by the old customization model of previous Outlook versions. You can now extend or replace any Outlook form. Excess, because the new customization model not only allows you to extend a form, but it also lets you completely replace a form in its entirety in favor of your customized version. Table 6-3 describes each type of supported form region, from simplest to most complex, and explains how you can use them in your solutions.

Table 6-3. *Supported Form Region Types*

Form Region Type	Description	Sample Scenario
Separate	Adds a new page to an Outlook form. This form region type would be a tab in previous versions of Outlook.	Use this type of form region to display additional data related to the Outlook item.
Adjoining	Adds a region to the bottom of the targeted Outlook form.	Use this type of form region to elevate data not typically displayed on the front page of a default form. For example, you could add a contact's personal data to a form region and display that person's date of birth, spouse's name, hobbies, and so on.
Replacement	Replaces the default page of the targeted Outlook form.	Use this type of form region to create a customized view for an Outlook item related to your solution.
Replace-all	Replaces the entire form. This type of form region is actually a composite of the Replacement form region and the Separate form region.	Use this type of form region to build a form completely suited to the purposes of your solutions.

DON'T ANNOY YOUR USERS—REFRAIN FROM USING TOO MANY FORM REGIONS

Form regions are a wonderful and welcomed feature for Outlook development. The possibilities enabled by form regions are powerful, but I recommend that you exercise restraint in your solutions, especially regarding the Replacement and Replace-all form region types. You don't want to annoy your uses by wasting their screen space. When considering adding a form region to your solution, just perform a little due diligence with your user base to ensure the data and/or features you intend to provide with the form region will be a welcomed feature.

As Outlook's popularity as a development platform continues to increase and add-ins targeting Outlook continue to proliferate, it is easy to envision a user running several add-ins at once. If each add-in provides a customized version of the default Contact form, for example, what will be the ramifications? Which form should display? How will the add-ins handle the conflict? When building your form regions, you need to think of all possible scenarios and perform thorough testing to ensure your add-in plays nice with others.

There are two development models for designing Outlook form regions. The first is to build the form region from scratch in Visual Studio. The second is to build the form region using Outlook's design tools and then import it into your VSTO Outlook add-in project. I will explain both methods by showing you how to build a custom form region that replaces the default reading pane.

Using Visual Studio to Build the ReadingPane Form Region

VSTO provides an Outlook Form Region template that you can use to quickly build a form region. This item template is really a wizard that asks you several questions about the type of form region you want and then creates a form region shell for you to customize further using Visual Studio.

For sample purposes, I'll show you how to build a Replace-all form region that you can use to read e-mail messages in the default inbox. This sample is overly simple and definitely not an improvement over the existing Outlook reading pane. That said, after building the custom reading pane, you will have good understanding of how to build a form region and display it within Outlook. Once you know how to perform this task, creating more complex form regions is an exercise left for you to do in working with Outlook objects and the .NET Framework.

To start building the reading pane, open Visual Studio, create a new VSTO Outlook 2007 project, and name it **CustomReadingPane**.

Designing the Custom Reading Pane

The custom reading pane is a `FormRegionControl` object containing only a button and a multi-line text box. The button allows the user to file the message viewed in the reading pane to a selected folder. The text box displays the body of the selected e-mail.

To build the ReadingPane form region, follow these steps:

1. Select Project ➤ Add New Item from the Visual Studio menu.

2. In the Add New Item dialog box, select the Outlook Form Region item and enter **ReadingPane** as the item's name. Click Add to initiate the New Outlook Form Region Wizard.

3. The first page of the wizard asks, "How would you like to create this form region?" (see Figure 6-10). You don't have a `.ofs` file, so choose the "Design a new form region" option. An `.ofs` file is a form region designed in Outlook. Click Next.

4. In the "Select the type of form region you want to create" screen, choose the Replace-all option. Click Next.

5. In the "Supply descriptive text and select your display preferences" screen (see Figure 6-11), enter **ReadingPane** as the value for the Name and Title fields. You want the form region to display only in the reading pane, so check the check box labeled Reading Pane. Leave the other check boxes unchecked. Click Next.

6. Specify what type of message class the form region will display (see Figure 6-12). The message class is the name of the form Outlook uses to display an item. For a Replace-all type of form region, you cannot use a default Outlook message class. Instead, you must specify a name for a custom. In this case, specify **IPM.Note.MODVSTO** as the message class name. Any message with the message class value will activate the custom ReadingPane form region. Click Finish to complete the wizard and add the form region to the project.

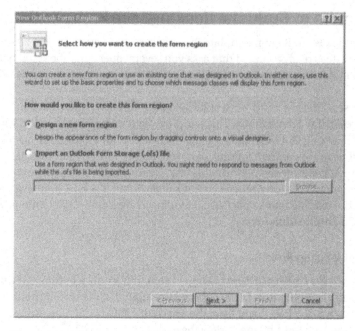

Figure 6-10. *Choosing a method for creating a form region*

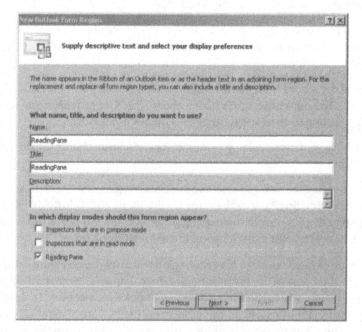

Figure 6-11. *Specifying the form region's display properties*

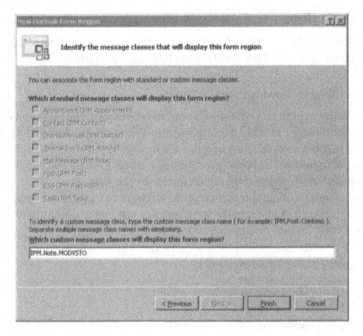

Figure 6-12. *Specifying the message type for the form region*

7. The ReadingPane form region's designer should be open in the Visual Studio. If not, go ahead and open it. Once open, add a Button control and a TextBox control to the form region.

8. Using Table 6-4 as a guide, edit the properties of the form region and its controls accordingly.

Table 6-4. *The Properties for the ReadingPane Form Region*

Object	Property Name	Property Value
FormRegionControl	Name Size	ReadingPane 600,335
TextBox	Name Size Location	txtBody 593,329 4,68
Button	Name Text Size Location	btnFile File Message 75,59 522,5

These steps are all that is required to design a form region. It is much like designing a Windows form or custom user control. However, none of the fields are mapped to any data. This requires adding a little bit of code.

Adding Code to the Reading Pane

The form region contains only two methods. The first executes when the form region displays in the Outlook UI. The second is the Click event for the File Message button.

The ReadingPane_FormRegionShowing Event

When the user selects a new item in an Outlook explorer, the contents of the new item display in the reading pane. A form region's FormRegionShowing event executes just before the form region becomes visible within Outlook. Think of it like a Windows form's Load event that executes as a form loads into memory. The FormRegionShowing event is the best place to take whatever action is required to set up the form region for use by the user.

In the case of the custom ReadingPane form region, you want to read the newly selected item's Body property and insert its value into the form region's text box to display to the user. Listing 6-8 contains the code for the FormRegionShowing event.

Listing 6-8. *The ReadingPage_FormRegionShowing Event*

```
Private Sub ReadingPane_FormRegionShowing(ByVal sender As _
    Object, ByVal e As System.EventArgs) _
    Handles MyBase.FormRegionShowing

    If TypeOf (Me.OutlookItem) Is Outlook.MailItem Then
      Dim mail As Outlook.MailItem = Me.OutlookItem
      Me.txtBody.Text = mail.Body.ToString

    End If

  End Sub
```

The selected item is available via the form region's OutlookItem property. You only want this code to attempt to read mail item types, so the code checks to ensure the passed OutlookItem is indeed a mail item. If it is, the code inserts the body of the e-mail item into the form's text box.

The btnFile_Click Event

Sometimes it's nice to have a feature more conveniently located. The File Message button (btnFile) implements convenient message-filing features that can also be found in the Outlook menu system. The custom form region has the advantage of residing directly in the reading pane, so it's easy for the user to see and use.

The purpose of this button is to allow the user to choose a folder to move the message to for filing (see Listing 6-9).

Listing 6-9. *The btnFile_Click Event*

```
Private Sub btnFile_Click(ByVal sender As System.Object, _
  ByVal e As System.EventArgs) Handles btnFile.Click

  Dim folder As Outlook.Folder
  Dim mi As Outlook.MailItem
  mi = DirectCast(Globals.ThisAddIn.Application. _
    ActiveExplorer.Selection.Item(1), Outlook.MailItem)

  folder = Globals.ThisAddIn.Application.Session.PickFolder()

  mi.Move(folder)
End Sub
```

The Click event works by creating a reference to the selected item and calling the PickFolder method of the current Outlook namespace session. PickFolder displays a dialog box that prompts the user to choose a folder in the Outlook folder hierarchy. After the user picks a folder, the code moves the selected e-mail message to it.

Adding Code to the ThisAddin Class

The last step you need to perform before you can run the reading pane solution is to capture the Application object's NewMailEx event. This event executes once for each new e-mail item received from a send/receive process. Because this event is accessed as part of the Outlook application object, you can use the ThisAddin class to write a method to respond its events.

Changing the Message Class as New Mail Arrives

As mail arrives in Outlook, the NewMailEx event fires for each item received. This event passes the EntryIDCollection as a string type. The value contained in EntryIDCollection is the unique string identifier for the newly arriving e-mail item. You can use the value to gain a reference to the item with a call to the namespace session object's GetItemFromID method (see Listing 6-10).

Listing 6-10. *The Application_NewMailEx Event*

```
Private Sub Application_NewMailEx(ByVal EntryIDCollection _
  As String) Handles Application.NewMailEx

  Dim mail As Outlook.MailItem
  mail = Globals.ThisAddIn.Application.Session. _
  GetItemFromID(EntryIDCollection)
  ChangeMessageClass(mail)
End Sub
```

Using the new mail's unique ID, grab a reference to the new mail item's object and then call ChangeMessageClass by passing the mail item reference as an argument.

Changing a Message Class So It's Visible in the Custom Form Region

Outlook uses forms to display an item's contents to the user. An item's MessageClass property provides the link between the form and the item. Outlook reads the value of this property, finds the related form in the Outlook Forms library, and displays the item. You change what form an item uses by changing the value of the MessageClass property to the name of the form you want to use. In this case, you want to set the value of all incoming mail items to use the custom message class name of IPM.Note.MODVSTO.

Listing 6-11 contains the code for the ChangeMessageClass procedure.

Listing 6-11. *The ChangeMessageClass Procedure*

```
Private Sub ChangeMessageClass(ByVal mail As Outlook.MailItem)
   Dim newClass As String = "IPM.Note.MODVSTO"

   mail.MessageClass = newClass
   mail.Save()

End Sub
```

This procedure expects a valid Outlook.MailItem as an argument. The procedure takes the passed mail item and resets its MessageClass value to the string that will cause the custom reading pane to activate and display. After changing its value, save the mail item to write the changes to Outlook.

Viewing the Custom Reading Pane at Runtime

Everything is in place to test the solution and see the custom reading pane execute in runtime. Follow these steps to build and test the add-in:

1. Press F5 to compile and run the add-in in Outlook.

2. Once Outlook displays, press F9 to send and receive e-mail. Alternatively, you can select Tools ➤ Send/Receive ➤ Send/Receive All from the Outlook menu.

3. As the e-mail arrives, the add-in will change the message class. Select a newly arrived e-mail to see its body display in the custom ReadingPane form region (see Figure 6-13).

Building a form region from scratch within Visual Studio is best suited when you want complete control of the design and development process. There is a cost, however, as you are required to write the code to bind the controls with Outlook data. There is another way to design a form region that eases control data binding.

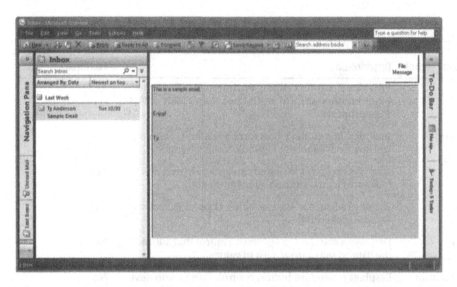

Figure 6-13. *Viewing an Outlook e-mail using the custom ReadingPane form region*

Using Outlook to Build the ReadingPane Form Region

Outlook provides you with the ability to build custom form regions without the use of code. Using the developer tool provided by Outlook, you can quickly extend a default Outlook form to display your custom form region in a matter of minutes. You can build the same types for form regions using Outlook as you can by using Visual Studio. A key difference is that form regions built within Outlook only support Visual Basic Scripting Edition (VBScript) for adding code behind the form. You need to import the form region into a VSTO project to take advantage of .NET code-behind capabilities.

Outlook Form Region Controls

A key advantage Outlook does offer when designing form regions is that it provides you with form region controls. These controls are specially designed to function like standard Outlook controls. For example, the Category control automatically provides the features implemented by the default Outlook forms. You can use the form region controls to build form regions that look and act like a user would expect a form to function within Outlook. Table 6-5 lists each of the form region controls and provides a short description of their usage. In addition, several controls leverage functionality specific to Outlook and are identified as such in the table.

Table 6-5. *Outlook Form Region Controls*

Form Region Control	Description	Outlook-Specific Features?
Body	Provides a rich-text editing environment. The control binds automatically to an Outlook item's Body or Message property.	Yes
Business Card	Included in a contact item form by default. This control is only available to Outlook contact items	Yes
Category	Displays an item's assigned categories. In default Outlook forms, this control resides at the top.	Yes
Check Box	Displays a Boolean state as either true (checked) or false (unchecked).	No
Combo Box	Displays a standard drop-down control that allows the user to select from a list of values.	No
Command Button	Displays a standard button control. This button deviates from a standard Outlook Forms button by supporting image displays and drop-down arrows (i.e., the buttons found in a contact item's phone numbers' section is a good example of this control).	No
Contact Photo	Displays the picture assigned to the item's assigned contact. This control only supports form regions that customize a contact item.	Yes
Date	Replicates the Outlook DataPicker control. You can set the control to display either the date or the time.	Yes
Frame Header	Displays a line separator that you can use to group sections of form region controls.	Yes
InfoBar	Displays metadata related to the item contained in the form region. Example data displayed in this control includes follow-up flags and formatting actions that Outlook applied to the item.	Yes
Label	Displays text and can automatically display the control using an item's header color as specified by the selected Office theme.	No
List Box	Displays a standard ListBox control containing a list of items. This control supports multi-item selection.	No
Option Button	Displays a standard radio button intended to be used as a group to select single values.	No
Page	Displays a form region as a page in an Outlook form. This control replaces the tabs used in previous Outlook forms.	Yes

Form Region Control	Description	Outlook-Specific Features?
Recipient	Displays a special text box that allows the user to enter recipient names and/or e-mail addresses. This control performs Outlook autocompletion and recipient lookups.	Yes
Sender Photo	Displays an e-mail sender's photo. This control autobinds to the sender's contact photo, if assigned.	Yes
Text Box	Displays a standard TextBox control. The text box can be a single line or multiple lines.	No
Time	Replicates the TimePicker control found in the default Appointment form.	Yes
Time Zone	Displays a drop-down control listing time zones. This control replicates the Time Zone control features in the default Appointment form that allow a user to specify the time zone for meeting's start and end times.	Yes
View	Displays items from an Outlook folder. You can specify which folder and view the control displays in the form region.	Yes

The VBScript limitation is not a problem if you import the form region into a VSTO add-in project.

Designing the Custom E-mail Form

A VSTO Outlook add-in automatically builds the code required to load a custom form region. Once you complete the New Outlook Form Region Wizard, all you need to worry about is implementing your business logic. In this example, you'll create a new form region using Outlook's developer tools and then import the form region into VSTO. Once imported, you can execute the add-in and immediately view messages with the IPM.Note.MODVSTO message class value in the new form region.

You can create this custom form by completing the following steps:

1. Open Outlook and select Tools ➤ Forms ➤ Design a Form from the Outlook menu.

2. In the Design Form dialog box, select the Standard Forms Library option from the Look In drop-down control. Select the Message form, and click Open to open the form in design mode.

3. In the Developer tab, click the Form Region button (see Figure 6-14) and select the New Form Region option to insert a new tab labeled (**Form Region**).

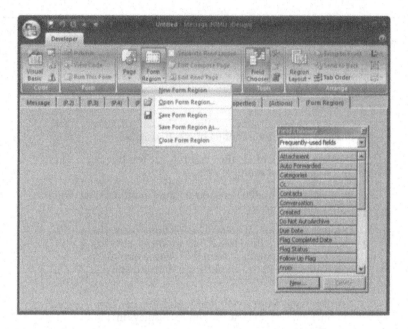

Figure 6-14. *Creating a new form region*

4. You want to utilize the Outlook form region controls to populate the form region. These controls are not included in the toolbox by default, so you must add them. Click the toolbox icon in the Developer tab to display the Outlook controls toolbox. Right-click the toolbox, and select the Custom Controls menu option to display the Additional Controls dialog box. All of the form region controls are prefixed with *Microsoft Office Outlook* (see Figure 6-15). Scroll down until you see these controls listed, and enable each one. Click OK to return to the form and see the additional controls in the toolbox window.

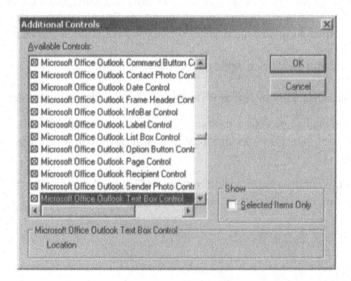

Figure 6-15. *Adding the form region controls to the Outlook controls toolbox*

5. Drag and drop both the InfoBar (`olkInfoBar`) and the Category (`olkCategory`) controls to the top of form region. The InfoBar control displays the metadata that Outlook tracks about an item, such as the date of receipt and the date and time of your reply. The Category control autobinds to the Category field of a `MailItem`.

6. Using the Field Chooser window, add the Message field to the form region. This action adds an Outlook Body control to the form and binds it to the Message field.

7. Export the form region as an `.ofs` file by clicking Form Region ➤ Save Form Region in the Developer tab. Enter **ReadingPane2.ofs** as the file and click Save. You might want to make a note of the location, as you'll need this file for the next step.

8. Create a new VSTO Outlook 2007 add-in project in Visual Studio and name the project **CustomReadingPaneOFS**.

9. Import the `ReadingPane2.ofs` file by selecting Project ➤ Add New Item from the Visual Studio menu. Choose the Outlook Form Region item from the Add New Item dialog box, enter **ReadingPane2** as the name, and click Add to initialize the New Outlook Form Region Wizard.

10. Choose "Import an Outlook Form Storage (.ofs) file" in the initial wizard screen. Browse to the location where you saved the `ReadingPane2.ofs` file and select it. Click Next.

11. Choose Replacement as the form region type and click Next.

12. Enter **ReadingPane2** into the Name and Title fields for the form region. Leave only the ReadingPane check box enabled. Click Next.

13. You want to take advantage of the same message class you created in the previous sample, so enter **IPM.Note.MODVSTO** as the custom message class. Click Next to complete the New Outlook Form Region Wizard and add the form to the project.

Nothing else is needed to run the add-in and view messages using the ReadingPane custom form region. You can test this sample by pressing F5. Messages with the correct message class value will display in the Outlook reading pane inside the custom form region (see Figure 6-16).

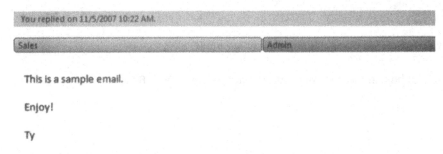

Figure 6-16. *The .ofs version of the ReadingPane form region displaying an e-mail message in Outlook*

Building the Quick Search Add-In

Outlook includes the new Table object that you can use to perform fast searches across the Outlook data store. The Table object is a read-only object that contains a collection of Outlook items that match the search criteria you specify. The Quick Search sample add-in illustrates how to use the Table object to perform searches in Outlook and display the results to the user.

The remainder of this section provides a walk-through for building a VSTO Outlook 2007 add-in. You can follow along by creating a new project in Visual Studio and naming it **QuickSearch**.

Designing the Quick Search Ribbon

The Quick Search add-in utilizes a custom Ribbon that allows users to enter their search criteria and then execute the search with the click of a button. To build the add-in's Ribbon, follow these steps:

1. With the QuickSearch project open in Visual Studio, add a new Ribbon control to the project by navigating to Project ➤ Add New Item ➤ Ribbon (Visual Designer). Name the ribbon **SearchRibbon**, and click Add to add the Ribbon to the project.

2. Add Group, EditBox, and Button controls to the Ribbon so that it resembles the one shown in Figure 6-17.

Figure 6-17. *The Quick Search Ribbon in design mode*

3. Edit the Ribbon and its control properties according to Table 6-6.

Table 6-6. *Quick Search Ribbon Control Properties*

Control	Property Name	Value
Ribbon	Name RibbonType	Search Ribbon Microsoft.Outlook.Appointment Microsoft.Outlook.Contact Microsoft.Outlook.Journal Microsoft.Outlook.Mail.Compose Microsoft.Outlook.Mail.Read Microsoft.Outlook.Post.Compose Microsoft.Outlook.Post.Read Microsoft.Outlook.RSS Microsoft.Outlook.Task
RibbonTab	Label	Quick Search
RibbonGroup	Label	Search Criteria
RibbonEditBox	Name Label SizeString	txtSearchString Find 111111111111111111111111111
RibbonButton	Name Label ControlSize	btnSearch Find It! RibbonControlSizeLarge

A few properties bear explaining. The `RibbonType` property specifies which Outlook Inspector types will display the custom Ribbon. In this sample, the Ribbon will display in the Appointment, Contact, Journal, Mail Compose, Mail Read, Post Compose, Post Read, RSS, and Task Inspectors.

The `SizeString` property functions as the width of the EditBox control. The control's width at runtime will equal the size of the string value you specify. The `ControlSize` property determines if the Button control displays a large image above the label (`RibbonControlSizeLarge`) or if it displays a smaller image to the right of the button (`RibbonControlSizeRegular`). In this solution, go with the large button to make it obvious to the user.

Adding Search Code to the Ribbon

The user enters a string into the edit box and clicks the Find It! button to initialize a search. This add-in performs a search against the `ActiveExplorer` object's current folder. Let's start with the code behind the btnSearch Button control.

The btnSearch_Click Event

Listing 6-12 contains the Click event for the Ribbon's Find It! button's Click event. This event starts the search process with a call to the Ribbon's GetTableSearch procedure. This procedure actually performs the search using the passed string provided by the txtSearchString EditBox control.

Listing 6-12. *The btnSearch_Click Event*

```
Private Sub btnSearch_Click(ByVal sender As System.Object, _
    ByVal e As Microsoft.Office.Tools.Ribbon. _
    RibbonControlEventArgs) Handles btnSearch.Click

    GetTableSearch(Me.txtSearchString.ToString())
  End Sub
```

The GetTableSearch Procedure

The GetTableSearch procedure, shown in Listing 6-13, accepts a string that will be used to search against the folder where the item in the active Inspector resides. The code searches the subject string for all items in the folder by calling the folder object's GetTable method. GetTable returns a Table object filled with all the items that meet the search criteria.

Listing 6-13. *The GetTableSearch Procedure*

```
Private Sub GetTableSearch(ByVal SearchString As String)
    Dim objTable As Outlook.Table
    Dim objColumns As Outlook.Columns
    Dim objFolder As Outlook.Folder
    Dim objFindValue As String

    objFolder = Globals.ThisAddIn.Application. _
     ActiveExplorer.CurrentFolder

objFindValue = "@SQL=" & Chr(34) _
      & "urn:schemas:httpmail:subject" _
      & Chr(34) & " ci_startswith '" & _
        txtSearchString.Text & "'"

    objTable = objFolder.GetTable(objFindValue, Outlook. _
      OlTableContents.olUserItems)

    objColumns = objTable.Columns
    objColumns.Add("From")
    objColumns.Add("Received")
    objColumns.Add("Importance")
```

```
  Dim objForm As New SearchResults()
  objForm.ResultsData = CreateDataTable(objTable)
  objForm.Show()
  objForm.Activate()
End Sub
```

The syntax for a GetTable call is

```
Folder.GetTable(Filter, TableContents)
```

The Filter parameter must be a string that uses either the Jet query syntax or the DAV Searching and Locating (DASL) syntax. The Jet syntax is the SQL-like syntax you used in the FCSW. This format requires the field name and the filter value for performing a search. DASL works with the schemas of the Outlook objects. The documentation of these schemas is not easy to find, but you can do it if you know the trick (see the sidebar, "How to Find a DASL Field Name").

In the sample, you search the subject field to return items that begin with the passed search string. You can perform a *contains* search by switching the ci_startswith keyword for ci_contains. You want the search results to include the sender's e-mail address, the received date, and the item's importance. These properties are not returned by default with a Table object, so you can add them to the table by calling its Columns collection's Add method.

Wrap up the procedure by instantiating the SearchResults form and assigning a DataTable object to the form's ResultsData property. The CreateDataTable function in this example and the related MakeColumn function are modified versions of the function from the FCSW. They work together to convert the Table object containing the search results into a valid DataTable object. Listing 6-14 contains the CreateDataTable and MakeColumn functions that have been modified for this solution.

Listing 6-14. *The CreateDataTable and MakeColumn Functions*

```
Private Function CreatedataTable(ByVal table As Outlook.Table) _
  As System.Data.DataTable

  Dim objDataTable As New Data.DataTable
  Dim objRow As Outlook.Row
  objDataTable.Columns.Add(MakeColumn("Importance"))
  objDataTable.Columns.Add(MakeColumn("From"))
  objDataTable.Columns.Add(MakeColumn("Subject"))
  objDataTable.Columns.Add(MakeColumn("Received"))
  objDataTable.Columns.Add(MakeColumn("MessageClass"))
  objDataTable.Columns.Add(MakeColumn("EntryID"))
  Do Until table.EndOfTable
    objRow = table.GetNextRow
    Dim objDataRow As Data.DataRow = objDataTable.Rows.Add()
    objDataRow.Item("Importance") = objRow("Importance")
    objDataRow.Item("From") = objRow("From")
```

```
            objDataRow.Item("Subject") = objRow("Subject")
            objDataRow.Item("Received") = objRow("Received")
            objDataRow.Item("MessageClass") = objRow("MessageClass")
            objDataRow.Item("EntryID") = objRow("EntryID")
        Loop


        Return objDataTable


    End Function



    Private Function MakeColumn(ByVal name As String) As _
        Data.DataColumn

        Dim objColumn As New Data.DataColumn
        With objColumn
          .Caption = name
          .ColumnName = name
          .AllowDBNull = True
        End With

        Return objColumn

    End Function
```

Building the SearchResults Form

The SearchResults form is a standard Windows form containing a DataGridView control only. This form's purpose is to display the records contained in its ResultsData property (see Figure 6-18).

You can build this form by adding a new Windows form to the project and then dropping a DataGridView control onto the form's design canvas. The settings for the form are

- Name=SearchResults

- Size=475,300

- Text=Search Results

HOW TO FIND A DASL FIELD NAME

Not only are the DASL field names not obvious, but not a lot of documentation exists that lists each and every field you may want to search against. Still, you can overcome this lack of information with a registry entry that enables an obscure Outlook feature known as the Query Builder. First, follow the steps outlined in the Microsoft article, "How to Use the Query Builder for View Filters and Advanced Searches" (http://support.microsoft.com/kb/default.aspx/kb/307922) to add the necessary registry settings.

Once enabled, you can access the Query Builder in Outlook from the Customize Current View dialog box as follows:

1. Select View ➤ Customize Current View from the Outlook menu to display the Customize View dialog box.

2. Click the Filter button to display the Filter dialog box.

3. Click the Query Builder tab.

4. Select a field from the Field button and specify a filter criteria and value.

5. Click Add to List to add the filter criteria to the Query Builder.

6. Select the SQL tab. You'll see the schema name for the property specified in steps 4 and 5.

The settings for the grid control are

- Name=dgResults

- AllowUserToAddRows-False

- AllowUserToDeleteRows=False

- AllowUserToOrderColumns=True

- ReadOnly=True

- SelectionMode=FullRowSelect

- Dock=Fill

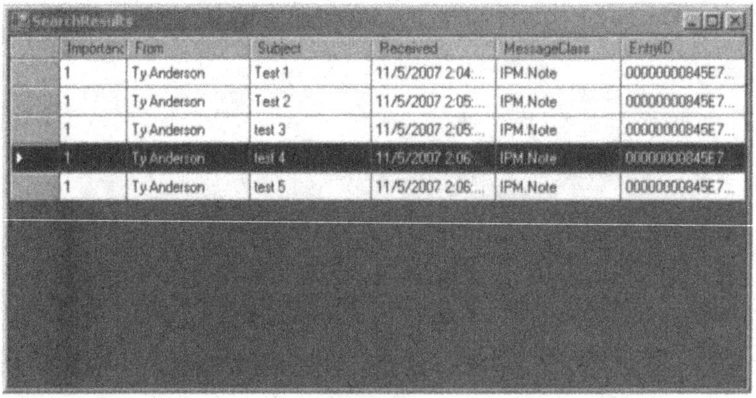

Figure 6-18. *The SearchResults form filled with result items*

Listing 6-15 shows the code for the form. The form contains one custom data table property, ResultsData, which sets the DataSource property of the data grid. The other method in the form is the CellDoubleClick event for the form's DataGridView control. This event uses the entry ID of the selected row as the parameter for the GetItemFromID method. This method is accessible via the Session object. The event completes by displaying the found item to the user.

Listing 6-15. *The SearchResults Form Code Class*

```
Imports System.Data.OleDb
Imports System.Windows.Forms

Public Class SearchResults
  Private _dt As System.Data.DataTable
```

```vb
Friend Property ResultsData() As System.Data.DataTable
  Get
    Return _dt
  End Get
  Set(ByVal value As System.Data.DataTable)
    _dt = value
    dgResults.DataSource = _dt
  End Set
End Property


Private Sub dgResults_CellDoubleClick(ByVal sender As    _
  System.Object, ByVal e As System.Windows.Forms. _
  DataGridViewCellEventArgs) Handles dgResults.CellDoubleClick

  If dgResults.SelectedRows.Count > 0 Then
    Dim dgRow As DataGridViewRow = dgResults.SelectedRows(0)
    Dim objMail As Outlook.MailItem

    objMail = Globals.ThisAddIn.Application.Session. _
      GetItemFromID(dgRow.Cells("EntryID").Value)

    objMail.Display()
  End If

End Sub
End Class
```

Summary

VSTO provides the tools you need to work with Outlook objects and data. Outlook's extensibility options, combined with its user popularity, make it a great platform for your solutions. This chapter covered several strategies that are useful when developing Outlook add-ins with VSTO. The StorageItem object is a new Outlook item ideally suited for storing information useful to the operation of your add-in. Form regions give you the capability to customize Outlook forms (including the ReadingPane form). Outlook provides the Table object along with the GetTable function. Together, these two objects allow you to incorporate Outlook search queries within your Outlook add-in solutions.

CHAPTER 7

■■■

Building SharePoint Workflows

In simple terms, software exists to automate processes. With the advent of the PC, software has served as the bridge that allows users to automate processes. The latest software has trivialized tasks that only a generation ago took much more time and effort. For example, authoring and formatting reports, building complex financial models, and creating graphics can all be done now in the blink of an eye.

These examples reside in the domain of the individual. For example, writing a report is typically done by one person typing away one key at a time. Sure, you can collaborate with another person or a team of people, but the task of creating the report is a singular task.

After someone produces the report, you need to coordinate and collaborate with others. This is the realm of SharePoint workflows. This chapter will

- Provide a SharePoint workflow overview

- Show you how to design workflows using the Visual Studio Workflow Designer

- Show you how to build sequential workflows

- Show you how to build state machine workflows

A Workflow Primer

As the name suggests, a *workflow* is a sequence, or flow, of tasks that achieve a predetermined end. In essence, a workflow serves to model actual processes, or work, in the real world. This work can be performed by computer systems, individuals, groups of people, or any combination thereof.

In SharePoint, the term *workflow* refers to business workflows performed by people: either groups of people or lone individuals. SharePoint serves as the automation engine connecting people to a software system that provides a rich workflow framework. SharePoint hosts the workflows and guides people to a series of steps predefined by a workflow developer.

Workflows Wait, React, and Persist (vs. React and Wait)

The heading says it all. I would argue that all software sits around and waits for something to happen. For user applications, that something is typified by the user clicking a button. Once the user clicks the button, the application reacts and springs into action to perform the chosen task. Most of the time, the tasks are individual in nature and linked only in the mind of the user compelling the application to act. Once the application shuts down, it has no memory of the user's workflow or state of mind (nor does it particularly care).

■**Note** Both Windows SharePoint Services (WSS) and Office SharePoint Server support workflows. For the sake of simplicity, I use the term *SharePoint* to refer to both flavors of SharePoint.

Comparatively, SharePoint workflows guide the user through a workflow. It is SharePoint who decides what to do next. Take, for example, a generic document-approval process that requires a manager to approve a document before it may be sent to a client. In this scenario, the document author would upload a document into a SharePoint document library. This uploading action would initiate a SharePoint workflow that creates a task for document review and approval. Once a manager reviews the document and marks the task as complete, the workflow sends an e-mail notifying the author of approval. While waiting for the manager to act, SharePoint waits and saves the workflow state to the SharePoint database.

Figure 7-1 illustrates the document-approval process. As a workflow progresses, SharePoint is working behind the scenes, managing the state of the workflow and its related information. It is enough to know that as a workflow progresses, SharePoint constantly hydrates (or awakens), executes, and dehydrates (or puts to sleep) the workflow.

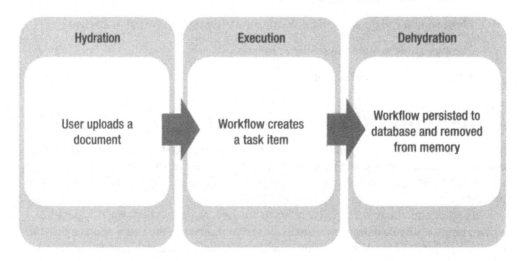

Figure 7-1. *The iterative process of the SharePoint workflow*

When the user uploads the document, SharePoint initializes the workflow and registers it against the uploaded item. This process is known as *hydration*, and it ensures that all objects and related information are available in memory.

Once hydrated, the workflow can take the appropriate action as defined by the workflow template. This can be simple, such as creating a task in a task library (as in the document-approval example), or much more complex, with multiple steps and workflow branching (including If…Else statements and more). When SharePoint takes action on a workflow, it is in execution mode.

After the workflow creates the task, SharePoint dehydrates the workflow instance and removes it from memory. During dehydration, all information concerning the workflow (such as the current step, the workflow item, and the workflow properties) is serialized and stored in the SharePoint database.

The workflow remains in the dehydrated state until the required event (marking the completion of the approval task) occurs. This event causes SharePoint to wake up and hydrate, or *reinitialize*, the workflow. Once hydrated, SharePoint repeats the process of executing a task and dehydrating.

Key Workflow Terminology

SharePoint workflows have a few key terms that, once understood, help shed light on how workflows operate. You could build a workflow without this knowledge, but you would be missing out on the finer details and nuances of a workflow. Figure 7-2 illustrates their relationship of these key terms to each other.

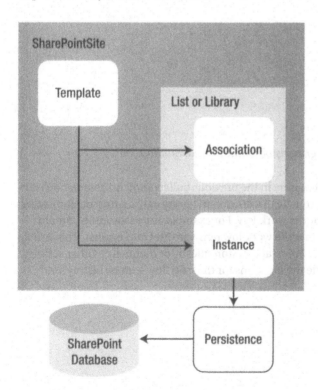

Figure 7-2. *How key SharePoint terms relate to each other*

These key terms are defined as follows:

- *Template*: A template is the actual workflow feature. You can build templates using SharePoint Designer or Visual Studio. Within Visual Studio, you use the Workflow Designer to build the workflow steps, direct the flow of the steps, and attach custom logic (see Figure 7-3). The template is installed in SharePoint. The resulting template is then installed in WSS and associated with a document library or listed in a SharePoint site.

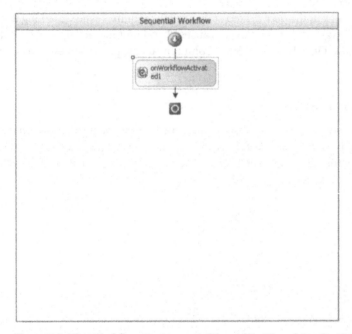

Figure 7-3. *The Workflow Designer visible within Visual Studio 2008*

- *Association*: I gave the definition away in the previous bullet point. An association is the object that binds a workflow template to a document library or list. An association stores the parameters and settings for the workflow. For example, the association contains information regarding the list that the workflow template executes against. The association also defines when the workflow starts (automatically or manually). Other settings stored in an association include the locations for the workflow's tasks, history, and approvers.

- *Instance*: An instance is born whenever a workflow association initializes against a list item. The instance is the combination of the template and the association. SharePoint utilizes the information and logic contained in the template to execute against the targeted item. Once an instance exists, the workflow is, in essence, alive.

- *Persistence*: I touched on this earlier when discussing workflow hydration and dehydration. Workflows can run for an indeterminate amount of time. They can execute in minutes or run for months. Given the potential for longevity, it makes sense to remove the workflow from memory and free up server resources. Persistence occurs anytime a workflow pauses to wait for user interaction. In the earlier example, the workflow persists while waiting for a manager to complete the approval task.

Hopefully these terms provide some teeth to what SharePoint is doing in the background. Again, knowing this terminology doesn't make a big difference in your ability to build a solid workflow, but it does shed some conceptual light on the matter, which isn't bad either.

Next up is the workflow architecture and how it operates within SharePoint.

SharePoint Workflow Architecture

Workflows in SharePoint are really just Windows Workflow Foundation (WF) applications hosted by SharePoint. WF provides the ability to integrate workflow logic into all types of applications. This support includes not only SharePoint sites but also WinForm, WebForm, and console applications, to name a few. The SharePoint workflow templates available in Visual Studio are preconfigured to set up SharePoint as the workflow host. This is a big advantage over building workflows in other application types, such as WinForms, simply due to the reduction in code and effort to build a viable workflow host. With VSTO, you only need to worry about building the workflow model, adding your code, and deploying the workflow feature to a SharePoint site.

MORE ABOUT WORKFLOWS

This chapter covers what you need to know to build and deploy a SharePoint workflow that implements a simple logic flow. Becoming an expert on this topic requires knowing how to build custom workflow forms (with InfoPath or ASP.NET), how to build custom workflow activities, when to use the various workflow controls, and more.

The topic of SharePoint workflows is deep and deserves a book of its own in order to provide enough coverage. This is why my fellow Apress author, David Mann, wrote the book on SharePoint workflows: *Workflow in the 2007 Microsoft Office System* (Apress, 2007). I recommend obtaining a copy of this book, as it provides the depth of information required to take this topic further.

■**Note** MSDN has an entire portal dedicated to WF content. It resides at `http://msdn.microsoft.com/ en-us/netframework/aa663328.aspx`. Here you will find a guided tour, sample code, webcasts, tutorials, and more.

Figure 7-4 shows the technology components involved to enable SharePoint workflows. On the outer rim is WSS, which serves as the application host for WF. WSS also exposes the workflow runtime engine that executes workflow templates according to the rules and logic present in the template. In addition, the runtime includes the base host providers needed to perform tasks such as persistence and messaging. Figure 7-4 does not include the Visual Studio Workflow Designer, as it is included as part of WF.

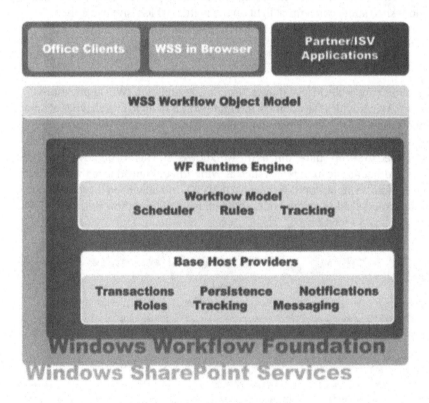

Figure 7-4. *The SharePoint workflow technology stack*

TOOLS REQUIRED FOR BUILDING SHAREPOINT WORKFLOWS

Developing SharePoint workflows will most likely require additional technologies not included in Visual Studio by default. To make sure you're ready later in this chapter when you build a couple of workflows, here is the list of components you'll need to install on your system:

- *Microsoft .NET Framework 3.5*: This version of the .NET Framework includes WF. Download it at `http://www.microsoft.com/downloads/details.aspx?FamilyId=333325FD-AE52-4E35-B531-508D977D32A6`.

- *Windows SharePoint Services 3.0 SDK*: This download includes tons of great stuff related to SharePoint development. The key items for this chapter are the SharePoint workflow Visual Studio project templates. Download it at `http://www.microsoft.com/downloads/details.aspx?familyid=5ddf902d-95b1-4640-b9e4-45440dc388d9`.

- *WSS or Office SharePoint Server*: You should develop workflows on a system that runs either WSS or Office SharePoint Server.

Components of a SharePoint Workflow

You use the Workflow Designer to model, or build, a workflow using Visual Studio 2008 (see Figure 7-5). Inside the designer, a workflow resembles a diagram created in a tool such as Microsoft Visio (although the Workflow Designer is not related to Visio in any manner). In fact, if you're familiar with Visio, you might agree that building the flow is indeed extremely similar creating a diagram in Visio. One of the key differences, however, is that the objects you add to the Workflow Designer are code objects, and Visual Studio writes code each time you add an object or change a property.

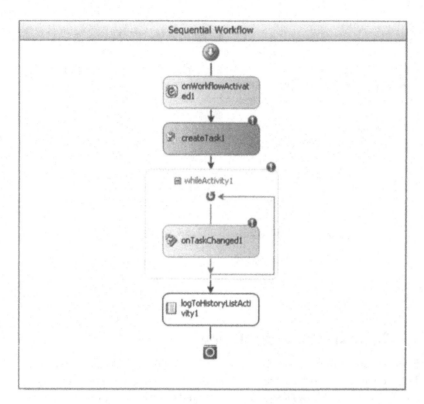

Figure 7-5. *Workflow methods and event handlers displayed in the Workflow Designer*

Note Figure 7-5 displays a bang character (an exclamation point) in the top right-hand corner in three of the workflow elements. The bang signifies that the attached element is not 100% configured. As you build a workflow and add values to their required properties, the bang character will disappear. The display of the bang is a nice feature on Microsoft's part, as it helps you see which items require additional work to complete the workflow.

SharePoint workflows execute code and wait for a user to complete an action that triggers the next workflow step. Workflows provide two types of objects that define what type of action to take and when to execute it. These are known as *methods* and *event handlers*, respectively.

The following list defines the main components used to design a workflow and link the various workflow actions to SharePoint items:

- *Methods*: Methods perform actions like CreateTask, SendMail, or InvokeWebService. For example, a method will create a task in the workflow's associated task list and then hook up the required event handler as defined in the workflow template. In Figure 7-5, the method is the blue square.

- *Event handlers*: Event handlers cause a workflow to dehydrate and persist its data to the database. Once persisted, the workflow waits for the user to execute an action that wakes up the workflow and forces it to hydrate and execute the next defined method. In Figure 7-5, OnTaskChanged is an example of an event handler. Event handlers are green in the Workflow Designer.

- *Business logic*: Business logic is the code you write that executes within the defined methods and event handlers. Just like in a WinForm application, the objects in the Workflow Designer expose events where you can attach code. Code should be attached to the methods and events defined in the Workflow Designer. In addition, you can add methods and classes to the workflow project in the same manner as you do with other Visual Studio projects.

- *Correlation tokens*: Correlation tokens are unique identifiers that link a SharePoint item with methods and event handlers that execute against it. Figure 7-6 illustrates this relationship. In the figure, the correlation token maps both the CreateTask method and the OnTaskChanged event to the workflow task created by CreateTask.

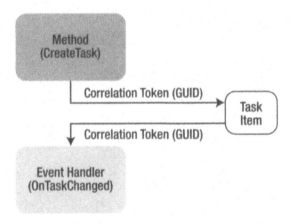

Figure 7-6. *Correlation tokens link a SharePoint item with workflow methods and event handlers.*

Two Types of SharePoint Workflows

SharePoint supports two types of workflows: *sequential* and *state machine*. Sequential workflows follow a linear path from start to finish. As an item moves from one stage of a sequential workflow to another, it can take variant courses of action depending on your logic. However, the workflow does not return to a previous stage or step.

State machine workflows can revert to previous stages. These stages are called *states*. A state machine workflow does not follow a linear path. Instead, it jumps from state to state, depending on the logic you implement. Like sequential workflows, state machine workflows having a starting point and an ending point. The key difference is that what happens in between the start and end is not predetermined.

Building a Sequential SharePoint Workflow

In this section, I will explain how to build a simple sequential SharePoint workflow. The scenario in this example is based on the life of a financial statement auditor who performs his work by testing accounting documents in order to validate account balances found on a financial statement. A good example is the cash balance found in a balance sheet. The auditor performs the steps shown in Figure 7-7 and then documents the results. Once done, the auditor marks the steps as complete, and the manager reviews the work.

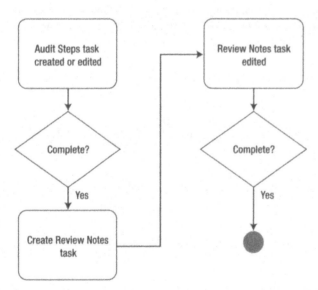

Figure 7-7. *The sample review process to be automated by the sequential workflow*

The sequential workflow in this section automates the process of creating a task item to notify a manager that an audit step is ready for review. The workflow waits for the task to be marked as completed before completing the workflow.

Creating the Sequential Workflow Project

Building workflows in Visual Studio isn't as code-intensive a task as compared to other project types. As a result, this walk-through is filled with "do this, do that" instructions. I provide a plethora of screen shots to mirror the narrative.

To create the sequential workflow application, open Visual Studio and complete the following steps:

1. Create a new project by selecting the SharePoint 2007 Sequential Workflow project template available in the New Project dialog box (see Figure 7-8).

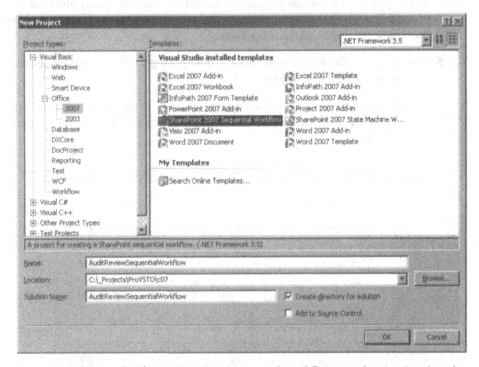

Figure 7-8. *Selecting the SharePoint 2007 Sequential Workflow template in Visual Studio*

2. Name the project **AuditReviewSequentialWorkflow** and click OK.

3. Visual Studio uses a wizard to prompt you to input a friendly name for the workflow as well as the URL for the targeted SharePoint site. In the New Office SharePoint Workflow dialog box shown in Figure 7-9, enter the URL of a SharePoint team site you want to use for this workflow. On my system, I have set up a team site with `http://teamsite/audit` as the URL. Leave the friendly name for the workflow as is, and click Next.

4. The second New Office SharePoint Workflow dialog box, shown in Figure 7-10, allows you to specify which lists in the target site to use in the workflow. The workflow requires a document library or list that will be associated with the workflow template you will create. In addition, you need to specify a list to contain workflow history items and workflow tasks. The history list will store workflow event information, and the task list will store user tasks created and tracked by the workflow.

   For this sample, I created task lists in the Audit team site named Audit Steps and Review Notes. Both of these are standard task lists without any further customization. You can create similarly named task lists, or you can use default lists already provided in the site. If you follow my example completely, specify **Audit Steps** as the target list, and specify **Review Notes** as the task list. Click Next.

5. The last New Office SharePoint Workflow dialog box provides options for defining when to start the workflow (see Figure 7-11).

   For this workflow, leave the default options enabled, as you want to start the workflow anytime a user creates a new item in the target library associated with the workflow. Click Finish.

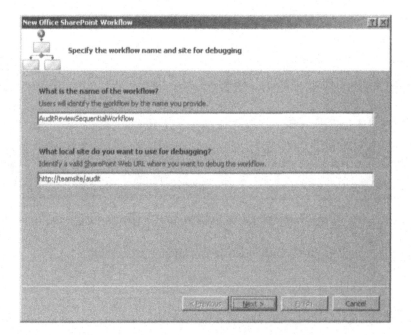

Figure 7-9. *Setting the initial workflow properties*

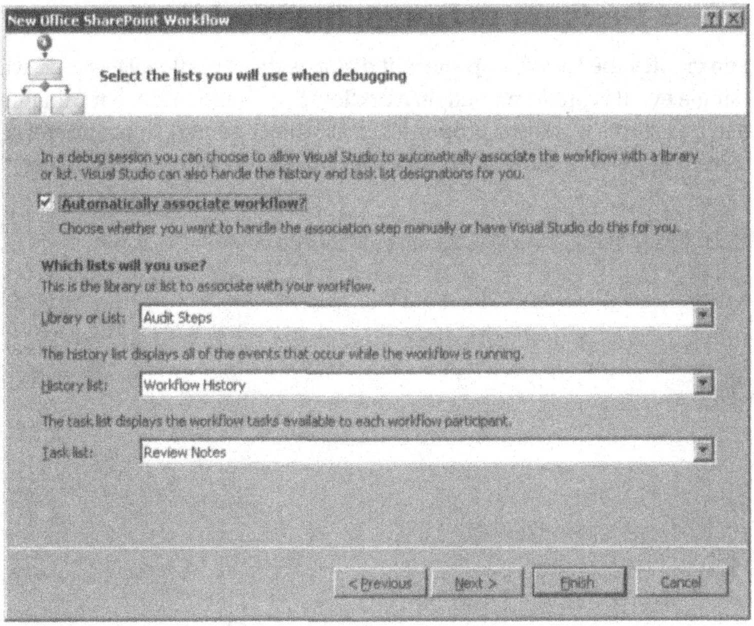

Figure 7-10. *Selecting the lists to be utilized by the workflow*

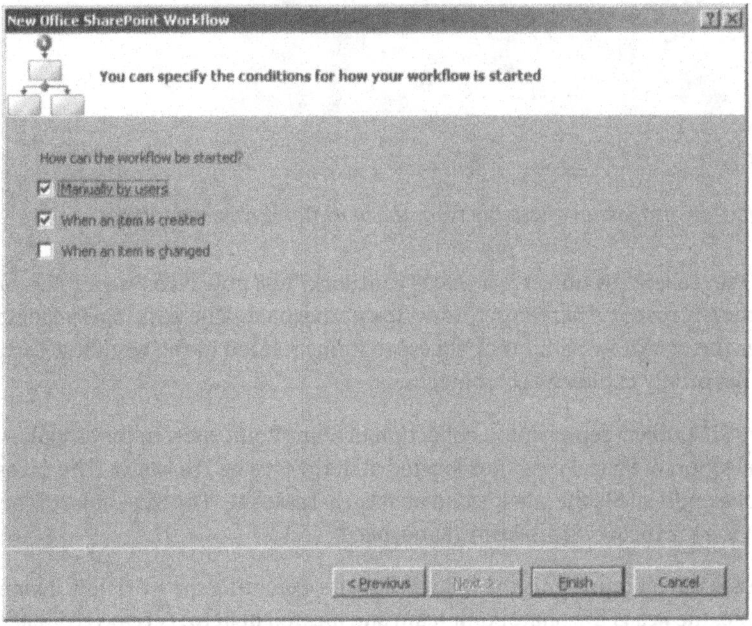

Figure 7-11. *Specifying workflow initialization settings*

Using Workflow Designer to Design the Workflow

After Visual Studio creates the workflow project, it displays the Workflow Designer, which contains only a single event handler named onWorkflowActivated. This event initializes a workflow instance and stores workflow properties in an object named, appropriately enough, workflowProperties. Figure 7-12 shows the properties made available via this object.

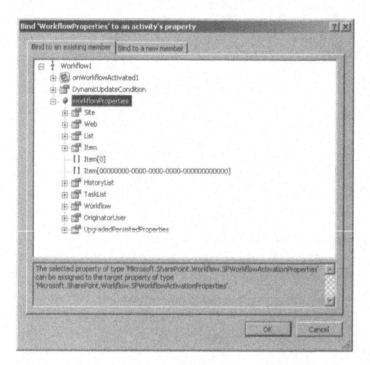

Figure 7-12. *Workflow properties available from the workflowProperties object*

The workflowProperties object is a SharePointWorkflowActivationProperties object and is part of the Microsoft.SharePoint.Workflow namespace. The workflowProperties object provides the workflow with quick access to items related to the workflow instance. The following list briefly explains each object:

- Site: The Site object represents a collection of SharePoint sites. In the sample, the Site is the collection of SharePoint sites located at http://teamsite/audit. The Sites collection for the audit site is the site located at http://teamsite. The Site object is an SPSite object in the Microsoft.SharePoint namespace.

- Web: The Web object represents the SharePoint site executing the workflow instance. In the sample, the Web is the SharePoint team site located at http://teamsite/audit. The Web object is an SPWeb object in the Microsoft.SharePoint namespace.

- List: The List object is the list that is associated with the workflow instance. In the sample, the list is the Audit Steps task list. The list is an SPList object in the Microsoft.SharePoint namespace.

- Item: The Item object is the SharePoint item that is the focal point of the workflow instance. It is an SPListItem object in the Microsoft.SharePoint namespace.

- HistoryList: The HistoryList object is another SharePoint list (SPList object). It is specified in the workflow project settings as the location for storing workflow history events.

- TaskList: The TaskList object is a SharePoint task list (SPList object). This list is specified in the workflow project settings as the location for storing tasks created by the workflow. In the sample, the task list is the Review Notes task list.

- OriginatorUser: The OriginatorUser object initiates the workflow. It is an SPUser object.

- UpgradedPersistedProperties: The UpgradedPersistedProperties object is a HashTable object that stores a collection of field names and values of fields edited by the workflow.

Note For the full details of each property provided by the SPWorkflowActivationProperties object, I recommend viewing the full object model on MSDN at http://msdn.microsoft.com/en-us/library/ microsoft.sharepoint.workflow.spworkflowactivationproperties_properties.aspx.

You can also use these objects to access other items with the site or site collection if needed. You're not limited to only accessing items involved in the current workflow instance. For example, you can use the Site object to access other lists within the site. You can use the List object to edit other items in the associated list. The point is that you can use the workflowProperties object as an entry point for accessing data throughout SharePoint.

Designing the Custom Workflow

After activation, the sequential workflow project waits for the item to be marked as 100% complete. You need to test for this situation by implementing an IfElse workflow activity. Figure 7-13 as a guide for where to place the objects.

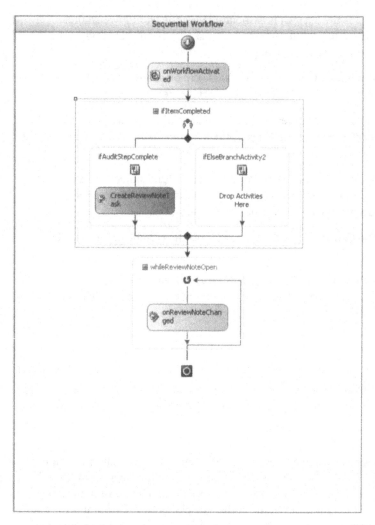

Figure 7-13. *AuditReviewSequentialWorkflow displayed in the Workflow Designer*

To begin building the workflow template, open the Workflow1.vb file in the Workflow Designer and complete the following steps:

1. Drag an IfElse activity from the Windows Workflow v3.0 toolbox tab and place the activity underneath the onWorkflowActivated event handler. Rename the object **IfItemComplete**.

2. Rename the ifElseBranchActivity1 to **ifAuditStepComplete**. The left side of the IfElse activity will respond if the If condition result is True. Leave the right side alone, as you won't take any action if the result is False. You'll configure the condition test in a subsequent step.

3. Drag a CreateTask activity from the SharePoint Workflow toolbox tab and place it within ifAuditStepComplete. Name the activity **CreateReviewNoteTask**.

4. Create a new correlation token for the CreateReviewNoteTask method activity by entering **ReviewNoteToken** in the `CorrelationToken` property. Once you enter the token name, press the Enter key. This action creates the correlation token and displays a "+" next to the `CorrelationToken` property. Click the "+" to expand the property and display the `OwnerActivityName` subproperty. Specify **Workflow1** as the owner of the correlation token.

5. Set up class properties to store the `TaskID` and `TaskProperties` properties for the task that the CreateReviewNoteTask activity method created. You can use the property window to create an object (of type `GUID`) in the workflow class that will store a reference to the created task and make it available to other steps in the workflow. Select CreateReviewNoteTask in the designer, and open the `TaskID` property by clicking the ellipsis button that displays when you click in `TaskID` property field (see Figure 7-14). Click the "Bind to a new member" tab. This tab allows you to specify a name for the property and select whether to create a field or property. In the "New member name" field, enter **CreateReviewNoteTask_TaskID**. Choose Create Field as the member type and click OK.

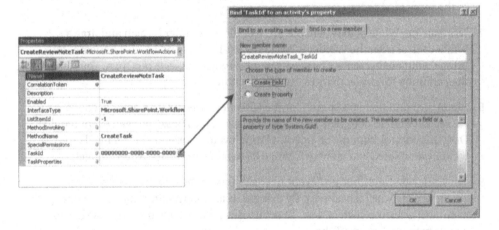

Figure 7-14. *AuditReviewSequentialWorkflow displayed in the Workflow Designer*

Note When creating new binding members, you have the option of creating a field or a property. In the case of the `TaskID`, choosing to create a field results in the creation of a public class-level object. Creating a property results in the creation of a private class-level object that is exposed through property methods.

6. You need to follow the same process from step 5 to create an object for the TaskProperties property. Select the CreateReviewNoteTask activity method, and open the property dialog box by clicking the ellipsis button. Follow the same steps as in step 5, but specify **CreateReviewNoteTask_TaskProperties** as the field name. Click OK to add the field. Just like the TaskID property, the TaskProperties property is bound to a variable residing in the Workflow class. This object is the SPWorkflowTaskProperties object, and it stores workflow task properties such as Title, Description, DueDate, and AssignedTo.

Note Full details of the SPWorkflowTaskProperties object are available on MSDN at http://msdn.microsoft.com/library/microsoft.sharepoint.workflow. spworkflowtaskproperties_properties.aspx.

After creating the task, the workflow needs to wait for a user to mark it as complete. The While activity forces a sequential workflow to wait. Set a condition in the While activity; as long as the condition is True, the While activity will continue to wait. Once the condition changes to False, the child activities contained in the While activity will execute in the sequential order.

7. To create the While activity, ensure the Workflow Designer is open and drag a While control from the Windows Workflow 3.0 Toolbox and place it beneath the IfItemCompleted activity. Change its name to **whileReviewNoteOpen**. You'll specify the condition for this activity in the next section.

8. When the condition you specify for the whileReviewNoteOpen activity changes to False, you want to complete the workflow using an OnTaskChanged event handler. Drag this control from the SharePoint Workflow toolbox and place it inside the whileReviewNoteOpen activity. Change its name to **onReviewNoteChanged**.

9. The onReviewNoteChanged event needs to link to the task created by the CreateReviewNoteTask activity. By using the same correlation token, the change event will track the correct task. To set up this link, change the CorrelationToken property to **ReviewNoteToken**.

10. To complete the workflow design, create one last object to store task properties. In this case, you need an SPWorkflowTaskProperties object to store the updated workflow task. Select the onReviewNoteChanged activity and select the AfterProperties property. Open the property dialog and create a new binding member field in the same manner as steps 5 and 6. Name this field **onReviewNoteChanged_AfterProperties**.

The design of the workflow is now complete. However, it still needs conditions for the IfElse and While activities, as well as some code to encapsulate the workflow's business rules. These topics are the focus of the next two sections.

Defining Conditions

Conditions are code statements that return a Boolean value. Conditions determine when a given activity occurs within the workflow. For example, an IfElse activity has a left and right If block (see Figure 7-15). Each block relies on a condition to determine which path to execute. In the case of the IfElse activity, the top node does not contain a condition. Instead, each side of the IfElse activity contains a separate condition. When True, the condition triggers its related IfElse activity.

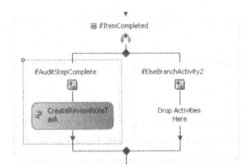

Figure 7-15. *The left and right blocks of an IfElse activity*

There are two types of conditions you can use in your workflows. The first type is a *code condition*. This type of condition is a custom code function you write within the workflow class. The function must return a Boolean value. Since you can write complex functions, a code condition is perfect for implementing complex business rules. The second type is a *declarative rule condition*. This type is a simpler condition and more suited to a simple situation where the workflow evaluates the value of a single property.

Creating a Code Condition

The AuditReviewSequentialWorkflow project utilizes two conditions: one of each type. You can implement these conditions as follows:

1. Open the workflow in the Workflow Designer. Select ifAuditStepComplete, and set its Condition property to Code Condition.

2. Expand the Condition property to display its child Condition property. The child property contains the name of the code method that the condition needs to evaluate. Enter **IsItDone** as the method name.

3. Now you need to create the IsItDone method. Open the workflow's code window by selecting View ➤ Code from the Visual Studio menu. In the code window, add the code found in Listing 7-1.

Listing 7-1. *The IsItDone Method*

```
Private Sub IsItDone(ByVal sender As System.Object, _
 ByVal e As System.Workflow.Activities.ConditionalEventArgs)
  Dim item As SPListItem = workflowProperties.Item

  Dim percent As Double = item("PercentComplete")
  If IsNothing(percent) Then percent = 0

  If percent = 1.0 Then
    e.Result = True
  Else
    e.Result = False
  End If
End Sub
```

This method creates a reference to the workflow item (a task from the Audit Steps task list) and checks the value of its PercentComplete field. If the task is 100% complete, then the method returns True. If value is less than 1, then the method returns False.

Creating a Declarative Rule Condition

The While event of the workflow uses a declarative condition to determine when to stop waiting and execute the onReviewNoteChanged event. To add this condition, complete the following steps:

1. Open the workflow's code window and add the following line of code just below the class declaration:

```
Private _OpenReviewNote As Boolean = False
```

This Boolean object specifies if the Review Notes task created by the workflow is open. Custom code that you'll add in the next section changes this value anytime the onReviewNoteChanged event handler executes.

2. Select the whileReviewNotOpen activity, and set its Condition property to Declarative Rule Condition.

3. Expand the Condition property to display its child elements. Select the ConditionName and open it by clicking the ellipsis button.

4. In the Select Condition dialog box (see Figure 7-16), click New to open the Rule Condition Editor window.

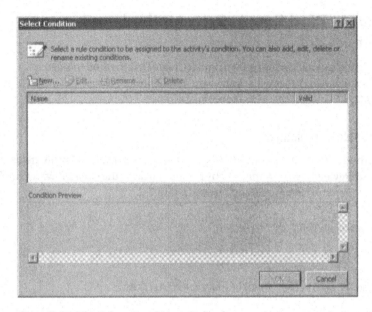

Figure 7-16. *The Select Condition dialog box used to create a declarative rule condition*

5. In the Rule Condition Editor window (see Figure 7-17), enter

```
this._OpenReviewNote == True
```

Click OK to twice to return to the Workflow Designer.

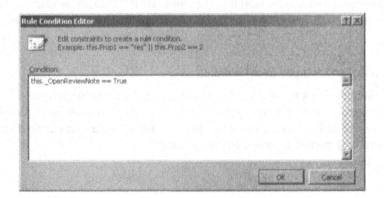

Figure 7-17. *The Rule Condition Editor dialog box*

As long as the value of the _OpenReviewNote object is True, the While activity will continue to wait. Once it is False, the workflow will continue to the onReviewNoteChanged event handler.

Attaching Code to Workflow Activity Methods and Event Handlers

Although you've designed a workflow and added both a CreateTask method (named CreateReviewNoteTask) and an OnTaskChanged event handler (named onReviewNoteChanged), they both require code.

Adding Code to a CreateTask Method

The CreateTask method does create a task, but it's a good idea to set values for the fields in the task. Attach the CreateReviewNoteTask method by double-clicking the CreateReviewNoteTask in the Workflow Designer and adding the code from Listing 7-2.

Listing 7-2. *The CreateReviewNoteTask Method*

```
Private Sub CreateReviewNoteTask_MethodInvoking(ByVal sender As System.Object, _
  ByVal e As System.EventArgs)
  Dim relatedItem As SPListItem = workflowProperties.Item

  CreateReviewNoteTask_TaskId = Guid.NewGuid
  CreateReviewNoteTask_TaskProperties.Title = "Review Note for: " & _
    relatedItem("Title")
  CreateReviewNoteTask_TaskProperties.DueDate = Date.Now.AddDays(7)
  _OpenReviewNote = True
End Sub
```

This code creates a reference to the workflow item and uses its Title property to create the title for the newly created task. In addition, the code creates a new GUID value for the task and sets the due date.

Adding Code to an OnTaskChanged Event Handler

As long as the Review Notes task remains open (i.e., the PercentComplete property is less than 1), the workflow will react to any change made to it. The onReviewNoteChanged event handler handles the reaction. When this event handler executes, it checks the changed values of the task to determine if the task is completed (see Listing 7-3).

Listing 7-3. *The OnReviewNoteChanged Event*

```
Private Sub onReviewNoteChanged_Invoked(ByVal sender As System.Object, _
  ByVal e As System.Workflow.Activities.ExternalDataEventArgs)

  If onReviewNoteChanged_AfterProperties.PercentComplete = 1 Then
    _OpenReviewNote = False
  End If
End Sub
```

Using the `AfterProperties` of the onReviewNoteChanged event, you can check for the `PercentComplete` property and quickly determine if the percentage is 100%. If it is, the code will set the class-level `Boolean` object, `_OpenReviewNote`, to `False` to signal that the Review Notes task is complete.

Remember that the whileReviewNoteOpen activity checks the value of `_OpenReviewNote`. If `_OpenReviewNote` is `False`, whileReviewNoteOpen will cease to wait, and the workflow will be completed.

Debugging the Workflow

Debugging a SharePoint workflow is now as easy as you would hope and expect. Just press F5, and Visual Studio will deploy the workflow to the target SharePoint site and associate it with the target list. You can then trigger the workflow by adding a new item to the Audit Steps task list.

Building a State Machine SharePoint Workflow

In this section, I will cover how to build a simple state machine SharePoint workflow. The scenario in this example is similar to the one from the previous example. Once again, the scenario that forms the basis of this example is from the accounting and auditing world.

Setting Up Workflow Lists in the Audit SharePoint Site

For this workflow sample, you will use a standard SharePoint team site located at http://teamsite/audit. This is the same site as in the previous example. Feel free to use the same site you utilized in the previous example, or, if you prefer, create another team site. It really doesn't matter. What does matter is that you make a modification required for the example state machine.

This workflow associates to the Audit Steps task list. The workflow will utilize the values in the Status column to determine what state to place the workflow in. To modify the Status column for this workflow, complete the following steps:

1. Open the SharePoint site located at http://teamsite/audit. If you have a different location, navigate to the desired URL.

2. Navigate to the Audit Steps task list, and click Settings ➤ List Settings from the list menu (see Figure 7-18).

3. In the Columns section of the Settings page, click the Status column. In the Edit Column page for the Status column, change the choices found in the "Type each choice on a separate line" field to be **Not Started**, **In Progress**, **Ready for Review**, and **Approved** (see Figure 7-19). Click OK to save the modification.

After completing these steps, the Audit SharePoint site is now ready to serve as the target of the state machine workflow. The example scenario is similar to the one implemented in the sequential workflow. The key difference is that the workflow can jump haphazardly from state to state. It does not follow a linear path. Instead, anytime you edit the associated item in SharePoint, this workflow will read the value of the Status column and set the workflow state to the one corresponding to its value. The workflow looks like Figure 7-20.

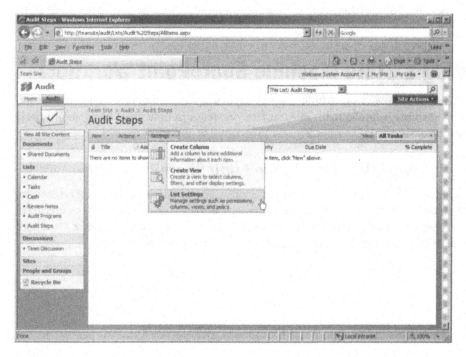

Figure 7-18. *Selecting the List Settings menu option from the Audit Steps task list*

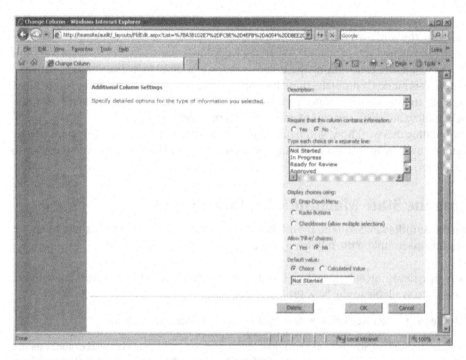

Figure 7-19. *Settings the value choices for the Status column*

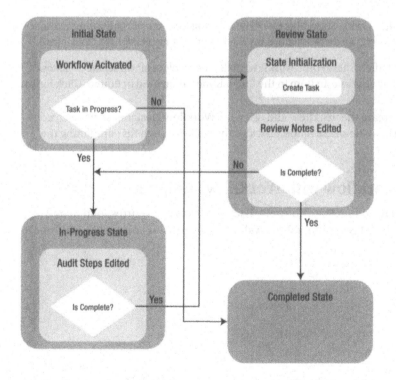

Figure 7-20. *The workflow for the AuditReview state machine workflow*

When the workflow begins, it checks the associated task item to determine if it is at least in progress. If it is, the workflow moves to its in-progress state. If the task isn't in progress, the task moves to the completed state and ends. When the workflow's state is in progress, the workflow waits for you to edit the task. Editing the task causes the workflow to hydrate and execute its logic. If the task is marked complete, then the workflow moves to the review state. When initialized, this state creates a Review Notes task in the task list. Whenever you edit the review note task, the workflow moves to the completed state and the workflow ends.

After building this workflow, you'll understand how state machine workflows move from state to state, how to respond to a state's initialization event, and how to add event handlers to a state activity.

Creating the State Machine Workflow Project

To create the AuditReviewSequentialWorkflow state machine workflow application, open Visual Studio and complete the following steps:

1. Create a new project by selecting the SharePoint 2007 State Machine Workflow project template available in the New Project dialog box.

2. Name the project **AuditReviewStateMachineWorkflow** and click OK.

3. In the New Office SharePoint Workflow dialog box, enter http://teamsite/audit as the URL of the SharePoint site for this workflow. Leave the friendly name for the workflow as is, and click Next.

4. In the second New Office SharePoint Workflow dialog box, select AuditSteps as the library or list. Accept the default values for the history list and task lists. Click Next.

5. In the last New Office SharePoint Workflow dialog box, select all three check boxes to start the workflow anytime an item in the target library is created or edited. Click Finish.

Visual Studio will create the workflow and open the Workflow Designer so you can complete the workflow design. The next section provides the walk-through for completing the design.

Designing the Workflow with Workflow Designer

For this workflow, you need four state controls. These controls each correspond to one of the possible values in the Status column. Let's walk through the creation of each state one at a time.

Adding the Four Workflow States

Before fleshing out each of the individual workflow states, it will ease your efforts if all state activities exist. If each already exists in the Workflow Designer, you can create the state transitions even if the transition state is only a stub.

You can create the workflow states by completing these steps:

1. In the Workflow Designer, select the Workflow1InitialState control. Change the control's name to **stateInitial**.

2. Drag three additional State controls onto the Workflow Designer surface. You can place them anywhere for now. The designer will automatically reposition them later.

3. Change the names of the three controls to **stateInProgress**, **stateReview**, and **stateComplete**.

4. Right-click the stateComplete control and click Set as Completed State to specify it as the workflow's final state.

With these four state controls in place, you're now ready to build the workflow logic.

Creating the Initial State Activity

When Visual Studio created the workflow project, it placed a State activity control on the Workflow Designer. This activity is the start of the workflow. This state contains logic for determining if the workflow item is in progress. If it is, the workflow will transition to the in-progress state.

To configure the initial state activity, complete the following steps:

1. In the stateInitial control, select the eventDrivenActivity1 activity and change its name to **event WorkflowInitialized**.

   Within state controls live one or more sequential workflows. These sequential workflows are wrapped by a special workflow activity known as an EventDrivenActivity. These activity types provide the mechanism for defining an event handler that will cause a given state to react.

2. Double-click the eventWorkflowInitialized event in the stateInitial control. The Workflow Designer will "expand" to display a sequential workflow (see Figure 7-21). Once an event triggers, the workflow will follow the sequence within the event's workflow. In the case of this workflow, the sequence will move to the stateInProgress or the stateCompleted states.

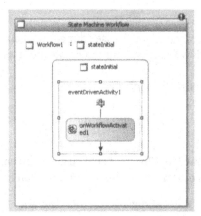

Figure 7-21. *The eventWorkflowInitialized's initial workflow sequence*

3. No changes are required for the onWorkflowActivated1 activity. What is needed is an IfElse activity underneath onWorkflowActivated1. Drag one from the toolbox onto the correct location in the Workflow Designer. Change the name of the IfElseBranchActivity1 to **ifInProgress**. Change the name of the IfElseBranchActivity2 to **ifNotInProgress**.

4. IsItemInProgress in the child `Condition` property. Hit the Enter key; the workflow's code window will display to show a stubbed-out IsItemInProgress method.

5. Edit the IsItemInProgress method to match Listing 7-4. The method creates a reference to the workflow item and then checks the value of its Status column. If the value is anything other than "Not Started" or "Approved", the item is considered to be "In Progress".

Listing 7-4. *The IsItemInProgress Method*

```
Private Sub IsItemInProgress(ByVal sender As System.Object, _
  ByVal e As System.Workflow.Activities.ConditionalEventArgs)
'reference the item triggering the worfklow
Dim relatedItem As SPListItem = workflowProperties.Item

  'Check the status field, if not started or approved
  'the item is in-progress.
  Select Case relatedItem("Status")
    Case "Not Started"
      e.Result = False
    Case "Approved"
      e.Result = False
    Case Else
      e.Result = True
  End Select
End Sub
```

6. Select the ifNotInProgress activity and set the Condition property to **Code Condition**. Expand the Condition property and enter **IsNotStarted** in the child Condition property. Hit the Enter key; the workflow's code window will display to show a stubbed-out IsNotStarted method. Modify the method so that it matches the code in **Listing 7-5**. This method is identical to IsItemInProgress except that it returns True if the Status column's value is "Not Started" or "Approved".

Listing 7-5. *The IsNotStarted Method*

```
Private Sub IsNotStarted(ByVal sender As System.Object, _
  ByVal e As System.Workflow.Activities.ConditionalEventArgs)

  Dim relatedItem As SPListItem = workflowProperties.Item

  'Check the status field, if not started or approved
  'the item has not started
  Select Case relatedItem("Status")
    Case "Not Started"
      e.Result = True
    Case "Approved"
      e.Result = True
    Case Else
      e.Result = False
  End Select
End Sub
```

7. Now that the conditions are set properly, open the Workflow Designer and drag a State control from the toolbox. Place it within the ifInProgress activity and rename it **setStateInProgress**. Change its TargetStateName property to **stateInProgress**.

8. Drag a Terminate control onto the designer and place it within the ifNotInProgress control.

Once you complete these steps, the work for stateInitial is complete. You can return to the top level of the workflow by clicking the Workflow1 link in the top left-hand corner of the Workflow Designer (see Figure 7-21).

Creating the In-Progress State Activity

The in-progress state needs a single event that will monitor any changes in the workflow item. The workflow within this event will transition the workflow to the stateReview state when the item is completed. You can add the required event by completing these steps:

1. In the Workflow Designer, right-click the stateInProgress control and select AddEventDriven from the context menu.

2. The Workflow Designer will expand to show the activity sequence for the newly added EventDrivenActivity2 activity. Change the name of this activity to **eventAuditStepChanged**.

3. From the toolbox, drag an onWorkflowItemChanged control to the designer and place it within eventAuditStepChanged. Change its CorrelationToken property to **workflowToken**. This token links the event to the item that triggered the workflow.

4. Drag an IfElse control from the toolbox and place it beneath the onWorkflowItemChanged1 event.

5. Select the ifElseBranchActivity and change its name to **ifComplete**. Change the Condition property to **Code Condition**. Expand the Condition property and input **IsComplete** in the child Condition property. Hit Enter, and modify the IsComplete method to match the code in Listing 7-6. This method checks for a value of "Ready for Review" in the workflow item's Status column. This value signifies the item is ready for manager review and should be transitioned to stateReview.

Listing 7-6. *The IsComplete Method*

```
Private Sub IsComplete(ByVal sender As System.Object, _
  ByVal e As System.Workflow.Activities.ConditionalEventArgs)

  Dim relatedItem As SPListItem = workflowProperties.Item
  'check the status column
  'return true if equals "Ready For Review".
  Select Case relatedItem("Status")
    Case "Ready for Review"
      e.Result = True
    Case Else
      e.Result = False
  End Select
End Sub
```

6. To set up the transition, drag a SetState control into the ifComplete control. Change its name to **setStateReview** and specify **stateReview** as the value in its TargetStateName property.

Once you complete these steps, the work for stateInProgress is complete. You can return to the top level of the workflow by clicking the Workflow1 link in the top left-hand corner of the Workflow Designer. You can now complete the workflow by configuring the review state.

Creating the Review State Activity

The review state requires two events. The first is an initialization event for the state. This event executes before any other event the state might contain. In it, the workflow creates a task item in the workflow's associated task list. The second event is an onTaskItemChanged event. This event monitors the created task item. If the task is completed, the event will transition the workflow to the completed state (stateComplete). If the task is not completed upon modification, the workflow will transition back to the in-progress state (stateInProgress).

You can follow these steps to complete building out stateReview and the workflow:

1. In the Workflow Designer, right-click stateReview and select AddStateInitialization. The designer will expand to display the sequence for this event.

2. Drag a CreateTask control and place it within stateInitializationActivity2. Rename the control **createReviewNote**. Create a new correlation token for the task you'll create by entering **ReviewToken** in the CorrelationToken property. Expand the CorrelationToken property and select stateReview in the OwnerActivityName property.

3. Create a new field for the TaskID property of createReviewNote and name it **createReviewNote_TaskId1**.

4. Create a new field for the TaskProperties property of createReviewNote and name it **createReviewNote_TaskProperties1**.

5. Double-click createReviewNote and modify the displayed event to match the code in Listing 7-7. This method creates a new task item and sets its Title property.

Listing 7-7. *The createReviewNote_MethodInvoking Event*

```
Private Sub createReviewNote_MethodInvoking_1(ByVal sender As System.Object, _
    ByVal e As System.EventArgs)

    Dim relatedItem As SPListItem = workflowProperties.Item
    createReviewNote_TaskId = Guid.NewGuid
    createReviewNote_TaskProperties.Title = "Review: " & relatedItem("Title")
End Sub
```

6. Select the stateReview link in the top-left corner of the Workflow Designer to return to the workflow's top-level.

7. Right-click stateReview and select AddEventDriven. After the designer displays the sequence for this event, change the event name to **eventReviewNoteChanged**.

8. From the toolbox, drag an onTaskChanged control to the designer and place it within eventReviewNoteChanged. Change its CorrelationToken property to **ReviewToken**, which links this change event to the task by the code in Listing 7-7.

9. Drag an IfElse control from the toolbox and place it beneath eventReviewNoteChanged.

10. Select the ifElseBranchActivity1 and change its name to **ifComplete**. Change the Condition property to **Declarative Code Condition**. Expand the Condition property and input **this.onReviewNoteChanged.AfterProperties.PercentComplete == 1** in the child Expression property. This condition will check the edited task's PercentComplete field. If the value equals 1, the expression result is True.

11. Select the ifElseBranchActivity2 and change its name to **ifStillInProgress**. Change the Condition property to **Declarative Code Condition**. Expand the Condition property and input **this.onReviewNoteChanged.AfterProperties.PercentComplete < 1** in the child Expression property. This condition will check the edited task's PercentComplete field. If the value is less than 1, the expression result is True.

12. Drag a SetState control and place it within ifCompleted. Change the control's TargetStateName property to **stateComplete**.

13. Drag a SetState control and place it within ifStillInProgress. Change the control's TargetStateName property to **stateInProgress**.

The AuditReview state machine workflow is now ready for testing. You can press F5 to compile and deploy the workflow to SharePoint and take it through its paces.

Summary

VSTO provides the ability to design SharePoint workflows within Visual Studio. Using VSTO, you have the ability to develop both sequential workflows and state machine workflows visually, thanks to the Workflow Designer. The Workflow Designer simplifies the process of designing a workflow by allowing you to diagram the workflow in a manner similar to Microsoft Visio. In fact, you can complete most of workflow development, including drawing workflow objects on the designer and configuring properties, simply by clicking the mouse.

Methods and event handlers are different types of workflow activities that carry out different steps in a workflow's hydration, execution, and dehydration cycles. Correlation tokens link workflow activities with SharePoint items such as tasks and documents. To implement custom logic in the workflow, you attach code to methods and event handlers. When writing workflow code, VSTO provides you with the workflowProperties object, which stores references to relevant objects involved in the workflow such as the SharePoint item that triggers the workflow, the SharePoint site, the workflow task list, and the workflow history list.

■ ■ ■

CHAPTER 8

Building Office Business Applications

Microsoft Office has been a viable development platform for years. With Office 2007, Microsoft has refocused its efforts to increase the footprint of Office as a pillar of business solutions by marketing Office applications as the perfect extensions to Line of Business (LOB) applications. LOBs are traditional applications such as accounting, enterprise resource planning (ERP), supply-chain management, and sales force automation. Basically, LOBs are the applications that businesses need to run effectively.

Office Business Applications (OBAs) are application solutions that use Office products to extend LOBs and present LOB data in the context of a business role or task. For example, you could build an Outlook add-in that allows a client account representative to work with data residing in the company's sales system without leaving Outlook. Furthermore, you could extend Outlook and provide features for closing opportunities in the sales system and converting them to billable projects in the company's accounting system. This is exactly what I'll show you how to do in this chapter.

Building the Account Rep Sample OBA

The sample OBA you will build in this chapter will integrate Outlook with an accounting system and a custom sales pipeline database. To keep everything simple and ensure you have access to all software in the sample, the accounting system is Microsoft Office Accounting 2008, and the custom sales database is the sample AdventureWorks database that works with SQL Server.

■**Note** The sample in this chapter works with both AdventureWorks 2005 and AdventureWorks 2008. If you're using SQL Server 2005, you can download AdventureWorks 2005 at http://www.codeplex.com/ MSFTDBProdSamples/Release/ProjectReleases.aspx?ReleaseId=4004. If you're using SQL Server 2008, you can download AdventureWorks 2008 at http://www.codeplex.com/MSFTDBProdSamples/ Release/ProjectReleases.aspx?ReleaseId=16040#ReleaseFiles.

Account Rep OBA Architecture and Business Rules

The Account Rep OBA runs within Outlook as a VSTO add-in and supports a simple work-flow. The sample scenario is one where an account rep is the main contact between a company and a client. The account rep works with the sales team to help win projects. In addition, the account rep works with the accounting department to ensure it bills the correct amounts and so on. In this sample, you'll build a workflow that allows an account rep to create accounting projects from sales opportunities.

Figure 8-1 shows the workflow starting from the sales pipeline system.

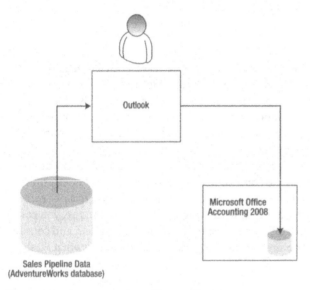

Figure 8-1. *The Account Rep OBA architecture*

Opportunity data resides in the pipeline system and can be imported into Outlook at any-time from the add-in. When imported, Outlook stores customer records as Outlook contacts. When a user opens an Outlook contact, the add-in retrieves any related opportunity records from the sales pipeline database and displays them in a custom action pane (see Figure 8-2).

The account rep can convert an opportunity to an accounting project by selecting the desired record and clicking the Convert Opp to Project button available in the Ribbon (see Figure 8-2).

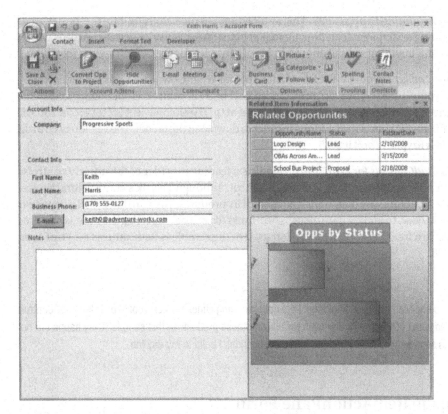

Figure 8-2. *The custom action pane displaying an account's related opportunities*

Setup and Prerequisites

Before you begin building the Account Rep add-in, you will need to download and install all the components I mention in this section. For your convenience, I have included all the links and, where necessary, some comments regarding the setup.

I'll go ahead and assume you already have Visual Studio 2008 installed and that you have the VSTO templates as well. With this assumption out of the way, here is a list of what else you'll need to build the Account Rep sample OBA:

- *SQL Server Express 2008*: The freely available SQL Server Express will run the Adventure-Works database. You can download SQL Express at http://www.microsoft.com/Express/Download. A default installation will suffice.

- *Sample AdventureWorks database*: The AdventureWorks database is no longer included with a SQL Server installation. The sample databases are now available on the CodePlex web site. To install the AdventureWorks database, run the installation file, and the setup program will do the rest. AdventureWorks is available for download at http://www.codeplex.com/MSFTDBProdSamples/Release/ProjectReleases.aspx?ReleaseId=16040. The file you want is named SQL2008.AdventureWorks_LT_DB_v2008.x86.msi.

- *Office Accounting Express 2008*: This application is a nice, nothing-but-the-basics accounting system. You can download it at http://www.ideawins.com/Downloads1.aspx. There isn't anything special about the install. Just accept the defaults when installing.

- *Krypton Toolkit*: Krypton is the labor of love of Phil Wright, owner of Component Factory. The Krypton Toolkit is free and provides a great library of controls for building professional-grade user interfaces. The toolkit is available at http://www.componentfactory.com. You will need to provide your e-mail address in order to download the toolkit. The version used in the sample is Krypton Toolkit 2.8.5.

- *Telerik RadControls for WinForms*: Telerik is a leading provider of third-party controls. This sample makes use of its RadChart control. Although Telerik's control libraries are not free, the company does offer free trials of its products. You can download a copy here at http://www.telerik.com/products/winforms/download.aspx. Registration is required to receive a free trial copy. The version used in the sample is RadControls for WinForms Q1 2008.

■**Note**   I feel compelled to let you know that I am not marketing either Krypton Toolkit or Telerik RadControls for WinForms to you. I don't receive any cash for utilizing these products in this sample. They happen to be included in this sample because I use them in the applications I build in my day job.

Building the ItemActionPane Form

The ItemActionPane (see Figure 8-3) is a custom Windows user control that lists an account's related sales opportunities and displays a graph of the opportunities according to status. The ItemActionPane utilizes a standard Windows DataGridView control to display any related opportunities, and it uses Telerik's RadChart control to display a graph.

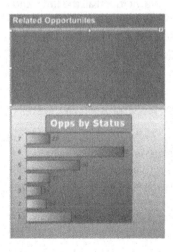

Figure 8-3. *The ItemActionPane in design mode*

To create the user control design, use Figure 8-3 as a guide and complete the following steps:

1. Create a new Outlook 2007 add-in project in Visual Studio 2008. Name the project **AccountRep**.

2. Add a new Windows user control to the AccountRep project and name the control **ItemActionPane.vb**.

3. Find the Krypton control group in the toolbox, and add a KryptonHeader control to the user control's design surface. Set the Dock property to Top, and set the PaletteMode to Professional - System. Change the Text property to Related Opportunities.

4. Add a DataGridView control and place it just below the KrytonHeader control. Change the control's name to **dgOpps**.

5. Add a Telerik RadChart control (available in the RadControls for WinForms toolbox control group) to the user control, and place it below the DataGridView control. Set the name for the control to **OppsChart**. Set the SeriesOrientation to Horizontal, and set the Skin to Gradient.

After completing these steps, you should have a form that more or less resembles Figure 8-3. If so, the control's design is complete, and you're ready to write the code that defines the control's behavior. Open the form's code view and add the following line to the Imports section of the form's class:

```
Imports Telerik.Charting
```

The control stores a reference to the contact that the user has selected using the Outlook UI. To keep this reference, the form uses a private, class-level ContactItem object. Add this line just below the class declaration line:

```
Private _contact As Outlook.ContactItem
```

The code in the ItemActionPane control is primarily concerned with retrieving data from the sales pipeline database and displaying it to the user.

The ItemActionPane_Load Event

The Load event, shown in Listing 8-1, retrieves any related opportunities from the sales pipeline database and displays them in the user control's DataGridView control.

Listing 8-1. *The ItemActionPane_Load Event*

```
Private Sub ItemActionPane_Load(ByVal sender As System.Object, _
    ByVal e As System.EventArgs) Handles MyBase.Load
    'find the SalesSystemId for the open Item by calling
    'the GetUserProperty function and specifying
    '"SalesSystemID" as the desired custom property.
    Dim id As Integer = GetUserProperty("SalesSystemID")
```

```
      'Use the SalesSystemID to return a listing of the
      'Opportunities from the Sales System.
      dgOpps.DataSource = SalesPipeData.GetOpportunitesList(id)

      'Hide columns we don't particularly want to see
      dgOpps.Columns("OpportunityID").Visible = False
      dgOpps.Columns("CompanyName").Visible = False
      dgOpps.Columns("Closed").Visible = False
      dgOpps.Columns("CustomerID").Visible = False

      'Set the column order for the columns that will display
      dgOpps.Columns("OpportunityName").DisplayIndex = 0
      dgOpps.Columns("Status").DisplayIndex = 1
      dgOpps.Columns("EstStartDate").DisplayIndex = 2

      'Refresh to force an update of dgOpps.
      dgOpps.Refresh()

      'Specify the data source for the Chart by
      'calling the GetOpportunitiesForChart function
      'from the SalesPipeData class.
      OppsChart.DataSource = SalesPipeData.GetOpportunitesForChart(id)
      'Specify the Label column for the chart & rotate it.
      OppsChart.PlotArea.XAxis.DataLabelsColumn = "Status"
      OppsChart.PlotArea.XAxis.Appearance.LabelAppearance.RotationAngle = 300
      'Bind the data returned from GetOpportunitiesForChart
      'to the chart.
      OppsChart.DataBind()
   End Sub
```

If a contact is associated with a record in the AdventureWorks sales pipeline database, then the contact will have a custom Outlook user property associated with it. The user property name is SalesSystemID, and it stores the unique ID of the contact that corresponds to the record in the sales pipeline database. The Load event calls the GetUserProperty method (which I explain in the next section) to retrieve the SalesSystemID from the currently selected Outlook contact. This event then calls the GetOpportunitiesList method (part of the SalesPipeData class, which I discuss later in this chapter) to retrieve all opportunities associated with the ID.

After the retrieving the data, the event sets the DataGridView control (dgOpps) to use the retrieved data and creates the required columns for displaying the data. The OppsChart configuration follows the same pattern as that of the DataGridView control, first retrieving the data and then configuring the control as needed.

The GetUserProperty Method

This GetUserProperty method (see Listing 8-2) does the job of retrieving the custom user property values. In this sample, the method accepts a string that represents the name of the desired property you want to retrieve.

Listing 8-2. *The GetUserProperty Custom Method*

```
Private Function GetUserProperty(ByVal UserPropName As String) As String

  Dim userProp As Outlook.UserProperty
  Try
    'Check to determine if Prop exists
    'all Outlook items have a UserProperties collection
    'containing all custom properties for that item.
    'We can use the Find method to search for custom property.
    userProp = _contact.UserProperties.Find(UserPropName)
    'If the custom property does not exist,
    'Find will return Nothing, so return an empty String
    If (userProp Is Nothing) Then
      Return ""
    End If

    If Find found the property, return its value.
    Dim value As String = userProp.Value.ToString()

    Return value
  Catch ex As Exception
    Return Nothing
  End Try

End Function
```

The code checks the class-level _contact object for the desired property. If the property exists, its value will be returned as the method's value. Otherwise, the method will return an empty string.

The RefreshData Method

The ItemActionPane provides the RefreshData method (see Listing 8-3) to allow other objects in the add-in to refresh the data in the task pane on demand.

Listing 8-3. *The RefreshData Method*

```
Friend Sub RefreshData()
  'Retrieve a listing of opportunities and set as the
  'data grid's DataSource, then refresh the data grid.
  dgOpps.DataSource = SalesPipeData.GetOpportunitesList(1)
  dgOpps.Refresh()
  'Refresh the chart too just to be sure.
  OppsChart.Refresh()

End Sub
```

The method uses the Friend modifier to allow other project objects to access and call the method. When executed, RefreshData updates the data in the DataGridView with a new call to the GetOpportunitiesList.

The OpportunityID Property

Not only does the ItemActionPane expose a method for refreshing its data, but it also exposes two custom properties: OpportunityID and Contact. The first of these properties, OpportunityID (see Listing 8-4), contains the ID of the current opportunity selected in the DataGridView control.

Listing 8-4. *The OpportunityID Property*

```
Friend ReadOnly Property OpportunityID() As String
   Get
      Dim oppID As Object
      Dim rowIndex As Integer

      'Check to make sure the user has selected
      'at least one cell in a row.
      If dgOpps.SelectedCells.Count > 0 Then

         'Grab the RowIndex of the first selected cell
         rowIndex = dgOpps.SelectedCells(0).RowIndex
         'Check the RowIndex against the RowCount
         'to avoid an out-of-bounds error
         If (rowIndex < dgOpps.RowCount) Then
            'grab the value of the row's OpportunityID column
            oppID = dgOpps("OpportunityID", rowIndex).Value
            'If there is a value, return it, else return 0.
            If oppID IsNot Nothing Then
               Return oppID
            Else
               Return "0"
            End If
         End If
      End If

      Return "0"
   End Get
End Property
```

After checking that the user has made a selection the grid, the code retrieves the value for the selected row's OpportunityID column. Since this property returns a value from the selected row, it is a read-only property.

The Contact Property

The Contact property (see Listing 8-5) is read/write property used to return and set the value for the class-level _contact object.

Listing 8-5. *The Contact Property*

```
Friend Property Contact() As Outlook.ContactItem
    'Property to set and return the class's _contact object
    Get
      'return the class's _contact object
      Return _contact
    End Get
    'set the class's _contact object to the specified value.
    Set(ByVal value As Outlook.ContactItem)
      _contact = value
    End Set
  End Property
```

By exposing the Contact property with the Friend modifier, you're allowing any object that references the ItemActionPane to access the contact item as needed.

Building the TaskPaneManager Class

Unlike Word and Excel, Outlook does not manage custom task panes for you automatically. The issue here is due to the inherent nature of Outlook and how it handles Explorer and Inspector objects. The ItemActionPane control will display with Outlook contact items. Because more than one contact can be open at a time, you need a class that will manage the ItemActionPane controls and allow you to determine which ItemActionPane control instance is attached to an Inspector window.

■**Note** Inspector and Explorer objects receive full coverage in Chapter 2. If you're unfamiliar with these objects, I recommend reading the explanations in Chapter 2, as they add context needed for this discussion.

The appropriately named TaskPaneManager class handles the management of ItemActionPanes. This class is called by the add-in's ThisAddin class (which I discuss at the end of this chapter) and adds a new ItemActionPane to the Inspector object passed to it. When the add-in user closes an Inspector window, the class removes the attached ItemActionPane control.

The TaskPaneManager contains the following namespace declarations:

```
Imports System.Collections.Generic
Imports Tools = Microsoft.Office.Tools
Imports Outlook = Microsoft.Office.Interop.Outlook
Imports Microsoft.Office.Core
```

The class declares two class-level objects: the Inspector object and the CustomTaskPane object:

```
Private WithEvents _inspector As Outlook.Inspector
Private WithEvents _taskpane As Tools.CustomTaskPane
```

These two objects store references to the Inspector object and the ItemActionPane control that the class will manage. Because each object is declared using WithEvents, the class is able to respond to each object's event.

The Constructor (New) Event

Whenever Outlook creates a new Inspector object, the Account Rep add-in creates a new instance of the TaskPaneManager class and passes a reference to the new Outlook Inspector object. Listing 8-6 shows the action that occurs in the class constructor event.

Listing 8-6. *The TaskPaneManager's New Event*

```
Public Sub New(ByVal Inspector As Outlook.Inspector)
    'declare a new ItemActionPane object that the TaskPaneManager
    'will track.
    Dim pane As New ItemActionPane
    'Set the pane's Contact property to the current item
    'contained in the passed Inspector object.
    'Also, cast it as a ContactItem
    pane.Contact = DirectCast(Inspector.CurrentItem, Outlook.ContactItem)
    'Store a reference to the passed inspector
    'for the TaskPaneManager to track in conjunction
    'with the ItemActionPane control
    _inspector = Inspector
    'add the ItemActionPane instance to the Inspector
    'and set its properties before displaying.
    _taskpane = Globals.ThisAddIn.CustomTaskPanes.Add(pane, _
        "Related Item Information", _inspector)
    _taskpane.Width = 345
    _taskpane.DockPosition = MsoCTPDockPosition.msoCTPDockPositionRight
    _taskpane.Visible = True
End Sub
```

The code here creates a new ItemActionPane and stores the value of the passed Inspector's CurrentItem in the pane's Contact property. Since the Contact property expects an Outlook ContactItem, a DirectCast is applied first. Also, the code creates an internal reference to the passed Inspector.

Next, the code adds the newly created ItemActionPane to the add-in's CustomTaskPanes collection while also storing an internal reference to the control. The method finishes its task by setting the display properties for the control.

The _Inspector_Close Event

Anytime an Inspector closes, you need to remove the ItemActionPane control from the CustomTaskPanes collection and destroy the reference to the ItemActionPane. The _Inspector_Close event (see Listing 8-7) performs this task by checking for the existence of an ItemActionPane control (which would be stored in the _taskpane object) and calling the Remove method of the CustomTaskPanes collection if one exists.

Listing 8-7. *The _Inspector_Close Event*

```
Private Sub _inspector_Close() Handles _inspector.Close
    'On close, we want to clean up the references to the
    'ItemActionPane and its Inspector
    Try
        'If there isn't a task pane, there is no point
        'attempting to remove it.
        If Not (_taskpane Is Nothing) Then
            'Remove the ItemAction pane from
            'the CustomeTaskPanes collection
            Globals.ThisAddIn.CustomTaskPanes.Remove(_taskpane)
        End If

        'Clean up the objects
        _taskpane = Nothing
        'remove the closing Inspector from the TaskPaneManagers
        'collection.
        Globals.ThisAddIn.TaskPaneManagers.Remove( _
            DirectCast(_inspector, Outlook.Inspector))
        'Remove the close event for the Inspector
        RemoveHandler _inspector.Close, AddressOf _inspector_Close

    Catch ex As Exception
        MsgBox(ex.Message)
    End Try
End Sub
```

In addition to removing ItemActionPane, the method also removes the event handler for the inspector's Close event.

The TaskPaneControl Property

The TaskPaneControl property provides other objects in the project with access to the class's ItemActionPane.

```
Friend ReadOnly Property TaskPaneControl() As Tools.CustomTaskPane
  'Return the stored reference to the ItemActionPane control.
  Get
    Return _taskpane
  End Get
End Property
```

This property is read-only and simply returns the control referenced in the class's _taskpane object.

Note You can find further details on the TaskPaneManager class on MSDN. I borrowed heavily from the concepts in the article, "Walkthrough: Displaying Custom Task Panes with E-Mail Messages in Outlook" (http://msdn.microsoft.com/en-us/library/bb296010(VS.80).aspx).

Building the Add-In Ribbon

The custom Ribbon for the add-in contains two buttons residing in a single RibbonGroup control. This Ribbon is only visible within the Contact Inspector windows. The commands it provides allow the user to 1) display the ItemActionPane to reveal related opportunities and 2) convert an opportunity selected in the ItemActionPane into a project in the accounting system.

Designing the Ribbon's Form Surface

Figure 8-4 illustrates the design for the AccountRep project's AddinRibbon control. This Ribbon integrates and displays with the Ribbon shown with Inspector windows that contain Outlook contacts.

Figure 8-4. *The AddinRibbon control at design time*

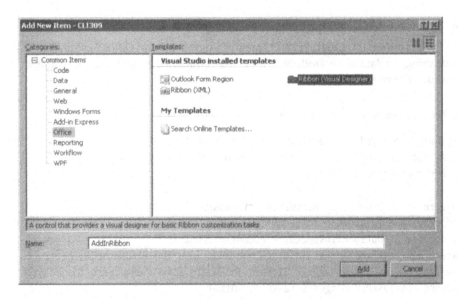

Figure 8-5. *Adding a new Ribbon designer to the AccountRep project*

Once added, complete the following steps to build the Ribbon's design:

1. Open the AddInRibbon's designer and add a RibbonGroup control. Name the control **Opportunities**, and set the Label property to **Account Actions**.

2. Add a RibbonButton control to the RibbonGroup created in step1. Name the button **btnCreateProject**, and set its label as **Convert Opp to Project**. If you'd like, you can add an image to the button, as shown in Figure 8-4.

3. Add the RibbonToggleButton control to the RibbonGroup. Name the button **btnToggleOpps**, and set the label as **Hide Opportunities**. Here also, you can add an icon to the button.

4. Select the Ribbon control's tab, and set **TabContact** as the value for the Name, ControlID, and Label properties.

5. Specify which Inspector windows will display the AddInRibbon. To complete this task, select the Ribbon control in the designer and select Microsoft.Outlook.Contact in the RibbonType property.

These steps complete the UI design of the Ribbon. The code for this component isn't extensive, so this section will be short and sweet. With the code view for the Ribbon open, add the following code to the Imports section of the class:

```
Imports Microsoft.Office.Tools.Ribbon
Imports Microsoft.Office.Tools
Imports Outlook = Microsoft.Office.Interop.Outlook
```

The btnCreateProject_Click Event

The Create Project button (btnCreateProject) creates a new project in Office Accounting Express 2008 using the data of the Outlook contact item contained in the Inspector window. Listing 8-8 shows the code for the button.

Listing 8-8. *The btnCreateProject_Click Event*

```
Private Sub btnCreateProject_Click(ByVal sender As System.Object, _
  ByVal e As Microsoft.Office.Tools.Ribbon.RibbonControlEventArgs) _
  Handles btnCreateProject.Click

    'Grab a reference to the Inspector object passed as
    'a property in e (RibbonControlEventArgs).
    Dim inspector As Outlook.Inspector = e.Control.Context
    'create a new TaskPaneManager instance and associate the inspector with it.
    Dim manager As TaskPaneManager = Globals.ThisAddIn.TaskPaneManagers(inspector)
    'reference the TaskPaneManger's TaskPaneControl
    Dim tp As CustomTaskPane = manager.TaskPaneControl
    'Check that we have reference to a control
    If Not (tp Is Nothing) Then
      'cast the control as an ItemActionPane control
      'and grab the pane's OpportunityID
      Dim pane = DirectCast(tp.Control, ItemActionPane)
      Dim id As String = pane.OpportunityID

      'Send opportunity data and create project
      'create a new Opportunity object and fill it
      'by calling the GetOpportunity method of the
      'SalesPipeData class and passing id.
      Dim opp As Opportunity = SalesPipeData.GetOpportunity(id)
      'Now use the retrieved Opportunity in the call to CreateProject.
      'CreateProject will create a new project in the Accounting
      'System and return the GUID of the new project
      Dim ProjectID As Guid = SBATools.CreateProject(opp)

      'If successful, update Opp in Sales DB and close it out
      'Refresh the ItemActionPane control to reflect the updated data
      'and alert the user that all went well.
      SalesPipeData.CloseOpportunity(opp.OpportunityID, ProjectID)
      pane.RefreshData()
      MsgBox("The new project was created successfully", _
        MsgBoxStyle.Information, "Project Created")
    End If
End Sub
```

The Ribbon can access its parent Inspector object from the Click event's RibbonControlEventArgs (via a call to e.Control.Context). Accessing the Inspector object from the AddInRibbon is important, because it enables you to access the ItemActionPane via the TaskPaneManager class.

Once you obtain a reference to the Inspector object's ItemActionPane control, you can grab the OpportunityID and retrieve the matching record from the sales pipeline database. Next, you create a project in Office Accounting by calling the CreateProject function that exists in the Accounting data layer (I discuss the class that is the Accounting data layer, SBATools, later in this chapter). This function returns a GUID that you can use to update the sales pipeline and close out the opportunity. Lastly, you update the ItemActionPane control and force it to requery its opportunity data to reflect the converted project.

The btnToggleOpps_Click Event

It is safe to assume that a user of the Account Rep add-in might not always want to see the ItemActionPane. The btnToggleOpps_Click event, shown in Listing 8-9, toggles the display of the ItemActionPane, allowing the user to display or hide the action pane.

Listing 8-9. *The btnToggleOpps_Click Event*

```
Private Sub btnToggleOpps_Click(ByVal sender As System.Object, _
  ByVal e As Microsoft.Office.Tools.Ribbon.RibbonControlEventArgs) _
  Handles btnToggleOpps.Click
    'Grab references to the Inspector via
    'the RibbonControlEventArgs parameter- aka 'e'.
    'Also reference the Inspector's TaskPaneManager class
    ' and its related TaskPaneControl.
    Dim inspector As Outlook.Inspector = e.Control.Context
    Dim manager As TaskPaneManager = Globals.ThisAddIn.TaskPaneManagers(inspector)
    Dim tp As CustomTaskPane = manager.TaskPaneControl

    'just make sure we have a TaskPaneControl before taking action
    If Not (tp Is Nothing) Then
      'set the control's visibility according to the
      'value of the ToggleButton on the ribbon.
      tp.Visible = TryCast(sender, RibbonToggleButton).Checked
      'Now change the RibbonToggleButton's label accordingly.
      If tp.Visible Then
        btnToggleOpps.Label = "Hide Opportunities"
      Else
        btnToggleOpps.Label = "Show Opportunities"
      End If
    End If
  End Sub
```

This event also grabs a reference to the Ribbon's parent Inspector object, which it uses to identify the correct instance of the ItemActionPane to show or hide.

The AddinRibbon_Load Event

When the form loads, the Account Rep add-in displays the ItemActionPane by default. Listing 8-10 contains the code for the AddinRibbon_Load event.

Listing 8-10. *The AddinRibbon_Load Event*

```
Private Sub AddinRibbon_Load(ByVal sender As System.Object, _
   ByVal e As RibbonUIEventArgs) Handles MyBase.Load
      btnToggleOpps.Checked = True
End Sub
```

Listing 8-10 contains the code that sets the Checked property to True and displays the action pane.

Building the Sales Pipeline Components

Outlook imports customer data from the AdventureWorks database and stores it as Outlook contact items. When a user opens a contact record, the Account Rep add-in queries the database to retrieve any active sales opportunities related to the opened contact. As already discussed, if opportunities exist, they will be displayed in a custom action pane.

The SalesPipeData class, shown in Listing 8-11, contains the data-layer code for retrieving customer and opportunity data. Instead of using ADO.NET to perform the data tasks, this class makes use of Language Integrated Query (LINQ). LINQ is part of the .NET framework and allows you to query data as typed objects (among many other things).

Listing 8-11. *The SalesPipeData Class*

```
Imports Outlook = Microsoft.Office.Interop.Outlook
'The pipeline object is the SalesDataDataContext.
'This object provides the CRUD (create, read, update, & delete)
'features needed in LINQ
Imports System.Data

Private Shared pipeline As SalesDataDataContext = New SalesDataDataContext

   Friend Shared Function GetAllCustomers() As Array
      'create an object to store the records returned from the
      'Customer table using a LINQ query to return the CustomerID
      '& CompanyName fields
      Dim custs = From c In pipeline.Customers Select _
               c.CustomerID, c.CompanyName Order By CompanyName
      Return custs.ToArray
   End Function
```

```vb
Friend Shared Function GetOpportunites() As Array
    'Query the Opportunities table and return all records
    'along with the specified columns.
    Dim opps = From o In pipeline.Opportunities _
            Select o.Customer.CompanyName, o.OpportunityName _
            , o.Service.ServiceName, o.DateCreated _
            , o.EstCloseDate, o.EstStartDate, o.EstEndDate, o.EstRevenue _
            , o.Notes _
            Order By OpportunityName
    Return opps.ToArray
End Function

Friend Shared Function GetOpportunity(ByVal OppID As String) As Opportunity
    'Use the passed OppID string to find the matching record
    'In the Opportunities table.
    'The use of First after the Query makes doubly sure
    'we only retrieve one record.
    Dim opp = (From o In pipeline.Opportunities Where _
            o.OpportunityID = OppID).First
    Return opp
End Function

Friend Shared Function GetOpportunitesList() As Array
    'Returns a listing of all records in the Opportunities
    'table that are not Closed
    Dim opps = From o In pipeline.Opportunities _
            Select o.Customer.CompanyName, o.OpportunityName _
            , o.EstStartDate, o.Closed _
            Where Closed = False _
            Order By OpportunityName
    Return opps.ToArray
End Function

Friend Shared Function GetOpportunitesList(ByVal Customer As Integer) As Array
    'Return all records in the Opportunitis list that are related to the
    'Pass Customer integer parameter. Also, don't include any records
    'that are marked closed.
    Dim opps = From o In pipeline.Opportunities _
            Select o.OpportunityName, o.Customer.CompanyName, o.Status _
            , o.EstStartDate, o.Closed, o.CustomerID,o.OpportunityID _
            Where CustomerID = Customer And (Closed = False) _
            Order By OpportunityName
    Return opps.ToArray

End Function
```

```
Friend Shared Function GetOpportunitesForChart( _
 ByVal Customer As Integer) As DataTable
  'Another query returning Opportunity records
  'This one returns on the columns needed for the
  'Chart.
  'Also the query counts the records and stores them
  'in a dynamic column called Total.
  Dim opps = From o In pipeline.Opportunities _
            Where o.CustomerID = Customer And (o.Closed = False) _
            Group By o.Status Into Total = _
            Count(o.OpportunityID)

  'Create a new table to store the records
  'retrieved in the LINQ query above.
  'This step makes it much easier to bind the data
  'to the chart.
  Dim table As New DataTable
  table.Columns.Add("Status")
  table.Columns.Add("Total")

  'Now that we have a table, loop through the
  'opps Array and a new row for each item in the array.
  For Each result In opps
    table.Rows.Add(result.Status, result.Total)
  Next
 'Return the table as the function value.

  Return table

 End Function

Friend Shared Function CloseOpportunity(ByVal OppID As String, _
    ByVal AccountingID As Guid) As Boolean
    'use a LINQ query to return the Opportunity with an
    'OpportunityID that matches the value passed in OppID.
    Dim opp = (From o In pipeline.Opportunities Where o.OpportunityID = OppID).First
    Try
        'using the record stored in the Opp object, close it
        'setting the Closed property to True. Set the date and
        'set the AccountingGUID to the value passed in the
        'AccountingID parameter. The accountingId links the
        'Opportunity to its corresponding project in the
        'accounting system.
```

```vb
        With opp
          .Closed = True
          .ActualCloseDate = Now()
          .AccountingGUID = AccountingID
        End With
        'save changes to the Sales database  (AdventureWorks)
        'by calling the SubmitChanges method of the pipeline object.
        pipeline.SubmitChanges()

        Return True
      Catch ex As Exception
        Return False
      End Try

    End Function


    Friend Shared Function UpdateAccount(ByVal SalesSystemID As String, _
                                    ByVal Company As String, _
                                    ByVal FName As String, _
                                    ByVal LName As String, _
                                    ByVal Email As String, _
                                    ByVal BusinessPhone As String, _
                                    ByVal Body As String) As Boolean
    'Create a reference to the customer account to update using a LINQ query..
        Dim customer = (From c2 In pipeline.Customers Where c2.CustomerID = 1).First

        'Set the properties of the customer object
        'by matching them to their corresponding parameter values
        With customer
          .CompanyName = Company
          .FirstName = FName
          .LastName = LName
          .EmailAddress = Email
          .Phone = BusinessPhone
          .Notes = Body
          .ModifiedDate = Microsoft.VisualBasic.Now

        End With
        'Save the changes to the database.
        pipeline.SubmitChanges()

    End Function
```

```vb
Friend Shared Function ImportSalesAccounts() As Boolean
    'create an accts object and use a LINQ query to
    'return Customer data from the sales database.
    Dim accts = From a In pipeline.Customers _
            Select a.CustomerID, a.CompanyName, a.FirstName, a.LastName, _
            a.Phone, a.EmailAddress, a.Notes, a.ModifiedDate
    'Create a reference to the Accounts folder in the
    'Outlook data store by calling the FindFolderFromPath method
    'residing in this class. The method uses the passed string and
    'returns the desired folder. If your folder is in a different
    'location, you will want to change the path.
    Dim fldr As Outlook.Folder = FindFolderFromPath( _
        "\\Personal Folders\Sales Data\Accounts")

    'Create ContactItems in Outlook that represent Customers in the
    'Sales system.
    'Start by looping through all records in the accts object.
    For Each name In accts
        'For each customer, create a ContactItem and add it to
        'the Accounts folder (fldr)
        Dim na As Outlook.ContactItem = fldr.Items.Add("IPM.Contact.Account")
        'Set the message class to use the Form Region's message class.
        na.MessageClass = "IPM.Contact.Account"

        'Now match the new ContactItem's properties with the corresponding
        'property values of the current Customer record.
        na.CompanyName = name.CompanyName
        na.FirstName = name.FirstName
        na.LastName = name.LastName
        na.BusinessTelephoneNumber = name.Phone
        na.Email1Address = name.EmailAddress
        na.Body = name.Notes

        'Attempt to find the SalesSystemID proeprty in the
        'ContactItem
        Dim up As Outlook.UserProperty = na.UserProperties.Find("SalesSystemID")
        'If no property exists then we create it.
        If up Is Nothing Then
            'create the property by adding it to the UserProperties collection
            'of the new ContactItem. Then set the value.
            up = na.UserProperties.Add("SalesSystemID", _
                Outlook.OlUserPropertyType.olText, True)
            up.Value = name.CustomerID
```

```
      Else
        'The property exists so just update its value.
        up.Value = name.CustomerID
      End If


      'Close the ContactItem and save it.
      na.Close(Outlook.OlInspectorClose.olSave)

    Next
  End Function

Friend Shared Function FindFolderFromPath(ByVal FolderPath As String) _
    As Outlook.Folder

  'This function parses the passed FolderPath string and returns the
  'the last foldername included in the string.

    Dim TestFldr As Outlook.Folder
    Dim FoldersArray As Object
    Dim i As Integer

    'Check the first 2 characters in the FolderPath string
    'Remove the "\\" characters if they exist.
    If Left(FolderPath, 2) = "\\" Then
       FolderPath = Right(FolderPath, Len(FolderPath) - 2)
    End If
    'Convert folderpath to array
    FoldersArray = Split(FolderPath, "\")
    'retrieve and store the first folder in the array
    ' we will retrieve the child folders until we find the
    'last folder specified by the FolderPath parameter.
    TestFldr = Globals.ThisAddIn.Application.Session.Folders.Item(FoldersArray(0))
    If Not TestFldr Is Nothing Then
      'We have the root folder, now go through the FoldersArray
       'find the desired folder and return it.
      For i = 1 To UBound(FoldersArray, 1)
        Dim SubFolders As Outlook.Folders
        'Reference the current folder's Folders collection
        SubFolders = TestFldr.Folders
        'get a reference to the next item in the FoldersArray.
        TestFldr = SubFolders.Item(FoldersArray(i))
```

```
                      'If we can't find a folder, return nothing and assume
                      'the passed FolderPath is incorrect.
                      If TestFldr Is Nothing Then
                          Return Nothing
                      End If
                  Next
              End If
              'If we have arrived here, we have found the last folder. So return it.
                  Return TestFldr
          End Function
```

GETTING STARTED WITH LINQ

If you're unfamiliar with LINQ, I recommend reading the content available on the LINQ Project page of MSDN (http://msdn.microsoft.com/en-us/netframework/aa904594.aspx). If you're in a hurry and want to find great code samples you can use now, I recommend a series of blog posts by Scott Guthrie. You can read the first post, "Using LINQ to SQL (Part 1)," at http://weblogs.asp.net/scottgu/archive/2007/05/19/using-linq-to-sql-part-1.aspx.

Great content exists outside of MSDN as well. Once you have a good grasp of LINQ, I recommend two articles by John Mueller: "Using Extension Methods with LINQ" (http://www.devsource.com/c/a/Languages/Extension-Methods-LINQ) and "Understanding and Using LINQ Expression Trees" (http://www.devsource.com/c/a/Languages/Understanding-LINQ-Expression-Trees).

For this class to work correctly, you need to add a LINQ to SQL class to the AccountRep project in Visual Studio. The LINQ to SQL class is a project item available from the Visual Studio Add New Item dialog box (see Figure 8-6).

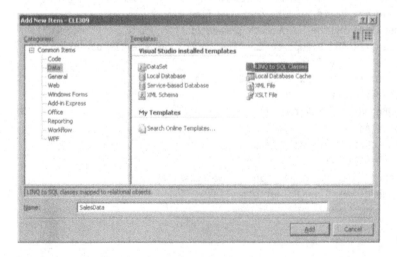

Figure 8-6. *Adding a new LINQ to SQL class*

Add a new LINQ to SQL class and name it **SalesData**. Once you add this class, create new class named **SalesPipeData** and insert the code contained in Listing 8-11.

Building the Office Accounting Components

The Microsoft Office Accounting 2008 application provides a robust set of APIs that allows you to easily integrate your solutions with accounting data. In the Account Rep add-in, you can tap into these APIs to create a new project for accounting purposes. This class is the last step in this add-in's process; it represents the closing of a sales opportunity (from the AdventureWorks database) by converting it into a valid project for the accountants.

Just as with the sales data class, you will use a class to handle the data access tasks as they relate to the Office Accounting application. In addition to the data access class, you have an additional class that allows you to load the Office Accounting data as needed. Listing 8-12 shows the utility class, LoadUtils.

Listing 8-12. *The LoadUtils Class for Loading Office Accounting Data*

```
Imports Microsoft.BusinessSolutions.SmallBusinessAccounting.Loader
Imports System.Reflection

  ' Store the SBALoader's strong name.
  'It will be needed when initializing the SBA objects
Const loaderFULLNAME As String = "Loader, Version=2.0.5201.0, " & _
  "Culture=neutral,  PublicKeyToken=31bf3856ad364e35"

  ' Define fully qualified name of Loader class
Const loaderNAMESPACE As String = "Microsoft.BusinessSolutions." & _
  "SmallBusinessAccounting.Loader.Loader"

Public Shared Function InstantiateLoader() As ILoader
  'Instantiates the Small Business Accounting loader object.
  ' Define variables
  Dim assem As Assembly              ' Loader assembly
  Dim ldr As ILoader = Nothing       ' ILoader object instance

  Try
    ' Load assembly by calling the Load method and
    'passing the loaderFullName as a parameter.
    assem = Assembly.Load(loaderFULLNAME)

    ' Instantiate the ILoader object
    'and cast the object as an ILoader.
    ldr = DirectCast(assem.CreateInstance(loaderNAMESPACE), ILoader)
    Return ldr
  Catch e As Exception
    Throw New TypeLoadException("Unable to instantiate Loader.", e)
  End Try
End Function
```

The LoadUtils class has the single purpose of loading the Office Accounting assembly. This process has the effect of opening the accounting system's data file for use in the Account Rep add-in.

A separate class, SBATools, utilizes LoadUtils to load an instance of the Microsoft Office Accounting 2008 APIs as well as the accounting data file. Listing 8-13 contains the code for the SBATools class.

Listing 8-13. *The SBATools Class for Handling Office Accounting Data Tasks*

```
Imports Microsoft.BusinessSolutions.SmallBusinessAccounting.Loader
Imports Microsoft.BusinessSolutions.SmallBusinessAccounting
Imports System.IO
Imports System.Data
Imports System.Windows.Forms


Shared Sub New()
 'create a reference to the SBA Loader object. This object provides
 'access to SBA objects.
   InstantiateLoader()
   'SBA uses Files that represent a set of accounting "books"
   'this call will open the desired books.
   LoadCompanyFile()

End Sub

Private Shared Function InstantiateLoader() As ILoader
   'instantiate the SBA loader and return it.
   Try
     ldr = LoaderUtil.InstantiateLoader()
     Return ldr
   Catch ex As Exception
     MsgBox("Unable to instantiate Loader object. Application must exit.", _
          MsgBoxStyle.Critical Or MsgBoxStyle.OkOnly, "Load Failure")
     Return Nothing
   End Try
End Function

Private Shared Sub LoadCompanyFile()
   'begin to build the path to the SBA accounting file
   'We start with the path to the user's MyDocuments folder.
   'then add the folders where the SBA files reside by default.
   Dim sbaFile As String = Environment._
    GetFolderPath(Environment.SpecialFolder.MyDocuments) & _

Path.DirectorySeparatorChar & "Small Business Accounting\Companies" & _
Path.DirectorySeparatorChar & "SampleServiceCompany2008.sbc"
   'create reference to the SBA loader
```

```vbnet
    ldr = InstantiateLoader()
    'Use the SBA Loader to grab a reference to the SBA Object Library
    sbi = DirectCast(ldr.GetSbaObjects(sbaFile).SmallBusinessInstance, _
        ISmallBusinessInstanceV2)
End Sub

Friend Shared Function CreateProject(ByVal Opp As Opportunity) As Guid
    'Create a new Project in the SBA file

    'Create new customer account object.
    Dim customer As ICustomerAccount

    'Step 1 - check if existing customer. If it lacks
    'an AccountingGUID, it is a new customer.

    If Opp.AccountingGUID Is Nothing Then
      'Step 1a - create customer account
      customer = SBAObjects.CreateCustomerAccount
      'Set the property values for the new customer & save
      With customer
        .Name = Opp.Customer.CompanyName
        .Active = True
        .AccountSince = Now
        .Save()
      End With
    Else
      'We are dealing with an existing customer record in SBA
      'Therefore retrieve it using the AccountingGuid property of the
      'passed Opp (Opportunity)
      customer = SBAObjects.CustomerAccounts.GetByGuid(Opp.AccountingGUID)
    End If

    'Step 2 - Create Project
    'a project is called a Job in SBA.
    'The object type is IJobAccount
    Dim job As IJobAccount
    'Create a new job and set its properties.
    job = sbi.CreateJobAccount()
    'use the same name as the related Opportunity
    job.Name = Opp.OpportunityName
    'Link the job to the Customer.
    job.Customer = customer
    job.Save()

    'Step 3 - Return Project ID
    Return job.Guid
End Function
```

The SBATools class calls the LoadUtils class to instantiate Office Accounting. Once instantiated, SBATools loads the accounting data. SBATools needs to execute these tasks before attempting to create a project. The CreateProject function creates a new project and links it to its related customer account. If this project is for a new customer, the function will create a new customer record before creating the project. The function finishes by returning the GUID for the new project. As discussed earlier, this GUID is then used to update the converted sales opportunity in the sales pipeline (the AdventureWorks database).

Tying It All Together in the ThisAddin Class

The ThisAddin class is the main VSTO add-in class. It fills the interface requirements for an Office add-in and is what Outlook calls when loading the add-in. So it is in this class's Startup event that you set up the objects needed for the Account Rep add-in to function properly. This add-in utilizes several class-level objects to maintain references to Outlook objects like the Inspectors collection and the Office CommandBarButtons collection. Listing 8-14 contains the class-level objects you need to add to the ThisAddin class.

Listing 8-14. *The ThisAddin Class-Level Objects*

```
Private WithEvents _inspectors As Outlook.Inspectors
Private WithEvents _inspector As Outlook.Inspector
Private WithEvents _explorer As Outlook.Explorer
Private _commandBar As Core.CommandBar
Private WithEvents _cbbSyncAccounts As Core.CommandBarButton
Private WithEvents _cbbNewAccount As Core.CommandBarButton
Public TaskPaneManagers As New Dictionary(Of Outlook.Inspector, TaskPaneManager)
```

The TaskPaneManagers object is a Dictionary object that allows you to track all instances of the TaskPaneManager class and their related ItemActionPane controls.

The ThisAddin_Startup and ThisAddin_Shutdown Events

The Startup method for the add-in performs the setup tasks of adding references to required objects and building the custom menu for the add-in in the Outlook Explorer window (see Listing 8-15).

Listing 8-15. *The ThisAddin Startup Event*

```
Private Sub ThisAddIn_Startup(ByVal sender As Object, _
    ByVal e As System.EventArgs) Handles Me.Startup
    'Reference Outlook's Inspectors collection
    'and the ActiveExplorer
    _inspectors = Me.Application.Inspectors
    _explorer = Me.Application.ActiveExplorer

    'Create a new CommandBar, name it, and set it as a temporary
    'CommandBar. We want it to reside in the normal Top position
    'within Outlook's UI.
```

```
_commandBar = Me.Application.ActiveExplorer.CommandBars. _
  Add("AccountBar", , , True)
_commandBar.Position = Core.MsoBarPosition.msoBarTop
_commandBar.Visible = True
'Create a new CommandBarButton and place it on the
'"AccountBar" commandbar just created.
'Specify the button type as Button.
_cbbSyncAccounts = _commandBar.Controls. _
  Add(Core.MsoControlType.msoControlButton, , , , True)

'Set the button's properties.
With _cbbSyncAccounts
  .Caption = "Sync Sales Account Data"
  .Style = Core.MsoButtonStyle.msoButtonIconAndCaption
  .FaceId = 487
End With

End Sub
```

After referencing the Inspectors collection, the method builds the add-in's command bar and a button that allows the user to import sales accounts into Outlook.

The Shutdown method (see Listing 8-16) is the best place for cleaning up the add-in's mess.

Listing 8-16. *The ThisAddin_Shutdown Event*

```
Private Sub ThisAddIn_Shutdown(ByVal sender As Object, _
    ByVal e As System.EventArgs) Handles Me.Shutdown
    RemoveHandler _inspectors.NewInspector, AddressOf _inspectors_NewInspector

    'When the add-in shuts down, we want to destroy references
    'to the Inspectors collection and the TaskPaneManagers class.
    Try
      _inspectors = Nothing

    Catch ex As Exception

    End Try

    Try
      TaskPaneManagers = Nothing
    Catch ex As Exception

    End Try
End Sub
```

All that you need to do here is clear the reference to the Inspectors collection and TaskPaneManagers object. Since the custom menu objects were created as temporary menus in the Startup method, you don't need to delete them, as Outlook will handle that for you.

The _inspectors_NewInspector Event

When the user opens an Outlook contact, you want to create a new instance of the
ItemActionPane and attach it to the contact's Inspector window. To do this, capture
the NewInspector event of the Inspectors collection (see Listing 8-17).

Listing 8-17. *The NewInspector Event*

```
Private Sub _inspectors_NewInspector(ByVal Inspector As _
    Outlook.Inspector) Handles _inspectors.NewInspector
    'Anytime a new Inspector opens in Outlook we want
    'to check the type of item in the Inspector.
    'if the item is a ContactItem, we take action to display
    'the ItemActionPane
    Try
      'Only show task pane for ContactItems
      If TypeOf Inspector.CurrentItem Is Outlook.ContactItem Then
        'Add a new TaskPaneManager to the TaskPaneManagers class.
        'The passed Inspector and TaskPaneManager will be tracked by
        'The TaskPaneManager class.
        TaskPaneManagers.Add(Inspector, New TaskPaneManager(Inspector))

      End If
    Catch ex As Exception
      MsgBox(ex.Message)
    End Try
End Sub
```

This event checks the CurrentItem property to ensure you're working with an Outlook
contact record. If you are, the event will instantiate a new instance of the TaskPaneManager
and pass a reference to the new Inspector object. The TaskPaneManager class will then attach
the ItemActionControl to the new Inspector before it displays. Both the new Inspector and
TaskPaneManager are added to the TaskPaneManagers object so you can track them and delete
them later when the Inspector window closes.

The _cbbSyncAccounts_Click Event

The Click event for the Sync Accounts button makes a call to the ImportSalesAccounts method
of the SalesPipeData class (see Listing 8-18).

Listing 8-18. *The cbbSynAccounts_Click Event*

```
Private Sub _cbbSyncAccounts_Click(ByVal Ctrl As _
  Core.CommandBarButton, ByRef CancelDefault As Boolean) _
    Handles _cbbSyncAccounts.Click
```

```
      'WHen the user clicks this button import all data from the
      'Sales datbase (aka AdventureWorks).
      'The ImportSalesAccounts method of the SalesPipeData class
      'will import the data as contact items in Outlook.
      SalesPipeData.ImportSalesAccounts()
   End Sub
```

After this call runs successfully, all the customer data found in the sales pipeline will exist in the user's Outlook data store in the form of Outlook contact items.

Summary

OBAs are a combination of at least one Office application and another application or system. OBAs turn Office into a front end for data from external systems and allow users to work with data in the familiar GUI provided by the Office applications. You can build OBAs that implement features from multiple external applications. In this chapter, I explained how to build an OBA that integrated data from a sales system and an accounting system. I also explained how to integrate data between the two systems and how to use Outlook as the front end for displaying data and for executing actions against the data.

CHAPTER 9

Deploying VSTO Solutions

Visual Studio Tools for the Microsoft Office System (VSTO) 2008 fully supports the ClickOnce deployment model. If you're new to Office development with VSTO, you might not be aware of just how big a deal ClickOnce support is to Office development. With previous versions of VSTO, solution deployment was anything but painless. In fact, it required understanding more about the .NET security model than you probably care to know. Thankfully, with VSTO 2008, those days are long gone, as deployment is now much simpler and much less painful.

ClickOnce Deployment Overview

ClickOnce refers to an application deployment and maintenance model in which you compile your solution and publish it to a location accessible to your user base (see Figure 9-1). The location could be a web site, a network share, or a CD or DVD. Users can then install the application locally on their systems, where the application can operate in offline scenario if the system loses its network connection.

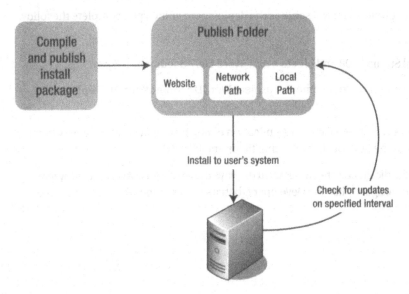

Figure 9-1. *The ClickOnce application deployment and maintenance life cycle*

ClickOnce also provides a maintenance model that includes features for downloading and installing application updates automatically. In addition, ClickOnce supports application *roll-backs*, which are useful if you need to revert to a previous version of an application for whatever reason—for example, if you've installed a bug-ridden, unstable update.

Note This chapter will focus on how to deploy a VSTO solution; it won't provide in-depth coverage of ClickOnce. The discussion of ClickOnce is from the perspective of Office and VSTO only. If you'd like to learn more about ClickOnce, MSDN has several articles covering the topic at `http://msdn.microsoft.com/en-us/library/t71a733d(VS.80).aspx`.

The remainder of this chapter will cover the details of VSTO deployment by providing a walk-through using a ridiculously simple VSTO sample solution.

Creating a Deployment Package

To illustrate a deployment scenario, you need a sample VSTO add-in. Because the focus here is on deployment, the sample add-in is a VSTO Word document add-in. The document contains a single content control that code in the add-in's StartUp event fills with a Hello World message.

Building the Sample Solution

To build the sample solution that will serve as the deployment guinea pig, complete the following steps:

1. Open Visual Studio 2008 and create a new Word 2007 document project.

2. In the New Project dialog, name the project **WordDocumentSampleDeployment**. Click OK.

3. In the Select a Document for Your Application dialog box, select "Create a new document." Accept the defaults in remaining fields and click OK.

4. After Visual Studio creates the project and displays the WordDocumentSampleDeployment. docx file in its designer, click the Developer tab that's visible in the Word Fluent UI (see Figure 9-2).

Figure 9-2. *The Developer tab displaying the available content controls*

5. Drag a RichTextControl (in the Controls tab, the control is labeled Rich Text) content control and drop it anywhere on the document surface displayed in the Word designer. Select the control and change its name to **CustomMessage**.

6. In the Solution Explorer, select the ThisDocument.vb file and open it in Code view by clicking the Code View button in the Solution Explorer toolbar.

7. Add the code contained in Listing 9-1 to the ThisDocument class.

8. Press F5 to compile and run the application.

Listing 9-1. *The ThisDocument_Startup Event*

```
Private Sub ThisDocument_Startup(ByVal sender As Object, _
    ByVal e As System.EventArgs) Handles Me.Startup

    Globals.ThisDocument.CustomMessage.Text = "Hello World"
End Sub
```

The ThisDocument_Startup event executes a single line that inserts the customary Hello World message just to show the application does something. This functionality more than meets our needs to use as a sample for deployment purposes.

Publishing a Solution to Its Deployment Location

You have the option to configure deployment options manually or using a wizard to create them automatically. The remainder of this section explains how to publish the sample application using each option.

Specifying Deployment Options Manually

The publish settings reside in the project properties (see Figure 9-3). To display the project properties, right-click the WordDocumentSampleDeployment project in the Visual Studio Solution Explorer and select Properties. After the Property Designer displays, click the Publish tab to view the project's deployment (or publish) options.

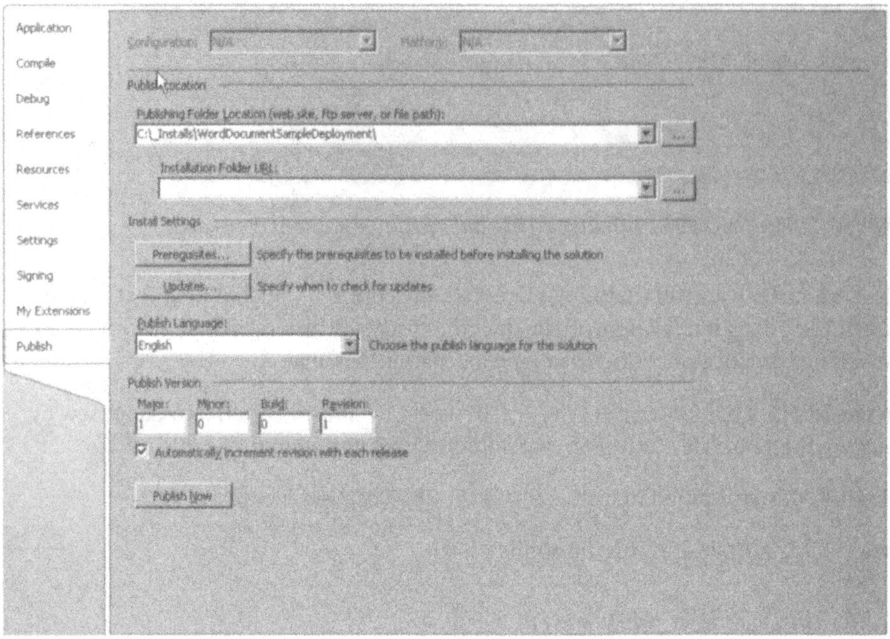

Figure 9-3. *The Publish tab displayed within Visual Studio*

The Publish tab allows you to fine-tune such deployment settings as the Publishing folder, Installation folder, how to handle project prerequisites, and more. Table 9-1 lists each element in the Publish form and describes their purpose.

Table 9-1. *Deployment Settings Available in the Publish Tab of a VSTO Project's Properties*

Form Field/ Control	Form Section	Description
Publishing Folder Location	Publish Location	The location where the deployment files should be published. The location can be a web site, a network file share path, or a local path. In addition, the path can be a fully qualified path or a relative path.
Installation Folder URL	Publish Location	The location the user will use to access the deployment package for installation on their system. The location can be a web site, a network file share path, or a local path. In addition, the path can be a fully qualified path or a relative path. This setting is optional.
Prerequisites	Install Settings	Opens the Prerequisites dialog box used to specify which prerequisite technology to include in the deployment package. This dialog allows you to cherry-pick whether or not to include technologies like the .NET Framework 3.5 and the VSTO 3.0 runtime. Also, you can use this dialog to specify the installation location for the prerequisites.
Updates	Install Settings	Opens the Customization Updates dialog box used to specify how often to check for application updates.

Form Field/ Control	Form Section	Description
Publish Language	Install Settings	The language to be used in the published deployment package.
Publish Version	Publish Version	The Major, Minor, Build, and Revision values for the solution build.
Publish Now	Publish Version	Creates a new build of the solution, creates a deployment package, and publishes the deployment package to the location specified in the Publishing Folder Location field.

To build a deployment package and publish it to its Publishing folder, complete the following steps:

1. In the WordDocumentSampleDeployment project's settings, specify a folder where the deployment files should be published. As shown in Figure 9-3, I specified C:_Installs\WordDocumentSampleDeployment\, but feel free to specify a location that makes sense to you.

2. Click the Prerequisites button to display the Prerequisites dialog box (see Figure 9-4).

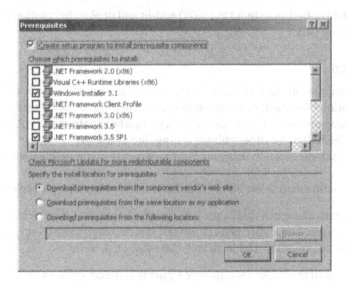

Figure 9-4. *Selecting options using the Prerequisites dialog box*

3. Check the "Create setup program to install prerequisite components" check box. Enabling this option forces Visual Studio to create a separate setup program that will check for the existence of selected prerequisite technologies. If any prerequisites are missing on the user's system, the program will install.

4. In the "Choose which prerequisites to install" section, select Windows Installer, .NET Framework 3.5 SP1, Microsoft Office 2007 Primary Interop Assemblies, and Visual Studio Tools for the Office system 3.0 Runtime Service Pack 1.

5. In the "Specify the install location for prerequisites" section, select "Download prerequisites from the component vendor's web site." Click OK.

6. Click the Updates button to display the Customization Updates dialog box (see Figure 9-5). Select the "Check every time the customization runs" option to force the VSTO add-in to check for a new version each time it runs. Click OK.

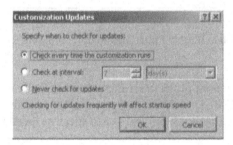

Figure 9-5. *Specifying update options using the Customization Updates dialog box*

7. Click the Publish Now button to build the VSTO add-in and deploy the solution to the specified Publishing folder.

Using the Publish Wizard

The Publish Wizard automates the task of specifying settings. It does not allow you to fine-tine the deployment options like the Publish tab of the project settings does. Instead, it streamlines the publishing process. The wizard asks you to input the path of the Publishing folder and the Installation folder. No other publish settings are available.

You can publish the sample solution using the Publish Wizard by completing these steps:

1. From the Visual Studio menu, select Build ➤ Publish WordDocumentSampleDeployment.

2. In the Publish Wizard dialog box (see Figure 9-6), specify the location to publish the deployment files. Again, I have specified C:_Installs\WordDocumentSampleDeployment\, but please feel free to publish to a folder of your choosing. Click Next.

3. On the second page of the Publish Wizard (see Figure 9-7), select From a CD-ROM or DVD-ROM.

   The Installation folder is the folder the user accesses to install the solution. By specifying CD-ROM or DVD-ROM, you're telling the Publish Wizard that the installation path is the same as the publish path. Click Next.

4. The last page of the Publish Wizard displays the publish location and declares itself ready to publish. Click Finish to publish the solution.

The Publish Wizard can be faster than setting publish settings manually; however, it does not provide access to all publish settings. That said, the Publish Wizard utilizes the settings specified in the Publish tab of the project settings form. A good practice is to specify the prerequisite and update settings and then use the Publish Wizard to quickly publish builds.

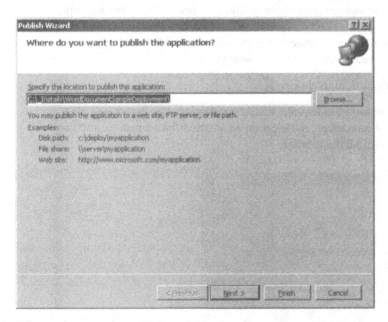

Figure 9-6. *Setting the Publishing folder location in the Publish Wizard*

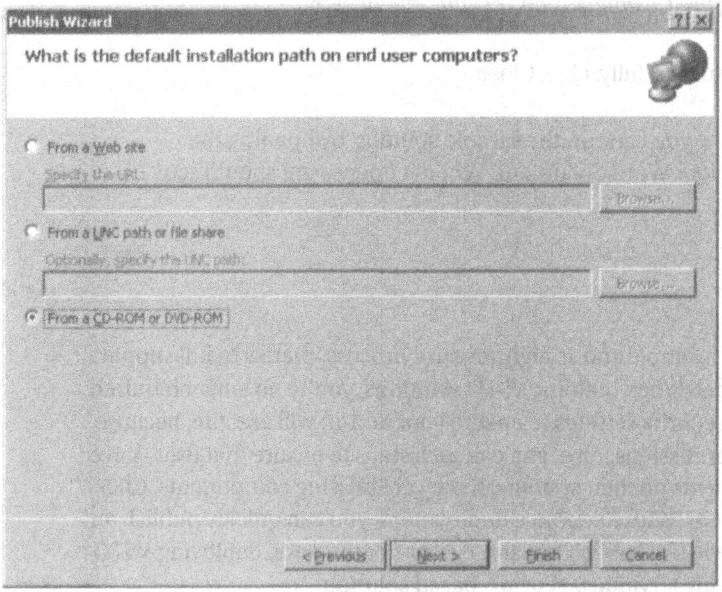

Figure 9-7. *Setting the Installation folder location in the Publish Wizard*

Installing the Add-In

After publishing the VSTO add-in to a Publishing folder, the user can install the solution by executing the deployment package's setup.exe file. This file installs the VSTO assembly so that it runs on the user's system against the target Office application or Office document.

To install the WordDocumentDeploymentSample solution, complete the following steps:

1. Navigate to the Publishing folder you specified in the project's publish settings (for example, C:_Installs\WordDocumentSampleDeployment\).

2. Execute the setup.exe file by double-clicking it.

3. The Microsoft Office Customization Installer dialog box displays (see Figure 9-8). The dialog box displays the solution name, the location where the solution resides, and the publisher. Click Install to install the solution.

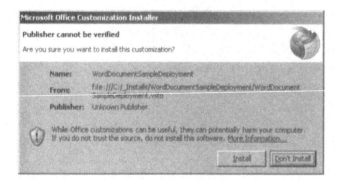

Figure 9-8. *The Microsoft Office Customization Installer dialog box*

4. After the solution installs successfully, click Close.

After you complete these steps, you can run the sample solution by opening the WordDocumentSampleDemployment.docx Word document. When it opens, you should see the Hello World welcome message.

Summary

Deploying VSTO solutions is now a simple and straightforward process, thanks to full support of the ClickOnce deployment model. When building VSTO solutions, you're no longer required to worry about configuring .NET security settings to ensure your add-in will execute, because ClickOnce sets the appropriate permissions. Also, you can take steps to ensure that users have the required prerequisite components on their systems. If they are missing components, Click-Once will download and install them. With ClickOnce deployment, you can quickly publish an installation package manually or via the Publish Wizard. No matter the path, deploying VSTO solutions is now as easy as deploying a Windows Forms–based solution.

Index

You Need the Companion eBook

Your purchase of this book entitles you to buy the companion PDF-version eBook for only $10. Take the weightless companion with you anywhere.

We believe this Apress title will prove so indispensable that you'll want to carry it with you everywhere, which is why we are offering the companion eBook (in PDF format) for $10 to customers who purchase this book now. Convenient and fully searchable, the PDF version of any content-rich, page-heavy Apress book makes a valuable addition to your programming library. You can easily find and copy code—or perform examples by quickly toggling between instructions and the application. Even simultaneously tackling a donut, diet soda, and complex code becomes simplified with hands-free eBooks!

Once you purchase your book, getting the $10 companion eBook is simple:

1. Visit www.apress.com/promo/tendollars/.

2. Complete a basic registration form to receive a randomly generated question about this title.

3. Answer the question correctly in 60 seconds, and you will receive a promotional code to redeem for the $10.00 eBook.

2855 TELEGRAPH AVENUE | SUITE 600 | BERKELEY, CA 94705

Offer valid through **05/09**.